Democracy at Dawn

Democracy
at Dawn

Notes from Poland and Points East

FREDERICK QUINN

TEXAS A&M UNIVERSITY PRESS
College Station

All photos from author's collection

The paper used in this book meets the minimum requirements
of the American National Standard for Permanence
of Paper for Printed Library Materials, Z39.48-1984.
Binding materials have been chosen for durability.

Library of Congress Cataloging-in-Publication Data

Quinn, Frederick.
    Democracy at dawn : notes from Poland and points East / by Frederick
Quinn. — 1st ed.
        p.   cm. — (Eastern European studies ; no. 5)
    ISBN 0-89096-786-5 (alk. paper)
    1. Post-communism—Europe, Eastern.   2. Europe, Eastern—Social conditions—
1989–   3. Europe, Eastern—Social life and customs.   4. Post-communism—Former
Soviet republics.   5. Former Soviet republics—Social conditions.   6. Former Soviet
republics—Social life and customs.   I. Title. II. Series: Eastern European studies
(College Station, Tex.) ; no. 5
HN380.7.A8Q56   1997   97-29954
306'.0947—dc21   CIP

Let justice flow on like a river
and righteousness like a never-failing torrent.
—*Amos* 5:24

Contents

Illustrations

Series Editor's Statement

So many years after the end of the Cold War, there do not exist enough ethnographies of the cultures, new nations, and diverse peoples freed from the yoke of Communism. For the most part, sociologists, psychologists, economists, and other social scientists have engaged in ideological and abstract theorizing about the future of the postcommunist world, concluding typically that "they" will soon become democratic and capitalist like "us." The present book by Frederick Quinn is a refreshing exception to these sterile exercises in social forecasting without a genuinely empirical base. Mr. Quinn is *not* a sociologist, yet his book performs an important descriptive function that most sociologists no longer perform—and one that therefore must be performed by other writers and disciplines. He gives us *concrete facts*, insights into "habits of the heart," and in general, an empathetic understanding of some of the peoples in formerly Communist nations from Poland to Romania, Moldova, Ukraine, and Kazakhstan, to name a few. In this regard, Quinn's approach and insights remind me of the writings of Georgie Anne Geyer, the award-winning journalist who also puts social scientists to shame with her sociological ethnographies of peoples all over the world, especially South America.

Why do we need the sorts of concrete facts that Quinn uncovers in this book? Because, if any meaningful "progress" is to be made in democratizing the many diverse peoples who were ruled by Communism, the serious analyst must understand why the Polish bus drivers on the buses Quinn took in Warsaw often drove past their scheduled bus stops if the lofty sounding phrase, "rational social order"—used carelessly by Western analysts—will ever become reality in postcommunist nations. The empty Western phrase "rule of law" must confront the specific situations Quinn cites in this book of how state constitutions and other legal phenomena were handled in ways that seem to illustrate anarchy.

This book uncovers for the Westerner a host of vivid, practical problems and issues: Why are airports so disorganized and dangerous in many postcommunist nations? What will many of these nations do about their minorities when many of them hold no traditions of minority rights? Why does the European Community preach reforms and democratic principles to formerly Communist nations but steadfastly refuse to let Poles and others sell their products in Western Europe? Why is Russia still perceived as a threat by so many formerly Communist nations? Perhaps at least as important, why does the United States see Russia differently, as a "partner for peace?" What will be the consequences of Ukraine's fundamental ambivalence toward Russia, namely, the desire by some of its citizens to sever all ties with Russia and become European as opposed to the desire of other citizens to become a part of Russia? How will formerly Communist jurists, politicians, and even laypersons grasp the American idea of a "government by the people?"

These are a few of the many pragmatic issues that Quinn uncovers with his remarkably engaging writing style. Most of what Quinn writes about Poland and other countries he visited applies to nations he did not visit, such as Croatia and Bosnia. It is a safe generalization that *all* formerly Communist nations, despite different degrees of "progress" toward the Western model of democratic capitalism, are experiencing problems, even social crises, that few Westerners understand. Quinn's book is a valuable first step toward understanding the everyday social reality of life in postcommunist nations. I hope that it will be followed by many more such studies.

Stjepan G. Meštrović
SERIES EDITOR

Acknowledgments

I am deeply grateful for the assistance of several people who measurably aided my work in Central and Eastern Europe, in addition to making their own highly professional contributions. In alphabetical order, they are:

James G. Apple, Giovanni Bucquichio, Robert Buergenthal, Mark and Carolyn Brzezinski, Lech L. Garlicki, Lloyd D. George, Audrey F. Glover, Luis López Guerra, Cynthia Holcomb Hall, Peter J. Messitte, Michael M. Mihm, A. E. Dick Howard, Anatoly Kogzev, Antonio La Pergola, John Norton Moore, George Marovich, Ergun Özbadun, Jacek Paliczeski, Charlotte A. Quinn, Edward Rafeedie, Harvey Rishikof, Andrzej Rzepliński, Erica Schlager, Herman Schwartz, Irek Stępiński, Helmut Steinburger, Dickran Tevrizian, and Allen B. Weinstein.

I thank the staff and members of the Venice Commission for Democracy through Law, ably chaired by Chief Justice Antonio La Pergola, for their valued professional collaboration and continuing contributions to advancing the Rule of Law.

This book is dedicated to Lloyd D. George, Cynthia Holcomb Hall, and Michael M. Mihm, all three members of (and the latter two chairs of) the International Judicial Relations Committee of the Administrative Conference of the U.S. Courts, who traveled with me to the extremities of the old Russian empire and to Peter J. Messitte who constantly provided sage counsel and skilled understanding to colleagues in the emerging judiciaries there.

Introduction

The sun shone in Austria on the afternoon of August 1, 1975. On car radio en route from Vienna to Prague I heard that President Gerald Ford and the leaders of 34 other countries gathered in Finland to sign the Helsinki Accords. I had just been assigned to the American Embassy in Prague where the Cold War's tensions were unabated. Ford's voice conveyed its usual matter-of-factness, blending hope and realism. His basic message about the Conference on Security and Cooperation in Europe was, "Let's give CSCE a chance." The great battle of the Accords, negotiated over the last several years, was borders versus human rights. Leonid Brezhnev was obsessed with obtaining international agreement on Europe's present borders, which included the Iron Curtain and Russia's World War II acquisitions. The United States and other western countries declined to accept the frontiers as binding, but pushed the Russians hard on provisions for freer expression and travel, family reunification, greater access to media, religious freedom, and wider cultural and educational exchanges.

The Communist governments were left high and dry; in their eagerness to advance the security issue they opened floodgates which, within a decade, would crack the Berlin wall. Communism's facade would be as gutted as the thousands of buildings left permanently under construction across the eleven time zones of the former Soviet Union.

In 1975 while a diplomat at the American Embassy in Prague, I prepared a one-page list of the Helsinki provisions and each month made the rounds of newspapers and the Foreign Ministry and asked, "How are we doing?" The answer was always a statistical one, so many more subscriptions to western publications permitted, such an increase in visas allowed, etc. It was grim business, for the numbers said nothing; for example, 800 subscriptions to the *National Geographic* were confiscated one month because of a paragraph in a story critical of communist border guards along the Danube River. Western journalists who wrote articles objectionable to the government were black-listed and could only revisit Prague as tourists. Dissidents were rounded up frequently and given long prison sentences. A rock group called "Plastic People of the Universe" was mercilessly pursued for its innocuous lyrics and music and accused of "hooliganism," a specific crime in the Soviet lexicon.

Vaclav Havel, chain-smoking and eternally dressed in a white knit fisherman's sweater, was one of the dissidents my wife and I knew. Playwrights like Havel could not have their productions staged. Artists generally gained a scanty living illustrating childrens' books under their wives' names. Christmas carols were not played on the local radio (though they were programmed for export on medium band radio to Germany). The bells in Prague's historic St. Vitus Cathedral were not rung on Christmas Eve since socialist workers needed their day of rest. Television showed only politically correct western films, such as those critical of the Vietnam War or portraying capitalism unfavorably. Upton Sinclair's novels, and those of Jack London, were widely translated; *Uncle Tom's Cabin* was universally offered in literature courses as a major American classic. Modern history courses divided in two parts; Europe Before its Liberation by the Soviet Union (1945) and Europe After its Liberation by the Soviet Union.

Travel to the West was severely restricted; if a wife received a scholarship to study in America, her husband had to remain behind as hostage. Or, if he accompanied her, the children could not leave the country. Artists could not travel to the West, but sporting groups were encouraged to do so. Thus a group of banned painters and graphic artists applied for visas as the "Wings of the Country" hockey team and spent two weeks in Switzerland visiting other artists and suiting up for an infrequent hockey match. Children applying for university admission were required to answer the question, "What was your parents' position in the 1968 uprising?" Church membership disbarred people from advancing to high positions in the government; many Christians became plumbers, electricians, carpenters and skilled workers, often establishing profitable careers. The government's work ethos, in the tradition of *Homo Sovieticus,* was, "They pretend to pay us and we pretend to work." It was in this setting the Helsinki Accords were signed, a grimly repressive world, which no one would have predicted would collapse.

I returned to central Europe 15 years later, from May 1993 to June 1995, spending two years as head of the Rule of Law programs of the Warsaw Office of Democratic Institutions and Human Rights (ODIHR), part of a regional international organization, then called the Conference on Security and Cooperation in Europe. The name was later changed from "Conference" to "Organization," a distinction without a difference, except that I had ordered a complete line of stationery for the office with the old logo.

My wife, Charlotte, was assigned to the American Embassy, Warsaw, as a political attaché working on NATO affairs. Over the twenty-five years of our marriage she had accompanied me to places like Yaounde, Cameroon (1966–68) and Prague (1975–78), abandoning excellent career situations as a professional historian, so I agreed in turn to move to Warsaw with her and Tigger, our German shepherd. ODIHR asked me to define a Rule of Law program, which built on my previous work with Chief Justice Warren E. Burger on the Bicentennial of the U.S. Constitution. We had helped countries writing new constitutions, sent expert speakers abroad on constitutional themes, and translated and distributed historical-legal publications to courts and schools abroad. I took the job, which kept me on the move for much of the next two years. I traveled by Russian internal airlines to Central Asia, Transcaucasia, the Baltic States, the Russian Federation, and the war-ridden Chechen Republic helping countries write constitutions and modernize their judicial systems.

As I traveled, I wrote this memoir, which is a personal narrative, not a traditional history or legal treatise. In places I have stopped the action and added imaginative sections written during the long, dark Warsaw winter, or in a drab hotel in a cement-block-and-Lenin-statue-capital of the former Soviet Union. The sequence is episodic, like life; my impressions are a series of strung-together experiences having their own internal unity. I recorded them, aware of the uniqueness of this two years in Central Europe's history. Successors will have different issues to deal with, different personalities to contend with and hopefully a more stable political-economic climate in which to conduct Rule of Law programs.

During my tenure there was demonstrable progress toward these goals. Issues of judicial reform were identified, constitutions and other fundamental laws analyzed, and each year more than 50 jurists from central and eastern Europe gathered in Warsaw to exchange professional experiences and improve their skills. We held professional seminars on subjects such as "The Changing Role of the Judge" or on topics specific to individual countries. We examined the role of different courts in Kazakhstan, where that country was considering alternatives to the judicial structure it inherited from Soviet times; free media in Kyrgyzstan, where that nation shut down two opposition newspapers and then evaluated the legal process for doing so; and federalism in Moldova and Georgia, two countries torn by protracted ethnic conflict and fractious regionalism.

What emerged from these contacts was an admiration for the professionalism of the judiciaries with whom I worked. They know what they want and how to get there, but they lack staff and libraries, and must daily fight their battles for independence. Many of the new constitutions will not last long and will need numerous amendments and constant revision, but that is to be expected in emerging countries with no real tradition of separation of powers, no real checks and balances, and much suspicion.

Americans need to shift perspectives drastically when considering constitutional change in central and eastern Europe, Central Asia, the Baltics, and Transcaucasia. For Americans, the constitution comes first, followed by the structure of government. Each country, we assume, has a season of innocence when wise founders appear and write just laws, but the countries I visited had their governments in place first, after which constitutions were written, or old Communist era documents modernized. Also, most of these countries lacked any tradition of an independent judiciary. The judge was a low level civil servant taking orders from an all-powerful procurator who in turn reported, not to a Minister of Justice, but to the legislative branch, as in Communist times. "Telephone justice," whereby a high government official would tell a judge in advance how to decide a case, was a fact of life.

A casual glance at the political-legal systems of these countries revels that the principle of separation of powers, central to mature democracies, has yet to become a political reality in most of these localities. Questions regarding the meaning and desirability of human rights and due process are also largely unanswered. Judges' salaries remain abysmally low and judicial education is lacking. Efforts to establish Rule of Law programs must confront the spread of organized criminal groups. These groups originate locally, but soon become transnational, driven by quick profits and the international demand for drugs and money. The list of obstacles to democracy's eastward struggle is daunting, but the case is more hopeful than it might appear initially. For one thing, there is widespread public discussion about what forms of government these countries might have. Actions of authoritarian leaders face public, even international scrutiny, through media, the growth of small but tenacious nongovernmental organizations, and the increased interest of international organizations in holding new member states to treaty commitments on Rule of

Law topics, especially human rights, free elections, and the creation of independent judiciaries.

Building a democratic civic culture requires more than a constitution. A legal infrastructure is needed including an able bar association, law schools, and an inquiring, informed media. Citizens must be active participants in public life, vote periodically to retain or reject their elected leaders, and have the freedom to form in political parties and civic associations. Without such an infrastructure, no independent judicial system will take root in a country. The constitutions of Afghanistan and Nicaragua were models of professional legal drafting, but were meaningless documents without the other ingredients of a democratic state. No nation in modern times has received more assistance in constitution drafting than Nigeria, but constitutional government in that once-prosperous African nation soon gave way to a succession of military tyrants.

"The Constitution," said James Madison, "reflects a fundamental conviction that governmental power is of an encroaching nature, and that it ought to be effectually restrained from passing the limits assigned to it." The battle in the emerging new European and transEuropean states is not to replace one monolithic power system with another similar structure, but rather to have popular, pluralistic democracy. That never comes easily. The gains of the mid 1990s are modest but real; compared to these countries' despotic pasts, they are revolutionary; compared to Western expectations, they are little more than initial steps. A note of cautious optimism is in order; these countries are unlikely to return to their authoritarian pasts, and if the road is unclear, and inefficiency, corruption, and inexperience are still part of the landscape, the jurists know in their hearts what is required and many work with vision, courage and determination for its realization; to them I express my deepest thanks and best wishes in their future work.

Democracy at Dawn

1

Warsaw, Moscow, Moldova

Our Neighborhood

May 25: Although the embassy administrative officer's letter welcoming us to Warsaw had described the house we would live in, for our first month in Poland we were assigned instead a one-bedroom apartment. Had we known this would be the arrangement, we would not have brought along Tigger, our ninety-pound German shepherd dog. Tigger made the flight in good shape and thinks we all live in a big kennel, with the bonus of long morning and evening walks. Many dogs live in this housing development, a gray five-story concrete building, one of ten in this immediate complex. "In Communist times" (a phrase Poles often use to describe a time when people rarely could buy cars or apartments), having a show dog was both a status symbol and a way of making a personal statement. So each morning we encounter Great Danes, a mastiff, poodles, cocker spaniels, and other German shepherds. Possibly five thousand persons inhabit the buildings, which represent middle-class housing, and other satellite cities radiate out toward the suburbs. Our complex has been under construction for ten years. A child who brought her dog, Sonia, to visit us said that she has lived here all her life. Three of the buildings are still under initial construction; workers' temporary sheds set up at the building site's edge look like they are here to stay. Many of Warsaw's buildings are of post-1945 construction, both because of urban growth and because Hitler ordered parts of the city systematically destroyed by artillery fire following the 1944 Warsaw uprising.

Animals from our complex are walked in a spacious oblong park near the housing development. The soil is sandy and overworked, the grass filled with weeds but also with beautiful blue and yellow wild flowers. On our return from a morning walk, we passed two apartments whose owners carefully planted flower gardens with large clumps of irises and borders of pansies and petunias. The buildings are residential, but we see no evidence of zoning laws; someone has turned a living room into a videotape rental store and another apartment into a barbershop. Stores are a good hike away, past the North Korean Embassy (a structure rarely used, since Polish–North Korean relations took a dive with the fall of Communism in this part of the world).

Our small third-floor living room opens onto a concrete balcony, where Tigger presides over the neighborhood. The room's three windows and glass door look onto Jana Sobieskiego Street, named for the eighteenth-century Polish king who defeated the Turks in Vienna. The street has three lanes on each side and a grass central divider, part of the historic Royal Way from northern to southern Poland. Traffic moves at breakneck speed; standing on a pedestrian crosswalk provides no safety, as a tiny Polish Fiat will try to sneak around from behind. Polish cars break down frequently and are parked in the grassy divider until the owner returns with a needed part.

One rainy morning I watched a frisky horse pull a long wooden cartload of cabbages down the Royal Way and, an hour later, return toward the country. The owner and his friend, looking as if they belonged in a Dutch seventeenth-century painting, *After the Rain*, chatted intently as a large red bus screeched to a halt behind them and a sleek Mercedes-Benz truck sped around them. Meanwhile, the attractive young horse carved out its own space in the fume-enshrouded road and pranced quickly through intermittent showers, eager to regain the comfort of its barn.

Except for three children who have taken an interest in Tigger, we know none of the building's inhabitants. Most stare at us as they approach, look beyond us when they are near, and glance over their shoulders toward us after passing.

People head for their cars carrying car radios in hand; otherwise radios are stolen regularly. Several nearby shops specialize in installing auto alarms; all but the smallest Polish Fiats have them, since car theft is rampant in Warsaw. At the housing development's other end is a used car lot, where the owner sleeps at night in a portable van, guarding his stock of twenty cars, small trucks, and buses. Nearby is an enclosed parking lot with a guard; residents pay extra for this service, more if they have Western European cars.

A black bird poises for almost thirty seconds in the air above the postage stamp–sized gardens across the street, then dives down on some small rodent emerging at sunset to search for food. Sometimes the bird sweeps in an elliptical motion to another site, holds itself stationary for a time, dives, and repeats the motion elsewhere over the field.

In a choice suburban neighborhood, about twenty acres of land have been made over into gardens. Probably, as the country prospers, they will give way to housing or commercial buildings, as a web of national, municipal, and local authorities cuts deals with German contractors, local architects, plumbers, and electricians. Meanwhile, there is a tiny kingdom of vegetable gardens, maintained by mostly elderly people. Each garden has a high wire fence and an elaborate door lock. Inside, there is often a small house with room for two people to stay overnight. Most compounds contain a few fruit trees, some tomato plants, and other vegetables, as well as space for flowers. Peonies and irises appear in the spring, then come a progression of summer blooms until October's dark skies arrive.

A Trip to the Veterinarian

May 27: In the late afternoon we took Tigger to the veterinarian for a shot against a heart disease prevalent in central Europe. Charlotte negotiated the transaction in Polish, including requesting a French vaccine, which the doctor kept in a yellow Donald Duck lunch box in his office refrigerator. The first time, a taxi had taken us across town to the veterinarian's office, and another, a small Fiat, had returned us, with Tigger's head out one window and tail out the other. This time, the return taxi refused to transport a dog, although the vet's office had called the taxi for us. I slammed the car door hard, and Charlotte was angry as well. Several Poles discussed the situation, and a truck driver courteously volunteered to drive us home in his small truck. Charlotte sat in front with the driver; Tigger and I were locked in the back, previously occupied by a load of excited chickens, which had left fresh droppings everywhere. We scrambled for the next ten minutes, as the closed truck bounced about Warsaw's uneven streets. When we arrived, Charlotte gave the driver a generous tip, and he kissed her hand in courtly Central European fashion; the dog and I picked ourselves carefully out of the cargo space, Tigger more gingerly than I.

Saturday Morning at the Russian Market

May 28: In the morning, Magosia (Charlotte's language teacher), her mother, and her sister go with us to the Russian market, across the river on its south side. The setting is a craterlike soccer stadium, built in the heyday of bread-and-circuses socialism. It seats eighty thousand persons in the open air, but it is rarely used, because it has neither electric lights for night games nor hot water for teams to shower. Wooden seats are warped and broken; a pair of badminton players on the field below are the only sportsmen in sight. Two rings of human vendors surround the stadium, one Polish and one Russian, selling everything from military knives to caviar, sable, and mink coats to Russian plastic toys that fall apart within hours. We push our way through the crowd to the entryway and are told that we need tickets, obtainable from vendors in one of two small Polish cars parked lower on the hill. Above us is the first ring, crowded with tents and umbrellas, under which are piled Indian, Chinese, Russian, and Polish clothing, shoes, purses, and cosmetics, most of the merchandise imitating well-known Western brands but not competitive in quality.

The upper ring is the Russian market; over three hundred merchants lean against the soccer stadium's top seats. Most are men in undershirts, but some are women dressed in Russian sporting clothes. Many made the seventeen-hour trip from Moscow, we are told, bringing whatever they could carry. Some vendors sell only junk, Russian machine parts, bits, drills, and tools. Others hawk Red Army binoculars, scientific instruments with elementary dials and knobs, caviar, icons ripped from church walls, army uniforms sold by deserting or demobilized soldiers, medals, velvet banners with Lenin's picture in the middle, clothing, and sometimes a battery-operated plastic toy tank. Fluorescent green water pistols are displayed at stalls, a sign that real weapons are obtainable. At the entrance, two sweaty central Asian males in gym clothes model ill-fitting mink coats with Hedy Lamar shoulders. Nearby, surrounded by piles of Russian industrial-strength women's undergarments, is a portly peasant woman in a T-shirt, with a piece of blue paper stuck to her nose to prevent sunburn. She wears a conical paper hat fashioned from *Pravda*.

Shoppers and vendors refresh themselves with fatty sausages, steamed cabbage, and piles of fetid sauerkraut. We purchase five inexpensive amber necklaces and two Gorbachev dolls, which open to reveal smaller figures of Yeltsin, Stalin, Lenin, and Marx, milestones in the bumpy progress of Russia's history.

After a morning at the market, we walk down Francuska Street, not far away, seeking the house into which we will move. It is opposite the Pakistan ambassador's residence, but the first embassy district police-man we encounter doesn't know the location and leads us to the central police booth for that part of town. The duty officer has neither map nor working radio. Street of the Defenders, Street of the Vanquishers, and Street of the Parliamentarians lead to Zakopianska Street, where the house is located, not far from Geneva and France streets. At the Cafe de Paris, we stop for lunch, but it is a bar where no food is served.

A Ride on Icarus

June 5: A supposed advantage of Communism was a public transportation system second to none. The argument was that, while workers might not own fancy Western automobiles, a good, quick bus system would move them to and from work easily. Buses are from Hungary, trams from the Czech Republic. The bus logo is an apt symbol: Icarus, who in Greek myth flew too close to the sun and fell into the sea in a cloud of wings and feathers. Most buses are two cars joined at the middle and swinging awkwardly along the streets. In heavy rain, buses leak badly, especially in the accordion-like rubber section joining the two halves. Driver's cabs sometimes are decorated; I rode in one with a driver's window surrounded by empty beer cans from many nations, a bouquet of fading red plastic geraniums on each side of the wheel, and a sign above the window, "Camel Cigarettes Trans-Saharan Rally, Poland."

Buses are top-heavy. Some drivers ease them effortlessly through traffic, while others clearly dream of driving race cars. I saw a woman with a loaded shopping bag land in the lap of another passenger when a driver took a curve too quickly. Drivers stop for only a few seconds, even in off-hour traffic; an elderly man shook his cane at the driver one Saturday morning as we rode into town, since the driver had not brought the bus to a complete halt while unloading passengers. At rush hour, perhaps fifty people crowd onto a bus with seats for one-third that number. One workday morning, our bus gave out while attempting the Belvedere Hill; passengers exited silently, walked up the hill in the rain, and reboarded the bus for the rest of the ride. Recently my bus stopped in mid-route; the driver locked passengers in and entered a nearby market for a liter of orange soda. One Friday evening, a drunk fell on my foot, successfully cradling his beer bottle and grinning. Another Friday, three No. 158 buses arrived simultaneously; I chose the third one and rode across Poniatowskiego Bridge in solitary splendor.

Passengers, except for holders of monthly passes, are required to punch tickets when entering the bus, pressing both ends in a small punch near the door. Drivers do not collect fares; inspectors circulate through buses, frequently checking tickets and fining passengers forty dollars if they have no ticket or one punched on another bus. On a rainy Saturday ride, one inspector, dressed casually as a street musician, showed me his badge, then quickly left the bus after checking a few fares. Tickets cost a fourth of what they would in Germany; most people purchase monthly passes. For two nights in a row, my standing place was under a ceiling exit which said in English, "In case of urgency press hard against the four seals, then discharge." The Warsaw bus map lists routes but not all stops, and we have experienced disasters, especially with the No. 503, an express bus that sped us past our apartment one humid evening just after we had made the vegetable run, continuing on to a housing development on the outskirts of town. Pickpockets stalk the busses; Charlotte saw one get punched in the eye by a student.

"Like Vienna in 1948"

June 11: I doubt that he sells much, although it is a choice location. The shop on the Old Town square offers modern reproductions of old maps. Nearby is a hand-operated press, which printed resistance leaflets during World War II but has not worked in decades. Since the shop is in the building's rear, the proprietor sits out front, reading *Literary Monthly* in a deck chair, chatting with tourists.

We talk about Warsaw's modern look after war's ravages and the dreariness of more than four decades of Communism. "All things considered, it's a bit like Vienna in 1948," I say, recalling *Life* magazine pictures of rebuilding the Austrian capital. Pleased with the comparison, the proprietor punches a key on a prewar cash register, and the drawer cranks open. There is no money in the machine, but a handful of old black-and-white postcards of photographs taken during the siege of Warsaw. A classic 1940s central European photographer had shot the pictures, someone with a superb eye for detail, background, and light.

Jerusalem Street, which we just crossed, now booming with new shops and busy crowds, was entirely rubble then. Polish troops in ancient metal helmets carry small submachine guns of an earlier time and race through piles of debris. Fires blaze from windows of an apartment building now housing a Polish-German export firm, a scene from a Renaissance painter's landscape of hell. Two nuns stare in horror at a Baroque church, sliced in two as with a knife, leaving piles of rubble on each side. The effect is like staring in a partially destroyed doll's house. A family dressed in heavy dark period suits and dresses walks behind a horse-drawn cart, fleeing the city with a few sticks of furniture and suitcases.

Present at the Creation: The Polish Political Science Association Meets

June 17: No Polish academic discipline took quite the pounding political science did. Its practitioners were watched closely by the party, who used political science as ideological justification for everything they did, buttressing their deeds with history, statistics, psychology, and social research. Today, a new generation of Polish political scientists is emerging. The fifteen who signed on as founding members of a new political science association wrote, "The Polish Political Science Association comes into existence at a time of profound systemic change in Poland. We now have new and unlimited possibilities to reflect on public matters and to conduct political research. Political science as it was taught in Poland over the last decades was the political science of the Communist party. . . . its content was rigorously controlled. This led to the deformation of political science, a deformation more profound than in other social science disciplines."

The association wants to write new textbooks, create civic education programs for all ages, and conduct independent analysis of Polish political life. Many of its members study voting patterns and electoral trends, new subjects in Polish political life. In late June, members of the new society gather in an Old Town conference center to hear what German, French, and British representatives have to say. I find the presentations predictable and the discussions guarded and polite. I am more interested in the coffee break conversations, in which I hear Poles say:

"Don't expect too much of us. We have only been independent a few years; our economy is a shambles, our political future by no means certain. We want to be a second France but don't think we are there yet."

"The remnants of communist ideology are different here than in some other countries, like Bulgaria or Czechoslovakia. It was easier to import books here and to travel to the West, and the party did not press for ideological purity the way it did in those countries. We face a secret enemy, which means you are never quite sure how much of a Communist the person in the next office was."

"What we need is a bookstore where you can go and wander and look at the latest titles from the West. There is an American library, but it is too expensive for us to copy articles from it. A professor here might make $350 a month. His wife must work, and probably he will hold two jobs, just to keep going."

"Our young people are filled with pessimism. There is no employment for them when they leave university. Also, cynicism is pervasive. We are used to taking care of our friends and family, but not defending the state. Many of us spent years trying to subvert state institutions. How can you expect us to create a civic culture in such a climate?"

Life's harshness is reflected in a display of photojournalists' work hanging in the conference hall, showing skinheads, despondent teenagers with nothing to do, gypsies living in barren camps, firemen extracting the bodies of two dead youths from a swimming hole while bystanders picnic on the shore. The most compelling photos are of a slaughterhouse, a metaphor for political society. Swarthy butchers, with profiles like aging party officials, pose proudly among carcasses, holding cuts of meat. The first shot is the slaughterhouse's entrance. A beautiful horse is turned upside down, held aloft by a metal device over one hoof; blood drains from the animal, which even in death retains its graceful lines. Next to it is a live young horse, standing free, yet held in a metal cage. Light at the door suggests the horse has just come from a run in the spring countryside. Suddenly he is aware the animal next to him is dead. The live animal is captured in the split-second between freedom and panic, but the outcome is never in doubt. The executioner stands nearby, ready with the fatal injection.

Stalin's Cathedral

Poles have a joke:
> Question: "Where is the best view of Warsaw?"
> Answer: "From the Palace of Culture."
> Question: "Why?"
> Answer: "Because then you don't have to look at the Palace of Culture."

As Chartres Cathedral dominates the landscape outside Paris, the thirty-story Palace of Culture and Science rises above Warsaw's skyline. From the late 1940s until several modern office buildings were erected in the 1980s, it loomed above the city's otherwise flat skyline. The Palace of Culture, a Stalinist secular cathedral, was designed to impress viewers several miles away, those approaching it, and those within it.

The structure, called "Stalin's Empire State Building," dominates almost any Warsaw vista. Entering it is an experience with several emotional stages. A block-long park and parking lot surround the building, reminding people how small they are and how grand is the socialist state. Next is the wedding-cake palace, its base six floors tall, with long, wide marble halls and reception rooms, suggesting Marxism's cultural achievement. A large art gallery and theater extend off the structure, as do two museums, a swimming pool, and restaurants. Elaborate stone carvings decorate the roof; chandeliers deck the halls, lighting the room's center brightly and leaving the corners in shadows. Just so, Russian politics contrasts light and shadows, as bright open spaces for parades and military displays are framed by dark corners where access is controlled tightly and conversations are held in secret. Between the Palace of Culture's cold marble halls and the huge park outside is an eight-column entryway accessible only through several small doors that allow only one person at a time to slide in under a guard's watchful eye. Vast scope and minute control—architecture mirrors Communist life. There is a faint Asian cast to the structure; not surprising, since the Soviet Union was a partly Asian country.

Leading to the tower are eight elevators, only two of which reach the thirtieth-floor Panorama. I join a delegation of sixth-graders crowding into the elevator, fourteen at a time. We walk around the windswept balcony, with its view of Warsaw. Pictures of the former city, leveled by German guns, are on display, along with propaganda pictures of the rebuilt city. The photographer's filter softened the drab government buildings; his lens caught happy families cavorting in then-new housing developments that soon would become a blight on the horizon.

Even on the thirtieth floor, one finds high stone ceilings, elaborate lighting fixtures, and above them yet another balcony and three-stage pinnacle. The visual message is clear: socialism reigns from a distance, close up, and within. It conquers heights but has its roots deep in the soil from which it springs. In the late 1940s, Poles were offered, as a gift from the Russian people, the choice of a subway system or this building; believing that a subway system had no future, they selected the massive Palace of Culture. The design is similar to that of comparable buildings ringing downtown Moscow. Smaller versions exist in Bucharest and

Prague. The latter is a former party hotel, the International, which Czechs call "Genghis Kahn's whorehouse."

The Diplomatic Life (An Entertainment)

Think of the diplomatic life and images come to mind of beribboned dukes, counts, and barons at receptions, sipping champagne from fluted glasses, conversing in gilded halls in French, German, and English.

The Gouzikistan National Day is none of that. The venue is the Orbis Hotel, a step up from the Stalinist-era Grand Hotel but a cut below the Marriott. In the Warsaw Pact's glory days, the now-frumpy twenty-story Orbis housed visiting delegations of Yugoslav soldiers or Cambodian workers, plus busloads of tourists from Sofia, Bucharest, and points east.

This National Day, the country's second, features trays of fried prunes wrapped in bacon, cubes of dried cheese, and canapés whose main ingredients are mayonnaise for bulk and pickles for seasoning. Gouzikistan's ambassador greets guests at the hotel ballroom's entrance, amid streamers in the red, white, and green national colors, flowing down from a "Canon Copies Faster" illuminated sign above the door. The ambassador, in a Bogart-in-*Casablanca* tuxedo, kisses the hands of female guests and gives men a Slavic embrace or a bone-crunching handshake, depending on the state of bilateral relations. When the guests assemble, he stands at the microphone and, in Polish and two Turkic languages, vigorously surveys his country's history and international relations. The folk-costumed hotel band then plays the post-Communist national anthem, "Long May the Eagle Soar." First the lead guitar haltingly establishes the melody; stringed bass, clarinet, and saxophone follow confidently. Those who know the words sing, "Lo, the eagle is soaring over freedom's new morning; Dawn's purple clouds, Fascism's shroud's overturning." Others hum the chorus: "Transcaucasian home, Transcaucasian home, Your children now are returning."

An older man daubs his eyes with a handkerchief that has seen him through a flu attack. Waiters pass with trays of lukewarm white wine, vodka, and canned gooseberry juice, a regional delicacy. By now there is a warm glow to the party, and guests slowly head for the exit.

Moscow: A Night at the Airport

On Sunday afternoon, July 4, I board a late afternoon flight from Warsaw to Moscow. My destination is the Moldovan Republic, where I am to speak at a conference on constitutional law and consult on the newly independent country's draft constitution. But first there is Moscow's Sheremetyevo Airport to traverse. When the plane lands, the air conditioning is turned off, and we wait for an armed guard to arrive and stare at disembarking passengers. Meanwhile, a line of at least two hundred Chinese forms at four passport control desks. I watch the clerk scrutinize each Chinese student's visa, line by line, comparing the student's passport photo and face with several up and down motions in the receding twilight.

After waiting a long time, I show my plastic-covered CSCE credentials and am led by a lanky guard, who, with a sweeping bow, motions me to a station. "I'm glad I don't have to go through all that," I think, looking beyond the airport's dust-streaked windows to a hotel where a hot bath and a good night's sleep await me.

The young guard opens my passport and takes as long as he had with the Chinese student's papers. Never mind, within minutes I will be out of here. He looks solemn and says, "Problem," motioning toward the lieutenant's office. Has the Russian Federation's Warsaw embassy left a line of the visa blank? Easy to rectify. I'll shrug my shoulders; Moscow police will respond with a Slavic gesture of hospitality and send me on my way. Meanwhile, I am motioned toward a family of Hungarian gypsies and a Taiwanese couple, while remnants of the planeload of young Chinese are processed. For the next hour, I sit next to the Hungarian mother, dressed in a suit of sequined blue denim and holding a recently born infant, who frequently cries. Her four-year-old daughter snaps an index finger painfully at a younger brother's nose and ears. He cries, and the mother hits him. Next he hugs his older sister, who pushes him down when the mother isn't looking, and when he cries, the mother hits him again.

Suddenly the police officer appears with the Warsaw flight's English-speaking captain. "Your visa has expired," he tells me. "You can return to Warsaw with us now or stay here. I think you should stay here." I ask if I can go to the hotel. This prompts the lieutenant, a bystander until now, to say "No" and confiscate my passport. "You can spend the night in the transit lounge," he says. "Come here at 7 A.M. The consul will be here, and your visa question can be regulated."

Not speaking Russian, I explore Sheremetyevo Airport on a Sunday night. A transit hotel is nearby, but, since the guard has seized my passport, I cannot go there. I want to cancel my hotel reservation but have no Russian coins or any idea how local phones work. "International Communications Center" says a sign in a corner of the transit lounge. The center is two ordinary telephones on a desk. Behind the desk is a young man with spiked blond hair and the Moscow version of an Italian summer jacket; he has a stopwatch, receipt book, and change for dollar bills. A French businessman calls his wife, an African student tries to phone home but cannot make connections, someone else complains that the young man starts the stopwatch before contact is made. During one such dispute, a Russian student dials the hotel for me.

With nine more hours to spend, I wander past the "Moscow Duty Free, 18% cheaper" sign, the Japanese sushi bar, the Irish Pub, the Baskin-Robbins ice cream stand open twenty-four hours a day, and the transit lounge, where fifty people are bedded down on the floor for the night, watching a Russian circus on television.

The upper floor first-class lounge is guarded by two dragons who roar indignantly at me as I appeal to their basic humanity and ask to sleep on a couch. Several rows of unfolded cardboard cartons allow Third World families to sleep on the balcony like a street in Calcutta. A foot extends from under a spread-out sari, and a tea kettle used for ablutions is left in the passageway; several travelers face Mecca for night prayers. An evening meal is shared, soup is poured from thermoses, while mothers wash laundry and hang it out to dry on the airport balcony. The airport's foul toilet has just been cleaned by a short, craggy-faced woman in a white worker's coat and hat, who yells at an Indian trying to enter. Stepping over sleeping bodies, I find the immigration office, a triangular-shaped room with a row of broken chrome and leather airport chairs and cracked circular rubber couches, the kind a Michigan university fraternity house might discard while modernizing. Aeroflot posters of Moscow in winter, a Pan Am poster, and two light boxes adorn the walls. Neither light box works; the transparency is gone from one; the other is of a 1960s hotel with a period Intourist bus in front. An energetic detective of medium height, one of three night-duty officers, welcomes me. I have no place to stay, I tell him; can I sit there? He says that the office will close in thirty minutes but, "Please stay awhile. Would you like some tea?" Although I decline, he brings me a glass of warm tea with a generous deposit of sugar in the bottom and a large fried egg sandwich, trimmed with dill and lettuce, part of the night staff's shared supper.

Meanwhile, a stream of African and Pakistani visitors enter. Some use the phone for local calls, others speak with the officer. This is a reconstructed version of his conversation with two young Africans:

"At three o'clock in the night you will come here. We will prepare everything. Do not disappear. If you do, the police will come for you. Where are you going to sleep?"

"Today I sleep on this side."

"Have you any luggage or not?"

"I have big luggage."

"Do you understand me or not?"

"I understand you actually."

"I know the situation you are in. You will not fly to your country, you will fly to another country, and you will solve your problems with another country. But, Sir, do not try to disappear."

"At three o'clock we are waiting for you. Do not worry."

"Try to help us and we will try to help you. Otherwise, there will be many problems with our country and your country."

A few minutes later, the police officer announces that he must close the office for the night. He is apologetic and brings us both glasses of chilled vodka, and me another sandwich. "There are many problems with Africans bringing in drugs and traveling under false documents," he says, adding that it is regrettable that several hundred people must sleep on the floor of Moscow's main airport at night. I thank him for the hospitality. "It is only what you would do if I visited your country," he replies, presenting me with an Aeroflot packet of five Moscow picture cards. "Be careful, there are bad people out there," he concludes, storing my luggage in his office.

I wander about, staring at the departure board; the 3 A.M. flight on which the Nigerians will depart is for Cotonou, Benin.

A temporary bed is provided by the cold marble floor in an isolated part of the departure lounge, but soon I am awakened by slamming metal grills, the duty-free shop closing for the night. And every half-hour the snap, crackle, and pop audio system announces departures to Kingston, Buenos Aires, and Dacca.

July 5: 7 A.M. Dawn over Moscow. At passport control office, the same guard I encountered the previous evening removes my passport from an ancient safe. We march up two flights to the "Consular Office." A chamber orchestra sleeps on the floor, instrument cases piled protectively in the middle, except for a stringed bass tilted against the wall, its owner curled up near it.

Behind piles of flimsy cardboard cartons marked "Taiwan" and "Fragile," in the office's corner is a pockmarked wooden desk with a stamp and stamp pad. There sits the consul, a disheveled man in a crumpled

suit and a grease-spattered tie, gatekeeper of the vast Russian bureaucracy. He asks when I will return to Moscow, quickly changes the visa
with the stroke of a ball-point pen, stamps the passport, and dries the
excessive ink with a tissue. He tells the Taiwanese man, "You must return in an hour." Later, at Moscow's domestic airport, the ticket clerk
informs me, "You must return in an hour." When I do, she is gone, and
her replacement, flustered, says my flight is boarding from a different
airport building.

Moscow international flights arrive at one airport; domestic flights
leave from another. The ride to the second airport is by a rickety small
taxi whose chain-smoking driver pilots it like a World War II fighter plane,
dodging between trucks and weaving through traffic. Police flag down a
late-model Italian car for speeding, and cars pull onto the berm, where
rust-covered trucks wait and private vendors pump gasoline into cars
and cans.

Smoked Fish for Breakfast

If Sheremetyevo International Airport presents difficulties, Domodedovo,
its domestic counterpart, belongs to one of the lower circles of Dante's
Inferno. It is 9 A.M., and a drunken young man lunges through the entrance. Inside, white-coated vendors sell warm beer, mineral water, tea,
fermented grain beer, and a selection of oversized, butter-soaked imitation French pastries. Clerks use hand-held calculating machines or wooden
abacuses. Almost all suitcases are wrapped in butcher paper tied with
loops of binding twine to discourage theft. As a gypsy boy taps rhythmi-
cally on my arm, begging for money, his mother thrusts a grease-covered
lithograph of the Blessed Virgin Mary toward me, asking for dollars.
Under one of the four hallway slot machines, a skinny cat sleeps; five
Central Asians hunch in a circle, snacking on a pile of smoked fish spread
on *Pravda*. The strong smell of Russian tobacco fills the air, along with
exhaust from outside trucks. I walk along the unlit, rain-specked corridor, looking for the gate marked "Chisinau," heading, I hope, for the
gentler South.

Opposite the gate are garbage bins from the airport employees' cafeteria; large crows pick purposefully through the scanty debris. On one
side is a plane marked "Air Moldova." The Moldovan national flag is
freshly painted over the former Soviet Union's hammer and sickle, the
outline of which remains visible. When the crew arrives, each carries stacks
of VCRs in both hands; on our return trip, they lug sacks of fresh veg-

etables to Moscow. Extra passengers, for whom there are no seats, stand patiently in the galley, grasping metal handles. On both flights we are served mineral water from a pile of plastic bowls, which are collected in a stack, then passed out again before landing.

Moldovan Constitutional Dilemmas

JULY 5–10: Moldova, with less than 1 percent of the former Soviet Union's population, is wedged between Romania and Ukraine. Moldova has a high population density, rich farmland, an industrial base, and a strategic location. Its infrequent intervals of free existence have been interlarded with long periods under Ottoman, Russian, Austrian, and Romanian hegemony. A small country, twice the size of Massachusetts, it is a land of gently rolling hills and tableland pointing toward the Black Sea. Although it was part of Romania, a German ally in 1939, Hitler still ceded it to Stalin in the Molotov-Ribbentrop Pact's secret protocol. Recaptured by Romania during World War II, it became the "Moldovan SSR" in 1944. The docile agrarian population was treated ruthlessly by the Russians; local institutions were dismembered. Russian immigration policy encouraged moving Russians in to the rich farmlands and deporting local peoples by cattle car to Central Asia. In early 1990, the Moldovan Popular Front won a parliamentary victory, eliminating total Communist control of the government. This was a year and a half before similar events occurred in Moscow. On August 27, 1991, following the Moscow coup attempt, Moldova declared independence from the crumbling USSR. The Russian 14th Army, headed by an outspoken, chain-smoking paratrooper general, Alexandr Lebed, remains omnipresent, muddling the delicate political equation while supporting the resident Russian population. A once-elite unit, it would defend the Motherland's southern flank against NATO and spearheaded Russian invasions of Hungary (1956) and Czechoslovakia (1968).

Chisinau, the capital, is a sprawling town of 500,000 people. The center has a Mediterranean or southern Russian provincial quality; most government buildings are within walking distance. Farm products are abundant, but long lines form for scarce consumer goods. The window of a downtown fruit-and-vegetable store displays an elaborate pyramid of cabbages; although stores are dark as caves, electric lights rarely are switched on during the day. A bookstore's newest acquisition is the Moldovan map and state seal, with a huge bull in the middle, but it also stocks older works, such as Voltaire's *Candide* in Romanian. Two calendars are for sale, one of the road police in action, the second mildly erotic. On the first calendar, a large police officer with a black American cowboy hat and a King Farouk mustache, whom our translator calls "Sergeant Sausage," grins confidently at the wheel of a blue police car. Behind him, in a semicircle, are a motorcycle, a van, a helicopter, and the caption, "There to Serve You." The erotic calendar shows a thin young woman, clad in *crepe de Chine,* standing in front of a historical portrait in a wood-paneled room, looking longingly at a bowl of lemons.

Moldovans walk with a slow lilt; little traffic moves on the wide, tree-lined boulevards; life's pace is easy, yet the two-year-old country risks being torn apart by ethnic conflict before it ever comes of age. Some Moldovan political sentiment exists for reunification with Romania, but that notion mostly reflects a politics of nostalgia. While respecting a long-standing cultural tie with their neighbor, Moldovans are familiar with Romania's deeply unsettled politics. Two additional complications in Moldovan political life are the presence of a self-declared independent republic along a sliver of land on the Dnistr River's east bank, and the so-called "Gagauz Republic," representing a sizable southern section of the country which has declared itself an autonomous republic within the Moldovan state. In the first instance, a sizable Russian population was angry at restoration of the Latin script and a requirement that government officials demonstrate fluency in Romanian as well as Russian. Romanian, with slight dialectical differences, is the Moldovan language, although nationalists on both sides will hotly contest this point.

The second major problem is the "Gagauz Republic," where southerners speak a Turkic language. An ethnic enclave whose ancestors wandered along the Black Sea a thousand years ago, the Gagauz retained their language but became Russian Orthodox Christians. This minority of 153,000 persons strives for political recognition and establishment of Gagauzia as a part of Moldova. Gagauz residents fear union with Romania; they also want economic, cultural, and educational autonomy within a Moldovan political framework. Possibly one thousand persons were killed in Moldova's internal disputes in recent years, five thousand were wounded, and one hundred thousand were displaced. No-one wants more violence.

Writing a post–Communist-era constitution has taken Moldovans a year and may take an additional year to complete. Earlier drafts were vetted through the American legal community. A Sorbonne law professor and the French Institute of Democracy in Paris also analyzed the document.

As we moved from office to office, I relayed to a series of parliamentarians these comments and those of other experts whom we asked to analyze the document.

Comments mirror the problems of most central European draft constitutions. They note the constitution's excessive length and the need for clarity about separation of powers. They ask for a fuller statement on the independence of the judiciary and rethinking the role of the procurator, a legacy of the Soviet legal system. Human rights protections are positively assured in one section of the constitution but are so qualified in subsequent paragraphs as to be of questionable value. This Russian legal heritage represents classic Soviet constitutionalism, giving with one hand and taking away with the other. The key phrase to watch for in such a document is "except when limited by law." The phrase usually appears near the article's end, restricting rights previously enumerated. Much extraneous material was included in early drafts, including a provision (later removed) that "a public authority can make use of any building basement for works of common interest on condition the damages caused to the soil, to the plantation, or houses as well as other damages are repaired."

Moldovans recognize the inadequacy of the draft document. As we talk, parliamentary commissions work on revisions. However, reform-minded jurists know that an old-boy party network is alive and well under new party names. Entrenched interests, especially in the powerful procurator's office, will not relinquish power easily. And Moldova is a small agricultural country, strongly represented in Parliament by rural forces resistant to change, including a Village Life bloc of right-wing deputies. Behind one deputy's desk is a glossy German-printed color poster of a popular folk singer with flowing shepherd's cape and wooden flute; in the blank space reserved for information about concert times is hand lettered, "He is one of us."

The Constitutional Law seminar is the brainchild of Sarge Cheever, an American Foreign Service Officer assigned to the Moldovan Mission of the Conference on Security and Cooperation in Europe (CSCE), and Florentina Blandu, an attractive, voluble American attorney of Romanian birth. Ms. Blandu volunteered to help Moldova modernize its judicial system through the American Bar Association's Central and East European Law Initiative, a program allowing American attorneys to assist in the democratic emergence of countries of Central and Eastern Europe. This initiative is one of the soundest additions to America's foreign policy in recent history, for it means that emerging countries of Central and Eastern Europe have the possibility of creating stable, independent, professional legal systems as part of their new political infrastructures. Not every country will use this resource wisely; some will try to keep their courts powerless, but many do use the expertise of American lawyers to reform judicial systems that were created in Communist times.

Most seminar sessions are led by Andrew Lester, who teaches constitutional law at an Oklahoma City law school. A high-energy, mince-no words litigator, Lester until recently was left to cool his heels in Kiev while the Ukrainian Ministry of Justice decided what to do with him. He jumped at the opportunity to weigh in on basic principles of constitutionalism at the moment when Moldova was writing its fundamental law.

The gathering opens on a hot summer day in a park on the edge of an artificial lake. Nearby is a sculpture garden which alternates benches full of intense young lovers with works of Socialist Realism. Atop an imitation Brancusi marble column, an artist has placed an aluminum handshake between two workers. A large bird's nest has been built above the metal hands, leaving straw trails and thick white droppings on the workers' fingers.

The initial constitutional law meeting is in a replica of a traditional wooden house, its large reception room decorated with local folk carvings. A sumptuous buffet of local wines and foods is laid for the hundred guests, who include the capital's eight-person resident diplomatic corps. The CSCE mission head goes first, delivering a four-page talk that is translated consecutively into the local language. Doors and windows are closed so that people can hear better. A parliamentary deputy replies with high points of Moldova's thousand-year history. Then Professor Lester begins his lecture. The center's management, being helpful, switches on the air conditioning. The motor's sound is like an ancient Iluychien prop plane taking off. Unaffected by the distraction, the trial lawyer continues as if in a courtroom.

The next day, we move to the massive Palace of Culture, with its heavy parquet floor and rows of local artists' original landscapes, bearing titles like *Hill in Autumn* or *Hill in Springtime*. I enter the wrong door and find myself in an auditorium that easily can seat two thousand persons. A local folk dance troupe does kick steps in two circles on stage, lit by a single light bulb; music is provided by a small boy with a shepherd's pipe, sitting on an overturned orange crate.

Our seminar meets around a U-shaped Communist-era table covered with green felt. Abundant bottles of mineral water or warm, sweet pear soda decorate the table. Fifty persons lean intently forward and discuss constitutional ideas each evening for the next two weeks. Lester's opening sessions are on separation of powers, federalism, checks and balances, and the need for an independent judiciary. My topics are comparative constitutionalism and the CSCE process. Some points:

—A blurring of civil law and common law approaches is taking place, especially in the European Court, where case law precedents are referred to increasingly. Many European judges rely on case law precedents to help shape decisions, especially on topics not covered in traditional codes, such as environmental, telecommunications, or commercial and banking law.

—Courts are being asked to rule on questions of social or political conflict, such as the status of minority groups, which cannot be resolved by the application of traditional legal principles. This represents a collision of law and history.

—Many new laws are coming on the books, often drafted by legislators instead of lawyers. Some are vague and difficult to apply. Organized crime laws, banking statutes, and intellectual property laws are some of the new fields that the former Warsaw Pact countries are having to contend with for the first time.

—All over Europe, countries are revising law codes to bring them into harmony with international human rights norms, such as the various CSCE accords.

Moldovans are attracted to the French experience, in part because they admire Romania, often promoted as "the France of the East." A deputy who is working on a law degree at Bucharest University says, "We have seven thousand students in Romanian universities; when they return, things will be different." The French prefecture system interests Moldovans because it provides a touch of local autonomy while keeping the strong hand of central control intact. Federalism is a code word for separatism to Moldovans, and we say, in numerous ways, that the two concepts are not the same, that federalism includes a separation of and sharing of powers between the center and the constituent parts, and that there is always creative tension in such a process.

"You Can Always Send Them Back to Spain"

A dominant question here, as in several other countries of the former Soviet Union, is what to do about minorities. How are their rights protected? Should a constitution enumerate individual rights and also group rights? Should it list traditional rights of persons, or should it also include social rights, such as the right to education, health care, employment, and social welfare benefits? Such issues are emotionally charged; some of our responses are greeted with puzzlement. Many important political questions are not constitutional issues, we say, and a lasting constitution must provide a statement of rights and the framework within which to resolve basic societal issues, rather than trying to solve every question. There is a difference between a constitution that provides the structure for a country's political system, and a long document that may be unenforceable and risks being revised every few years. This discussion, with slight variations, is repeated in several countries during the next two years. I share with them Quinn's Law: the longer the constitution, the shorter its shelf life.

At one point I use the example of Los Angeles's providing educational and social services for Spanish-speaking minorities. A local commentator says that the situation there is different from that in his country, because, if there are disputes between the Los Angeles government and Hispanic citizens, "You can always send them back to Spain."

Judicial Reform: "Our Judges Have Robes Now"

The chief justice of the Supreme Court, the minister of justice, several judges and parliamentarians, and independent lawyers meet individually with me. The minister of justice says that Moldova is the first of the former Soviet Union's now independent republics to abandon the two lay judges, a distinctive feature of Russian justice since Lenin's time. He adds with pride, "Our judges have robes for the first time."

While I expect meetings to be traditional courtesy calls, many last two hours. Below are some representative comments from a sampling of jurists and parliamentarians.

Judicial Modernization: "We Need Word Processors"

We realize our system has problems, but we think it has prospects. The Constitutional Court is separate from the rest of the court system now. It will deal with political questions and not judicial questions; if ordinary courts get into politics, you will have no justice. . . . We need a new criminal code. The Russians believed they could write one criminal code that could be applied everywhere in the Soviet Union without local modifications. . . . The procurator's role must be redefined and placed under the Ministry of Justice, although conservative forces oppose breaking it up and detaching it from the legislature. I'll be frank with you; I worked in the procurator's office; nobody there will give up power easily.

Our main task is modernizing the judiciary and we have made some progress. . . . The Ministry of Justice has taken over several old Communist party buildings; we have a good physical plant, but we need equipment. Jurists at every level work only with pens and pencils; the Chief Justice of the Supreme Court doesn't have a working typewriter. . . . There are no written records of many proceedings, we don't have paper. . . . We need word processing and reproduction equipment. We can agree about human rights issues; it's different building a functioning judiciary to protect them.

Now our judges must have contact with the West, to see your judges in action. Our judges were docile minor civil servants under the czar and the Communists, they must change their manner as well as their function.

Ratification

Ratification is an important issue. Should we hold a special constitutional convention? Some want parliamentary approval by majority vote, then a referendum. The present parliament has no legal right to act on the constitution. The Soviet Socialist Republic of Moldova doesn't exist now. This is a dead parliament. It has no authority, even in drafting our constitution. . . . We can't adopt the constitution in a normal manner. Two key parts of the country will stay out of the process because they cannot participate under present conditions. If it is adopted, they will say it doesn't apply to them.

Supplanting the Soviet Heritage: "Telephone Justice" Was a Fact of Life

Our legal specialists were trained in Russia. The priority in other countries was given to human rights, but we learned about group rights. . . . "Telephone justice" was a fact of life. . . . In one code I put in the office of inspector; the cabinet minister was terrified. Here was a person monitoring the law who could levy fines or bring court actions. That is new for us.

After fifty years of Soviet domination, our society was leveled.

Any person with initiative either encountered a wall in front of them or was suppressed. Initiative was punished. My brightest students were sent to remote villages, while mediocrities were given the main governmental posts. The result is that we have inherited an administrative apparatus which has executive skills but no vision.

The Russians are supposed to leave on January 1, 1994. Through humiliation, mistreatment, and intimidation, they beat our people down. It wasn't in the tradition of Moldovans to mistreat another nationality. Sometimes we think all our problems are because we are too yielding. . . . The choice is more important than Pepsi-Cola versus Coca-Cola; we are like a developing country. Our basic issue is our country's survival; we must find pragmatic solutions to these questions.

"Our Best Days Were after the Romanians Left and Before the Russians Came"

On Friday, July 9, the self-proclaimed Gagauz Republic is our destination, a two-hour ride away through rolling vineyards and pleasant farmlands. The presidency is a nondescript three-story municipal building, in front of which stands a brooding statue of Lenin in a huge winter coat. On each floor are macho young men in jeans, tight-fitting shirts, wide belts, and sidearms, the republic's armed forces.

The president receives us in his office, giving us a locally printed visiting card with a blue and gold band and a wolf standing on a ridge. In back of the president's desk is the only extant copy of the national flag. Three white stars symbolizing past, present, and future are pasted on a sky-blue background. A black timber wolf stands on a hill's crest against a golden circle bordered with red filigree designs in one corner. I ask about the wolf. An ethnologist who is a cabinet minister says that, according to a myth of the Gagauz peoples' founding, in a time of great difficulty a wolf led them to freedom. Ever since, wolves have been revered in local folklore.

Around the table sit the foreign minister, head of Parliament (a linguist), and several other officials. Behind the president's desk is a calendar from Turkey, from whom the Gagauz are trying to obtain scholarships and other assistance.

After each member of the government makes a five-minute presentation on basic positions, the rest ask questions about constitutions, listening intently and taking extensive notes. Questions of minority rights loom large for the Gagauz, who want peace and incorporation into the

Moldovan republic as an autonomous state, with constitutional guarantees of their special status. Gagauz report racial discrimination by Moldovans, some of whom refer to them scornfully as "Turks." A cabinet member tells of being expelled from her apartment by Moldovans; when she sought legal redress in Chisinau, she was told, "Get out of here, you Gagauz."

We gather at the town's only hotel for a lunch of Turkish meat stew and local cognac. The dining room is decorated with local folk themes, a brilliant blue silk wall featuring elaborately carved paneling of local woods. Except for pop music blaring from a portable tape-deck at the table next to us, this could have been a nineteenth-century rural noble family's parlor. As we leave, the president says, "Our best days were after the Romanians left and before the Russians came." The hotel staff gathers at the door with bottles of local brandy. "Do not forget us," says the linguist, waving as their tiny black car sputters back toward the small republic's capital; we speed northward in the mission's Volvo, soon crossing an unmarked border.

2

Warsaw, Berlin, London

Return to Warsaw

Warsaw, July 18: Wanting to experience everyday life in Warsaw, I have lunch not far from the office. The restaurant's decor is sparse, the clientele along in years, and the food steamed dumplings and knee joints from large farm animals. No waiters are in evidence, only an authoritarian dining room manager who ignores my request for help with the menu. Service is slow, the waits long; with my Polish dictionary, I translate the wall sign, "Welcome to Christian Charities Soup Kitchen for the Elderly."

Warsaw, July 19: We leave for church at 9:15 A.M.; the service starts at 10. After a brief wait, we board the No. 501 express bus but miss our stop. Instead, we arrive at the Hotel Forum, a mile from church. It is now 9:45; there is no alternative to taking a taxi, usually avoided because hotel and airport taxis are run by gangs who charge exorbitant fares. Warsaw's four thousand cabs are not regulated by the government and freely set their own rates; some drivers carry pistols and knives, fearing holdups and shootings. Nearby are two small taxis, but both drivers are asleep, so we take the first of three late-model cars lined up across the street. The driver has a Western-style silk print sport shirt and gold chains.

His placard says 30,000 zloty, or two dollars, the approximate fare for that distance. I ask if he has a meter, and he points to one, while turning on the late-model Audi's air conditioning, something we encounter in no other Warsaw cab. By the time he pulls into traffic, the meter jumps to 50,000, clicking furiously. The driver moves through traffic, and soon the tab is over 100,000 (six dollars); when we reach the church entrance, it is 380,000 (twenty-two dollars). I have only a 500,000-zloty note; the driver tries to cheat me out of the change by giving me a 1,000-zloty note instead of a 100,000 note, but I catch him. By setting his meter at four rotations instead of one, he quadrupled the price of our ride.

Our Office: "And the Wall Came A-Tumbling Down"

July 23: CSCE's office is located in the Privatization Ministry, formerly the Ministry of Heavy Industry. A six-story Stalinist-era concrete-and-steel structure, the building fills a complete city block and has its own two-person post office, small hotel, and basement cafeteria. Two guards sit at a desk in the entrance area, with a television set in front of them and a lithograph of Marshal Pilsudski, Poland's authoritarian interwar president, behind them. At another desk, an elderly man in a sport shirt sits behind a placard reading, "Information on Privatization." You have to go around a pillar to talk with him, and perhaps he has planned it that way for, being just beyond the flow of pedestrian traffic, his days are spent watching humanity pass while his pile of brochures remains untouched.

A small kiosk is built into the hallway, selling bus tickets, newspapers, soap, and toilet paper. Most people keep their own roll and soap bar, as supplies for each floor's restrooms disappear by late morning. The entrance area's marble floor is covered with rubber or metal-laced webbing. Its metal sections, like those covering a World War II temporary airfield, are of different heights. People step gingerly between squares or risk catapulting ahead while dreaming of privatizing state-owned industries.

Last year, to project a more favorable corporate image, the ministry refurbished its floors with three different floral carpet patterns produced locally for export. The designs were chosen to woo a Middle Eastern commercial mass market. Something went wrong in laying the carpet; large nylon ripples now cross the floor. Above the carpet, walls were covered with metallic imitation wooden strips, and each of the dark building's rooms was furnished with white Scandinavian lamps and word processors. Some German-Polish and other private firms have offices in the building; rumor has it that the minister pocketed their rent payments.

Our offices are on the third floor. Originally scheduled for completion in mid-May, work still remains now in late July. I spent a month moving from seat to seat with a portable word processor like a war correspondent; the day is filled with the sound of walls being built or torn down. Once workers misread plans and knocked a door opening in the wrong wall; later that week, a single metal pick stroke took out telephone and electrical lines for part of the building.

The most dramatic event is a morning-long dispute between workers and the building manager, after which the entrance wall is knocked down again and moved back seven centimeters. An elevator rider explained that the new wall was too close to the elevator door and nobody was willing to bribe the building manager to leave it in place. CSCE and the Polish Foreign Ministry dispute construction costs. Although the ministry is broke, it is responsible for furnishing the CSCE mission with adequate work space. Poles want to keep the office in Warsaw, despite constant efforts to move it to Vienna, but they do only the minimum necessary to support it. Since construction is at a standstill, the office director, Luchino Cortese, has advanced funds from CSCE's budget; the ministry now says there is a misunderstanding and CSCE is responsible for improvements. Additionally, the National Bank charges 1 percent of the office's annual balance as a special fee for holding the CSCE account. Throughout difficult times, the staff has been cheerful, bringing apples, cherries, flowers, and small cakes from home or nearby bakeries. This harmony disappears as the office grows larger and splits into factions.

Conference on Security and Cooperation in Europe (CSCE)

A bit of history. The CSCE process dates to the mid-1970s, when it began as a forum for East-West contact at the Cold War's height. The watershed event was the August 1975 signing of the Helsinki Accords, which opened Eastern Europe to the free flow of information, freed up travel, and increased acceptance of international human rights norms. With Communism's recent collapse, CSCE's fifty-three participating states were forced to rethink the organization's role. The Warsaw office—ODIHR, the Office of Democratic Institutions and Human Rights—is responsible for "human dimension issues," an awkward term which includes the protection of human rights, free elections, protection of minorities, and support of Rule of Law and democratic institutions. The origin of these activities is the 1975 Helsinki Accords, Basket I (European security issues) and Basket III (humanitarian issues). Baskets, a diplomat of the period argued, was a useful term, because no-one topic was more important than another, hence they fell into "baskets." Human rights standards were refined further in CSCE meetings in Paris, Copenhagen, and Moscow and at a second Helsinki Summit of 1992. At each meeting, definitions of human rights were expanded, and former Communist countries accepted those definitions as binding in domestic law. Qualifications diminished; increasingly clearer standards were expounded, and the map of Europe's human rights future is clearly laid out.

CSCE works through a laborious process, an annual meeting of heads of state or foreign ministers. These leading figures usually appear for a day or two, following weeks of pick-and-shovel work by their diplomatic staffs. Day-to-day governance of CSCE is through tedious monthly meetings of a Committee of Senior Officials, a permanent Vienna-based group, and a recently-appointed secretary general, Wilhelm Höynk, a senior German diplomat who had no previous substantive experience with human rights. He has an administrative role (political power rests with the chairman-in-office, who rotates annually) but will move quickly into any political vacuum and attempt to expand his power under the guise of coordination. "Don't do anything controversial" is Höynk's motto, although human rights work is generally confrontational and controversial, for it usually pits an individual or a minority group against a government and includes accusations of human rights and due process violations.

ODIHR helps countries write constitutions and modernize judicial systems, monitors elections, and trains nongovernmental human rights groups. The Warsaw office also supports field missions in Moldova, Latvia, Georgia, and Tajikistan. These CSCE missions are sensors, registering, much like foresters tracking smoldering brushfires, the extent of political and ethnic discontent. Such preventive diplomacy missions exert a stabilizing influence in places like Estonia, Moldova, and Tajikistan; they transmit reports of problems, such as conflict between factions over an election's outcome or minority unrest, to the next higher level, the Committee of Senior Officials. The work is not easy; all countries give lip service to democratization, but clear political will is not evident on many issues, and CSCE has no military or peace-keeping forces to use for leverage. The head of the Swedish Foreign Ministry's legal department, traveling to the former Yugoslavia for a difficult mission, said, "I was faced with an armed guard and I didn't even have a flag I could show him. All I had was my calling card."

Each year CSCE holds several public policy seminars, which are organized by ODIHR on human dimension issues suggested by the Committee of Senior Officials. The gatherings usually are held in the former Warsaw Pact conference headquarters on the town's edge. I do not know the origin of the term "human dimension," but I guess it is the Euro-English opposite of "military, scientific, natural," or some other "dimension." In any case, most discussions are about human rights and minority issues. Recent topics include work conditions for migrant workers, Roma (gypsy) populations, free media, minorities, and human rights standards in various countries. I found the seminars well-intentioned but mind-numbing in their execution; at various times I attempted to count the light bulbs in the main conference hall but never got beyond two hundred. Topics are vague, the sort diplomats might arrive at just before a coffee break and which become further muddled in translation. Delegates rarely move beyond set speeches. I once tried to lead an exchange on minority issues; when the discussion became lively, a Swedish delegate poured water on it with a twenty-minute talk on what Sweden is doing for its reindeer-herding populations. Next, a porcelain-faced monsignor, silent during the conference's first two days, saw this as the strategic moment to summarize a recent papal encyclical on social issues. By then it was lunch time, and I resolved I never would follow this format when I began holding Rule of Law programs.

OSCE, after twenty years, has performed an admirable role on paper and a less impressive role in reality. The hard-fought battles to create agreement on democratic governance and rule of law are revolutionary when their content is traced to the original CSCE documents. What is lacking is an institution capable of effectively monitoring and enforcing these acts. Success stories are not numerous and most OSCE missions assume an observer's role, reacting to events or reporting on them rather than actively contributing to their resolution. OSCE institutions lack a clear political mandate and the means to realize it, this by conscious decision of the sponsoring countries, the United States included. The result is easily observable in visiting an OSCE field mission where seconded diplomats, some more talented than others, wait in small offices or seek occasions to hit the road and observe a troop concentration or a dispute between peoples, waiting endlessly for instructions from Vienna to take the action needed to resolve a crisis. Low salaries, reduced benefits, and three-year-term appointments for most positions contribute to the organization's transitory nature.

ODIHR in Warsaw

ODIHR's office originally was established as the Office of Free Elections, beginning work in April 1991, with the arrival in Poland of its director, Luchino Cortese, former deputy director of the Italian delegation to the original CSCE talks. Cortese served in Moscow, Warsaw, and several Latin American countries before taking up this assignment, which required him literally to live out of a suitcase for three months in a Warsaw hotel. A traditional diplomat, he had little grounding in human rights but a gift for outlasting and outtalking opponents. The office's original mandate was to assist new countries of Central and Eastern Europe in holding free elections.

The early 1990s witnessed a post-Communist wave of parliamentary, presidential, and local elections, plus constitutional and other referenda. Countries asked basic questions: Who should vote? How are elections conducted? How are votes counted? How are election disputes resolved? ODIHR invited international experts from North America, Western Europe, and increasingly Eastern Europe, to training seminars for election officials in the former Soviet Union and nearby countries. The office sends election observers to countries like Albania, Bulgaria, Estonia, Georgia, Lithuania, Poland, and Romania. It reviews draft electoral laws and provides international commentary on the electoral laws of Albania, Bulgaria, and countries of the former Yugoslavia. In the West, election law is solidly established. Most basic questions about who can vote were settled long ago, but in the East, all this is new. Who can vote, what is acceptable political speech, who controls the electoral process— all are questions central in the political life of a new nation.

The office's elections role soon broadened in response to changing political demands. The number of CSCE member states increased with the breakup of the former Soviet Union and Yugoslavia. At the same time, states realized that free elections alone cannot guarantee democracy. A country must both demonstrate respect for human rights and cultivate a democratic infrastructure with independent legal institutions, free media, and respect for international human rights norms.

A Broader Role

CSCE's Council of Ministers, meeting in Prague in January 1992, expanded the Office of Free Elections into the Office for Democratic Institutions and Human Rights, making the office responsible for managing the "Human Dimension Mechanism," a rarely used means of resolving international disputes. Each participating CSCE state furnishes an official list of experts, upon whom the office may draw for missions to report on human rights problems. This is done by activating the Human Dimension Mechanism, which requires the support of CSCE member states. During 1992, the Mechanism was activated three times: first, by the United Kingdom on behalf of the European Community in relation to Serbia; second, by the same parties on Bosnia-Herzegovina; and third, by Estonia for a mission on its own territory, protesting Russian interference in its domestic affairs. It was not otherwise used in the two years I spent in Warsaw, although several countries talked about employing it. The "mechanism" sits on a shelf, waiting to be used.

CSCE's work is cumbersome; talks are long, results rarely dramatic. The organization cannot move beyond the political will of its sponsors, and international organizations are sluggish by nature. Preventative diplomacy requires patience in bringing parties together, perseverance in listening to their grievances, and persistence in seeking incremental solutions. This is not employment for those desiring quick, dramatic results. Peace-makers may be blessed, in the biblical image, but their place is rarely in the fast lane.

Cortese is short, with a squeaky high voice; elevator shoes do not add to his stature. His English is laced with phrases like "How may I say it. . . . They can go to the hell. . . . Exactly!" He describes himself as an old-fashioned ambassador, which means that, when we are trying to break into the closed countries of Central Asia with democracy-building programs, his approach is to fly across five time zones and hold a cocktail party for the resident diplomatic community and some local officials. Superb at flattering women, he listens intently to men, then does nothing. He arrives at the office promptly at 11 A.M. each morning and begins calls to Rome, which extend past noon. Rarely does he put an idea on paper. His modus operandi is a long, circuitous conversation, elliptically approaching the topic under discussion. "I only half agree with you" means the discussion is dead. Sitting in a dark office lit by two small desk lamps against the Warsaw dark, he moves documents among four foot–high piles, as there were no files in the office's first few years. Jack Zetculic, his American deputy, says, "We fulfill each others' national stereotypes." Cortese's conference strategy is to outtalk the opponent; a sign of victory is the other side wearily vacating the room while the director sits there, as loudly in command in late afternoon as in the morning.

The Polish staff he assembled is not strong, with three exceptions. Jacek Paliszewski, an elegant Polish ambassador from an old family, is both energetic at work and politically astute. Irek Stępiński, a former Polish airline's chief purser, pays excellent attention to administrative details. Katarzyna Syrzycka, a skilled and patient receptionist, fields, in several languages, nearly inaudible calls from telephones in various parts of the former Soviet Union. Some of the remaining staff will do anything for the boss and little for anyone else. Poles are used to formal hierarchies, lavishing flattery and attentiveness on the person on top and providing no support to anyone else unless forced to. I suppose that such work habits began in the dark periods of Communist rule, when coworkers couldn't be trusted and it was preferable to sabotage an office rather than make it a productive unit. Work habits are sloppy; since Cortese does not arrive in the office until late morning, there is a long settling-in period when tea is sipped, relatives called, and want ads scanned for cars and apartments. "I'm too busy" is a frequent response if a Polish support staffer is asked for aid. The director's secretary told Cortese's successor, Audrey Glover, "Call me any time, day or night." But when I called from the field to see if there were any messages, "Your secretary isn't here, call her tomorrow," the same woman replied briskly.

Office practices were both rigid and anachronistic. The budget office's Polish manager once told me that an American bank transfer statement was not valid because it contained neither a signature nor an official stamp. Signed, stamped bank statements disappeared with green eye shades and roll-top desks but remain important to Central European institutions. The office manager is a former Orbis tourist guide, the cashier a pastry waitress from the Bristol Hotel. All these staff members were hired by Cortese just before a generation of computer-literate young Poles, high on skills and hungry for jobs, came on the market. On those rare occasions when we can get him to focus on management problems, Cortese's favorite phrase is "I am shocked to hear this," his tone resembling that of a 1940s film maitre d'hôtel who has just learned that the band has canceled moments before Fred Astaire and Ginger Rogers are about to perform.

The director is gone much of the time, leaving me to develop the Rule of Law program, for which I am grateful. Unable to obtain a list of priority themes or countries from him or to secure agreement on the subsequently prepared list, I conclude that the most important task we can accomplish with limited resources is to help countries with writing their constitutions and training judges to be independent, professional jurists. Since most of these countries come from a civil law tradition, I form three-person teams to visit countries requesting help. Experts include a Polish judge, someone who has been through the refiners' fire of Communism; a Spanish, German, or French jurist, steeped in the civil law heritage, and an American or British judge, representing the authority of a sitting judge who must continually decide cases promptly, independently, and with integrity. Sometimes countries approach us with requests and others come from CSCE field missions, but most originate from my following the currents of judicial change in member countries and buttonholing ambassadors or ministers at international gatherings and soliciting their help in arranging programs tailored to their countries' needs. If I wait, like a traditional, cautious international bureaucrat, for business to come my way, these Warsaw years will be spent reading the *International Herald-Tribune,* drinking coffee, and watching the slow change of seasons from the office window.

No budget ever is given me for Rule of Law programs in my two years in Warsaw. Extrabudgetary funds come from Western countries such as Germany, Great Britain, and the United States (through its USAID democratization program); sometimes there is money left from the larger international meetings that are ODIHR's stock-in-trade. However, our expenses are minimal, as our American federal judge participants take no honoraria and travel on Russian internal airlines is cheap.

An Office in the Tower of Babel

Often I am asked, "What is it like to work for CSCE?" The organization's general indifference to substantive democratization programs in the conduct of its resident missions, and the growing bureaucratic ossification of its Vienna headquarters, make working for CSCE like having an office in the Tower of Babel. I discover this image one day in Vienna, after a particularly frustrating morning at the Hofburg Palace, where CSCE is in session. Across the courtyard is a Vienna art museum with its roomful of Breughel's paintings, including the "Tower of Babel." The Tower (Genesis 11:1–9) was a commendable idea at its inception: such towers once were powerful centers for trade, culture, and military strength. Nevertheless, the ruins of ancient Babylon's ziggurats suggest that such institutions did not last long. "The Lord dispersed them from there all over the earth, and they left off building the city" (11:8). Human pride caused the institution's destruction in the biblical account; the contemporary international reality is more complex but contains some of the same ingredients.

Confusion is endemic in international affairs, a component of almost all international organizations, with their political confusion of tongues. The successes of the Organization on Security and Cooperation in Europe (OSCE) are and will remain modest, unless there is a demonstration by the sponsoring nations of political will to identify and solve specific international problems.

A House on Zakopianska Street

Two months after arriving in Warsaw, we move into our house, a two-story semidetached stucco dwelling with finished attic and basement and a small yard. The owners, a Polish couple with a flower shop, received a ninety-nine-year lease on the property for a parent's services to the Communist party. The dark, high-ceilinged living room can seat six persons; as there is no dining room, a dining table is wedged into the lower stair landing. Our predecessors spent most of their time in the basement family room, a windowless bunker which we use as a storage room. The space reminds me—on those rare occasions when I enter it—of a World War II bomb shelter.

In Poland, security is a constant concern. On our house, there are four front-door locks, grills on all windows and doors, gate locks, and an internal alarm system. Until the embassy took these security measures, at least one American-embassy house was robbed almost weekly. Poland leads Europe in personal thefts and muggings. It is also high on vehicle thefts; at diplomatic parties, hosts routinely hire guards to watch cars and patrol nearby streets until guests leave. The American consul told us of spending an hour at a reception and returning to find that his car, with safety bar, had been towed away by a thief. Now it may be on its way to Russia in the back of a truck, covered with apples or potatoes.

Tigger claims the front terrace as his command post, providing a view of the street in front and the yard in back. A metal fence surrounds the property. On either side, older inhabitants fill garden space with piles of compost, wooden sticks, and old tires. Sections of a commercial car-washing machine, partly wrapped in heavy plastic, sit under a neighbor's apple tree. Some neighborhood houses are gloomy, with heavily curtained windows beyond chest-high weeds. Others are carefully painted, with well-maintained yards and flower gardens. At our street's end is a new house with a marble interior swimming pool; enough external lighting fixtures for a Saudi palace; a massive, multilevel living room; and a stretch limousine in the garage. Our gardener says it belongs to a Pole who owns five discotheques and married three different women. Next door lives the Guatemalan ambassador, a short, youngish woman who wears electric blue or green suits like the colors of birds on the state seal cemented above her embassy's front door. Sometimes she chats with us while walking her white-mustachioed poodle, but in the early evening she is all business. Tigger and I watch her being driven by, perched on a cushion on the mission Volvo's rear seat. She is a different person then, representing her country's interests at National Day receptions, looking solemnly ahead, as if rehearsing a démarche to the foreign minister.

In the morning, Tigger and I walk past a tiny rusted Polish Fiat, small as a circus clown's car, covered with plastic pails of large purple and white lilies, which engulf the driver who sits there much of the day, selling them for a dollar a stem. Down the street, a Mercedes-Benz is filled with sports shirts, piled high everywhere but on the driver's seat. At a vegetable and fruit stand, strawberry season is over, and red raspberries and gooseberries are almost gone, but containers of cherries and blueberries are stacked high. Warsaw is a city of small family-run stores, often overlapping in their merchandise. Within our half-hour walk are two watch and clock repair shops, three shoe repairmen, two hair dressers, a health food store, five grocery stores, two bars, and two stationery shops. The retail scene is reminiscent of America in the 1950s but is changing quickly. Consumer demands result in a reconfiguring of neighborhood stores all over the city.

Returning from a pleasant summer morning's walk, I find water cascading downstairs into the living room. Like the gravediggers in *Hamlet,* the embassy plumber and his assistant discuss what went wrong. The plumber's signature dress is a tight-fitting blue narrow-brimmed cap tilted upward like Moe's in *The Three Stooges.* Replacing a defective toilet bowl, they failed first to shut off the main water tap, hence the deluge. One plumber, as he departs, breaks the garage-door lock carrying the old bowl through the unopened door.

The Garbage Truck's Arrival

July 27: Each second Tuesday morning the garbage truck arrives, a crucial link with Warsaw's municipal services. Every residence is allotted three cylindrical metal cans, and the garbage men refuse to carry away anything not placed in them. I had several bales of waste paper from our move.

"Will they be on time?" I ask the newspaper vendor at our neighborhood kiosk. "Who knows," she answers, like Mother Courage, "It depends on the crew. It can be any time from 8 A.M. to noon." Garbage truck technology reflects 1950s socialist engineering: cans fit a hitch at the truck's rear, crank slowly to the top, and are dumped. A large metal bin detaches like a lifeboat from the trucks rear and two assistants push it through the neighborhood. Meanwhile, the truck chugs ahead, spewing smoke and clanking pistons, the driver descending at intervals to load a few cans or salvage empty bottles or discarded furniture.

When they reach our gate one worker remarks, "Much work," the other hauls boxes. In a hurry, they remove the boxes that face me, waiting for a gratuity. I dump out a handful of bills, worth a few dollars. One worker bows like a Hapsburg peasant, the other counts the bills and says, "Not enough." I add more notes with multiple zeros. Large plastic bags hang from the truck's sides containing empty beer bottles, clothing, and shoes. The garbage-men greet two chimney sweeps, clad in black uniforms with large silver belt buckles and coiled heavy metal wire lines strung over their shoulders, carrying long feather brushes.

Berlin

August 20: It takes eight hours to drive from Warsaw to Berlin, six of them in Poland. Main Polish roads have only two lanes with wide edges. If you pass a truck, it or the vehicle in the other lane should pull toward the side, allowing you to pass down the middle. Huge German trucks, horse-drawn farm wagons, speedy French and Italian cars, and tiny Polish Fiats, propelled by motors that sound like washing-machine motors, all plug along on the same highway. Cows graze on the road's edge; old men bicycle precariously along it, while villagers dressed for Saturday evening outings walk, their iridescent polyester fabrics bathed in exhaust fumes. At intersections, enterprising youths approach stopped cars to clean their windshields and lights. Near the border, roadside vendors sell Polish apples, onions, and mushrooms, as well as piles of garishly painted plaster gremlins and trolls, including an elf with a black patch over one eye. At the border, it takes cars an hour to cross, but trucks from Russia, Iran, and Bulgaria wait a day or longer, their drivers sitting by the roadside in undershirts, endlessly smoking, sipping tea, and listening to cassette tapes of Central European or Middle Eastern pop music. On the other side, I pulled into a sprawling, clean, well-lit installation, believing that it was the German passport control. Instead, it was a newly opened gasoline station.

I crossed the Iron Curtain many times when we lived in Czechoslovakia in the mid-seventies, and the memories remain two decades later. Dog patrols are gone, as are the barbed wire and the grim-faced young soldiers in Eastern Bloc uniforms. Today remnants of the Berlin Wall are being plowed under. My most enduring memory of our visit is the Checkpoint Charley museum, a collection of Berlin Wall visuals and memorabilia. Tiny cars, the sort used in circus rides, were used to secret people across the border. Weapons and uniforms of the German border guards, like props from a martial opera, are lined up beside license plates and flags from the now-defunct DDR, the German Democratic Republic. I spend several minutes before a realistic painting of a Protestant pastor who burned himself to death in 1975. He sat beside his small Communist-era car, wearing billowing black clerical dress and the confident facial expression of a Lutheran at peace with himself and the world. Two posters were laid on each side of the pastor, but these were quickly confiscated by Communist police who made a specialty of watching public squares for demonstrators. The slogans were never disclosed; reportedly, one was "Stop corrupting our children."

Our final destination is the remains of the main American military base in Berlin. Paint peels from walls of the buildings, once impeccably maintained; lawns formerly green and manicured have gone to seed; barracks are empty; and an abandoned picnic table stands beside a vacated house. From these bases NATO troops were poised to defend Europe from the Warsaw Pact invasion that never came. (The Polish border is sixty miles to the east.) Off Clayalle, named for the allied commander of the immediate postwar years, Gen. Lucius Clay, is Salvador Allende Haus. A military barracks now forms part of the Free University of Berlin. It is unseasonably cold, and a recording of taps sounds in the autumnal air. The few remaining soldiers and families pause briefly. I recall visits we made to the bases with our two small children during 1975–78, when we lived in Prague. I regret that the American military presence, pivotal in Europe's security for the last half-century, is coming to an end.

September 1: All around Warsaw are large poster ads for an American cigarette, L&M. They project a confident, youthful, virile man in jeans, carrying an electric guitar, smoking, and wearing a Boston Red Sox baseball cap. The German printer flipped the negative; hence the baseball cap's *B* is printed backwards, like a Cyrillic letter. An American advertising executive, here to help the Poles, said that several hundred large Pepsi-

Cola ads were displayed around town the week before the company's president arrived to launch a new product. The logo was printed backward; a hurried last-minute effort was made to replace the posters.

Ruffles and Flourishes

September 3: Our neighborhood's tranquillity is ruffled by stirrings across the street at the Pakistan Embassy residence, a building vacant since the ambassador and his daughter left in May. Now three cars appear in quick succession. A scurrying servant in flowing white robe races from one and, like a minor character in an Elizabethan drama, fumbles in a pale green plastic bag through bunches of keys, until he finds ones to open the house and garage gates. Within minutes, twenty persons gather at the flagpole, two sections of local water pipe welded together. The acting head of mission and his tall blonde British wife are followed by a distinguished-looking elderly man who is either the embassy translator or the former Polish ambassador to Pakistan, as well as three nervous young Pakistani men in unpressed white nylon shirts, possibly students at a local technical university. I do not know the occasion; the Pakistan National Day is March 23.

From a small battery-operated tape recorder, martial music crackles. The ranking diplomat slowly raises the green and white flag, and hesitant voices sing the country's national anthem. Next the mission limousine speeds to the gate with boxes of pastries. Everyone goes indoors, lights are turned on in the reception hall for the first time in months, recorded Pakistani popular music blares from open windows, and laughter wafts from under the ornate blown-glass chandeliers. At noon, the lights are extinguished and guests depart. As in the last act of a provincial ballet, the residence resumes its lifeless air to await the new ambassador's arrival, probably after Pakistan's fall election.

September 8: We thread our way through early morning traffic to the American Embassy, a nondescript building flanked by two lovely eighteenth-century palaces. The previous American Embassy once was housed in such a palace, torn down in 1950 during a dispute between the U.S. State Department and the local government over finding more office space for the embassy. The State Department, never big on historic preservation, replaced the palace with a grim four-story building resembling a Chicago trucking firm's regional headquarters. Windows are covered with reflective surfaces which prohibit secret agents from photographing in.

Curled by the sun, the windows' protective film splits in leprous fashion. Inside, five officers crowd in rooms designed for single occupants. A Marine Security Guard station, its thick Plexiglas windows capable of withstanding a bomb attack, rises like a monument in the reception room's center. Several unmatched chairs, discarded when various offices were remodeled in recent years, complete the decor. Walls are hung with warped, faded travel agency photographs. An aerial shot of the Jefferson Memorial is bowed like a radar screen after hanging several years in direct sunlight. Edges of frayed black cloth hang down through concrete ceiling squares.

Outside, more than one hundred Poles gather at another entrance, seeking visas. The embassy issues relatively few tourist visas, since many recipients do not return to Poland but end up working in America. However, each visa applicant is allowed an interview, and many people drive long distances and sleep in cars to claim a place in line. On a hot day, I saw two people faint. Imagine what it must be like with a crowd of two hundred people huddled outside in winter. Later, the consul tells me that he has requested funds for a protective shelter for applicants; finally, despite severe budget cuts, the money is approved.

The Prime Minister Arrives

September 27: Clouds of acrid smoke float through the former Warsaw Pact Conference Center, where more than three hundred persons from fifty-three member states of the Conference on Security and Cooperation in Europe (CSCE) gather for a three-week meeting. A sound of distant guns. Poland's prime minister will arrive soon. I run to the door, as spectral figures in battle dress and signature Polish army square caps race with rifles through smoke and silver haze. It is not an invasion, but a film crew shooting a war movie.

Shortly after the smoke blows away, the prime minister's blue car and two escort vehicles arrive. Recently, a rural policeman fired at the prime minister's motorcade as it sped through a village late at night, so guards are edgy. Prime Minister Hanna Suchocka, in her early fifties, acting much like an in-charge schoolteacher, speaks on human rights. She did her doctoral work at Crakow University on institutional protections of human rights and was a well-known human-rights activist before leading the government. Her term as prime minister will end soon. She is rumored to be in line to chair the parliamentary constitutional commission when it forms next month or to be offered the constitutional tribunal's presidency.

The World Turned Upside Down

September 28: That evening I walk down Nowy Swiat (New World Street) in spitting rain to a Polish Foreign Ministry reception for CSCE delegations. I like to walk about Warsaw; its older parts hold endless interest. I watch the filming of a television commercial, with an attractive young couple drinking Polish fruit juices at a breakfast table laden with foods few homes will ever see. This summer Polish farmers lost most of their crops, because the European Community (EC) wouldn't let Poland's lower-priced fruit and juices into the European market. Poles are required by the EC to reform drastically their political and economic laws and institutions, in hopes of eventual EC membership. Meanwhile, the EC maintains an absolute iron wall prohibiting Polish agricultural products from entering its markets.

The Royal Palace entrance hall is poorly lit, its gray marble floor slippery, its stairs slightly uneven and covered loosely with heavy carpeting folding over stairs. Up curved stairs, I enter the throne room, which had been meticulously redone, and then the large Baroque reception room, where the deputy foreign minister says that it will be at least five years before Poland's bid to join the EC is acted upon. Meanwhile, Poland's security goal is to join NATO and stabilize its relationship with the West. "Just look at what is happening in Russia to see why this is important," he observes, speaking of the impasse in which President Boris Yeltsin dissolved the parliament, which in turn declared him no longer president. "What do we have to do to prove to the West that we have left the past behind us and are part of Europe?" he asks.

After an hour at the reception, I call Charlotte, telling her I am coming home. In descending the stairs, I think of how rainy it is and wonder which bus to take; suddenly, the dimly lit scene at the stairs' bottom turns quickly, and I am on the ground, looking at the ceiling. The bottom step's rug was loose, and I slipped on it. As my leather shoe hit the slippery marble floor, my feet slid out from under me, and my right knee twisted. Two thoughts flash in my head: First, I wrenched a knee and will be unable to attend the meetings laid on during the conference. Second and more important, I will get up immediately and walk away quickly, and all will be well. When I try to stand, it is as if electric wires are wrapped around my right knee with the current turned on. Meanwhile, people leave the reception, walking past me on the stairs. Some ask if there is anything they can do, while other delegates step by me as if I do not exist and am not sitting there on the bottom step of the royal staircase. An ambulance is summoned, and I am hauled away. Since I am too long for the small ambulance, I hunch my way up between the driver and his assistant. We move slowly through night traffic to the Ministerial Clinic, the country's best hospital, a relic of Communist times when free medical care was available to all, but quality care was accessible only to a few. "This is the hospital for the elite; I could never get into it," says one of our employees, who underwent a knee operation himself in June and must soak his knee each evening for swelling.

The ministry hospital is dark as Poe's House of Usher on the outside. Four people carry the pallet inside; there is no emergency room. We head toward the X-ray room, then to a small, oblong cell on the fourth floor. It is 9 P.M.; I am alone in a dark metal bed I cannot adjust. On the nearby table, just out of reach, is a small lamp with a forty-watt bulb. Into the darkness, like the lead *basso* of an opera company, strides the head of the anatomy department at Warsaw University's Medical School. He is a commanding figure with leonine mane and a voice to match. After a minute's poking about my knee, he announces, "Your right thigh muscle is detached from the knee; we will have to operate this week." Meanwhile, the American Embassy physician arrives and tells the Polish medical team, now three persons, that embassy policy requires that all medical operations, except emergencies, be done in London or the United States, where the State Department has long-standing hospital arrangements. A subtle war breaks out. The eminent Polish surgeons say that they are well qualified to perform the operation and that the hospital is adequately equipped for surgery. I will have to decide. Dr. Gary Penner from the embassy clearly conveys the decision. One of the Polish doctors draws Charlotte aside and explains the case in Polish, hoping that we will reconsider. It is a momentary dilemma for me; in three decades in the foreign service, I have always tried to use local institutions. Now the choice is over my right leg. My heart says Warsaw, my body London.

A Constitutional Interlude

I spend two nights and two days in the hospital, watching light patterns change on the beige walls and listening to a tape of Bach choral works on my portable tape recorder. Fortunately, the grim setting is changed into an intellectually exciting one. The Constitutional Tribunal's vice president, whom I had known before, is also a patient, assigned the room next to mine. He has a lengthy draft article for an international law journal on the evolution of Poland's Constitutional Tribunal and asks me to comment on it. We work on the manuscript from 7 A.M. to 1 P.M., then resume after lunch and a nap. He makes some excellent points, but English is not his first or second language. The court was founded in 1985, in the height of Communist times, and has steadily carved out a role for itself despite numerous restrictions on its power. There are twelve judges, all nominated by Parliament for eight-year terms, and six vacancies occur this year, including the posts of president and vice-president. The court presently is situated in an annex to Parliament, two judges to a room, and the courtroom is in a sealed-off corridor nearby. It will take over the spacious old Military Library next year, but first a total renovation is required.

Decisions of the Polish Constitutional Tribunal can be rejected by Parliament, although this rarely happens, and lower courts rarely appeal constitutional issues to it, although they have the power to do so. There is a Supreme Court, really an appeals court in Western terms regarding such institutions. Notwithstanding, the constitutional court has carefully carved out a role for itself; among the Central European courts, only its Hungarian counterpart has more influence. The Czechoslovak court was off to an excellent start when the country split. The heavily politicized Russian court was dissolved for its anti-Yeltsin activities; the Romanians and Bulgarians have little to show for their efforts.

In the middle of the day, Jack Zetkulic, our office's deputy director, arrives with a Big Mac and french fries, plus a chocolate milkshake, all much appreciated, since lunch otherwise was a scoop of mashed potatoes and cherry sauce.

London Bound

October 4: Departure from the hospital at 7 A.M. Since I will not be operated on in Warsaw, the Polish medical staff has lost interest in me. Exit is in a wheelchair navigated by the night porter, who is flummoxed when we reach the top of the ground-floor stairs. He gives me a look: "Well, what do you want to do now?" Fortunately, the embassy driver takes charge, stops two passersby on their way to work, and the four persons carry the wheelchair down to the embassy station wagon.

At Warsaw Airport, the attendant cannot figure out how to extend the wheelchair's leg rest. Our luggage is piled on one cart, with my leg on top; one attendant pushes the wheelchair while another pulls the cart, and we head toward international departures. Twice the cart separates from the wheelchair; pain shoots through my knee. I take command, directing the two porters with my umbrella. I am placed in the first row, aisle seat, my foot hanging into the aisle. Fortunately, I brought my British umbrella to the diplomatic reception, and it went with me to the hospital. I hold the handle above my foot, preventing any of the hundred entering passengers from bumping my leg. Most passengers thoughtfully avoid it; several elderly ladies with multiple bags plow toward me; I steer their packages off, using the umbrella like a hockey stick. An Australian says, "Teach you to play football on the Continent, mate."

October 6: After surgery I leave the hospital to stay in a nearby hotel for a week to watch for blood clotting or infections, neither of which develops. I feel fine. During the week, I watch television news with scenes of Russia's President Boris Yeltsin confronting the Parliament, which is barricaded in the same "White House" from which Yeltsin held out against a coup a year ago. The number of deputies still in the building dwindles from a thousand to a hundred. They deliberate by candlelight, since all power is cut. Barricades are erected, and angry young people throw rocks at inexperienced riot police. Pro-parliamentary forces, composed largely of Communist hard-liners, monarchists, and anti-Semites, are given a day to surrender weapons, after which they will receive pensions, government jobs, and other payoffs. Instead, the parliamentarians urge followers to attack the riot police and seize the television building and the mayor's office. After some hesitation, the army backs Yeltsin and counterattacks, routing the defenders and firing at the White House floor by floor with tanks.

I think of the seminar on federalism I am supposed to attend in Moscow next week and wonder if it is still on. (It is canceled.) The meeting is supposed to be carried on Russian television with Yeltsin in the chair, discussing a blueprint for Russia's constitutional future.

3

Warsaw, London, Tiraspol, Venice

October 15: At noon Dick and Mary Howard and I visit the law school for lunch with the deans. Dick is here for the CSCE talks, taking time off from the University of Virginia Law School to be part of the American delegation. We discuss how Poland's legal system and legal education are changing in the wake of Communism's collapse. New courses have been added in European community law, international commercial law, and human rights law. The deans are especially interested in the role of a development officer at an American university, how alumni associations are formed, and how gifts are solicited. Formerly funded entirely by the state, law schools now scramble for money like all other Polish institutions.

A 1920s Driveway

October 27: The owner of our house brings a new furnace to replace an aging Russian model and to correct a driveway problem. The garage and inclined exit from it to the street were designed in the 1920s, when cars were smaller. Our medium-sized Toyota car scrapes on both entering and leaving. I draw a diagram, the embassy maintenance chief backs the car in and out, plumbers gather beside one wheel, the furnace repairers beside the other, measuring and commenting. Tigger sits on the top step, supervising.

Sensing a discussion, laborers who have been doing pick-and-shovel work on the sidewalk gather at the incline's top. Various combinations of boards are tucked in place and hunks of concrete removed. The house's owner returns later with new designs and workers. The problem is never solved, and for the next two years our car's bottom scrapes each time we enter and leave.

All Saints' Day

November 1: A national holiday in Poland. Red lamps with candles are placed all over the city at monuments for the war dead; cemeteries are filled with candles, an eerie sight on a dark autumn evening. During the weekend, thousands of people visit graveyards, scrub tombstones, polish metal, and cart away debris, a final cleansing before winter's onset. Modest picnics and socializing at grave sites follow the work. Special buses are laid on for all three days, a time for Poles to commemorate the dead of both world wars and departed family members.

Count Kinski's Treasures
(A Fantasy)

November 10: As we walked the dog through the neighborhood, I noticed a large prewar carriage house at the back of one property. The residence in front of it, of red brick with a yellow brick trim, once had occupied a large lot, carefully laid out with garden and trees. Now the lot was divided into four irregular parcels of land, two of them sporting nondescript gray 1950s Communist-era apartment buildings. Meanwhile, the manor house had been rebuilt to house three families, one on each floor. It was reasonably well maintained, the various owners repairing the roof or windows when they had money. However, the carriage house was in poor condition. Roof tiles had broken loose, weeds grew high around the edges, and paint peeled from windows and door frames. Surprisingly, set amid the crumbling walls, there was one ground-floor window of recent German design, with tasteful curtains on each side. Inside were new Italian halogen lamps placed beneath old European paintings.

Suddenly Tigger chased a cat into the driveway, toward the carriage house. The cat leapt into a clump of ferns behind a green Polish park bench of wrought iron and wood. Standing next to the 1930s bench was a slender man of medium height, in his sixties, with alert eyes and a thin patrician face and Van Dyke beard—the sort of face that appears on

French bank notes. "I am Count Kinski," he said, speaking slowly, with a pronounced 1940s English accent. "It is a foul afternoon, worse than the Scottish moors this time of year." He seemed pleased with the topical reference, "Won't you come in for a cup of tea?"

The sitting room was small but elegant, everything placed as if by a museum curator who had installed the show twenty years ago. The count sat in what clearly was his chair; a stack of *Le Monde* and *Frankfurter Allgemeine* newspapers were piled high on the inlaid eighteenth-century Italian table next to it; an ivory recorder and lute hung from the nearby wall. A recent issue of *Point de Vue* was on the footstool, held in place by a magnifying glass; the count had been following his European relatives' activities when Tigger burst upon the scene. The dog now reclined on a dark red and blue Persian carpet.

"Fortnum and Mason's Earl Grey," he said matter-of-factly, placing Meissen cups in front of us and offering a plate of small anise cookies. For the next hour, we talked of Polish culture and politics. The count had known most Warsaw musicians and actors of the last half-century, and his political observations were grounded in local history. Of the current prime minister, he said, "His family worked on my father's estates in Silesia. They were earnest and hard-working but not very imaginative, like most peasants of that era."

We said our good-byes, but the count continued, "Allow me to offer you a *digestif*; it comes from my cousin's vineyards in Tuscany. Besides, you might enjoy our family gallery." He stood up and motioned us to follow him behind a curtain that I thought would lead to a storage room, but descended instead to a rickety circular staircase and a subterranean chamber. "In the nineteenth century, this was Warsaw's most famous brewery," he said, his voice dark and thin from below the ground. "My father's wagons delivered as far west as Berlin." With a heavy click, a period porcelain light switch was turned on, illuminating, through a prewar lighting system, a long display room with circular ceilings and forty-foot-high walls of meticulously laid brick. "The Communists did not know about this," he said, "They thought they had confiscated all our property."

Ahead of us in a long room, generations of Kinski art collections had been amassed. Filling one wall were Albrecht Dürer's *Annunciation* and a set of vestments for a long-departed Hapsburg prelate, embroidered in colors of rose and gold. Opposite them were several works by the Russian Constructivist artists whom Stalin purged in the 1930s, some paintings by French Impressionists, and a table bearing Italian gold candelabra (commissioned by the Czar of All Russia) and an autographed manuscript of two early Chopin piano works. We lingered over four Dürer etchings and two Miros. "My uncle was ambassador to Spain," the count explained, "before the bad times." Beyond the principal collection was a forest of antlers gathered from Kinski estates and enough metal suits of armor to outfit a palace guard.

It was all I could do to absorb a hurried first impression of the large collection, and to register a lasting memory of the early German paintings and etchings. Sensing this, the count said, "I hope you will come again." Charlotte and I thought of inviting him to our house but realized he was by now a creature of his setting. "I rarely go out anymore," he said, anticipating us, "except in the summer to visit our place near the sea."

I looked back as we left. His thin profile was sharp against the yellow light, and he lifted his right hand in a brief wave, much like that of the Queen Mother on the BBC evening news. On the way home, we talked of what we had seen. Charlotte thought of some names of current cabinet members upon whom she would like him to comment. Meanwhile, Tigger plodded onward as if nothing was unusual.

I was away the following week and did not walk the dog. When I did, the next Saturday, it was another slate-gray Central European day; skies would remain like this until March. A mist rose from the Vistula River, making shapes in the landscape indistinct. When I came to the Kinski property, I stopped and thought of entering the driveway. It was supper time; lights were illuminated in the kitchens of all three floors of the main house, and the government-built apartments stood like pillars in the mist. I looked for the carriage house, but there was no light, only indistinct darkness. The dog and I advanced slowly down the driveway. There was the green bench, the ferns and weeds, but no carriage house, only an outline and overgrown traces of the place where a building once had stood.

Remembrance Sunday

November 14: A cold, clear day. Remembrance Sunday at the British War Memorial in a park near us. There, in May 1944, a Liberator bomber went down, one of several that fell in the liberation of Poland. The planes took off from Italy, flew for ten or twelve hours, dropped their supplies or bombs, then flew on to airfields in Russia, as they did not have enough fuel to return to their original bases.

The British ambassador, a skilled musician, has rehearsed a Polish military band to play the hymns. Wreaths are laid by the Australian ambassador (on behalf of the Commonwealth), the Polish Air Force commander-in-chief, the mayor of Warsaw, and a representative of the Polish War Veterans' Association, a true military hero who the British ambassador's wife said has become "a bit of a fascist." The Commonwealth ambassadors are present, as are about one hundred Poles, many of them aging World War II veterans, and resident British citizens. The service, especially the prayer by a World War I poet, has a haunting beauty: "They shall grow not old as we that are left grow old: age shall not weary them, nor the years condemn. At the going down of the sun and in the morning we will remember them."

Washington in December

December 5: I am in Washington for a two-day American Bar Association symposium organized by John Norton Moore, a leading figure in advancing the rule of law globally. Moore, who has just negotiated the Iraq-Kuwait border dispute, is one of the first major foreign-affairs figures to view international political stability as linked to the development of professional, independent judiciaries in emerging democratic states. The conference honors Ambassador Max Kampelman, who until recently headed the American delegation to the CSCE talks and who for several decades was a leading human-rights advocate. I visited with him shortly before going to Warsaw. Now I share observations on the status of the judiciary in Central and Eastern Europe:

> Where is democratic reform in Eastern Europe, especially as it affects Rule of Law issues? Each country and each legal system is different, but three generalities hold. First, Eastern European countries have over half a century's forced exposure to the Soviet legal system, in which courts were the willing agents of state and party. In discussions with jurists of the region, it is useful to stop the conversation and discuss meanings, when words such as "federalism," "separation of powers," "independent judiciary," and "judicial review" are used. An American professor recalls a lecture he gave in Moscow, describing the Western concept of "Rule of Law," which the translator, without missing a beat, called "socialist legality." A Russian jurist asked me if judicial review was a magazine's name. My point is not to chronicle again the Soviet system's shortcomings, but rather to say that even those most eager to change it simply don't know how Western democracies work.

Second, the judiciary is held in low esteem in most of these countries. Poland's new minister of justice says that his top priority is finding a billion zlotys to raise judges' and prosecutors' salaries. A well-known Polish constitutionalist told me that her salary, as a full professor of constitutional and administrative law, was the equivalent of $1,000 a month; but her husband, a Supreme Court judge, made good money, $2,000 a month. Both are university teachers as well, and that contributes to their income. Forty-eight percent of any Pole's wages go as taxes toward social-welfare benefits and another 20 percent as a value-added tax. That leaves this couple with little disposable income. When I visited Moldova, the chief justice of the Supreme Court showed me his outer office with two electric typewriters of an earlier generation, neither of which worked. The minister of justice said, "We can sit here all afternoon and discuss what is wrong with the institution of the Soviet procurator, but if you want real human-rights laws to work, you must first have a judiciary with self-esteem and an information processing system to track cases and record decisions."

Third, there must be a major Western effort to equip these judiciaries to become the third branch of government. Presently there is a substantial Western effort at writing banking, privatization, and investment laws, safeguarding the place of labor, building parliaments, and strengthening presidencies. There is also prolonged debate about individual rights, minority rights, and a panoply of social rights, ranging from the right to work to the right to a clean environment. Commendable as these initiatives are, they risk becoming proverbial houses built on sand, unless an independent judiciary is established so that it may function, first, as the arbiter between the executive and legislative branches, and, second, literally as the conscience of a nation.

I believe that the battle will focus on the role of the constitutional courts of the former Soviet Union and Warsaw Pact. The fate of these courts will be, *mutatis mutandis,* an index of the extent to which democratization catches hold in these countries.

As these courts emerge, we ask, what sorts of personnel will equip them? What terms of tenure and remuneration will they be given? Will their opinions be binding or advisory? Will they represent a supreme court to which lower courts' decisions are appealed? Will individuals have access to all levels of the judicial system? Or will the court's role be restricted to being a prestigious but relatively powerless body, along the lines of the French *Conseil consti-tutionnel?*

January 4, 1994: As I wait for Warsaw's No. 117 bus for the morning ride to the office, a greasy container for french fries, laced with globs of colored condiment, falls past my face. I look up to the leafless branches above, where a crow is visibly disturbed at losing his snack. He flies down to the ground and circles the container, but, finding me a threat, he refuses to pick it up until we board the bus.

The "Tiraspol Six" Murder Trial

January 10, 1994: Political trials were a feature of the Central European judicial landscape in Communist times. Last summer, the traditional Communist leaders who held power in the self-declared Dnister Soviet Socialist Republic orchestrated one such trial, held in a factory theater. With Professor Andrzej Rzepliński, a skilled human-rights advocate who monitored over two hundred trials in Poland, I head for Chisinau, Moldova, and for Tiraspol, capital of the "Dnister Soviet Socialist Republic," a sliver of land that once was part of the Soviet Union. Last summer, six Moldovan citizens were tried in Tiraspol for terrorism and murder; on December 9, 1993, one received a death sentence. The others received prison sentences of from two to fifteen years. Every aspect of the trial was flawed, from a botched investigation to human-rights violations, from misapplication of the law to turning the whole event into crude political theater. Our purpose is to examine the trial documents, talk with participants, and negotiate reopening the entire procedure.

Members of the Ilascu group, sometimes called the "Tiraspol Six," were arrested in Transdnistria between May 29 and June 5, 1992, and charged with antistate propaganda and the politically motivated assassination of two midlevel local functionaries. The timing of the arrests coincided with armed hostilities between the two regions, as several hundred civilians were arrested and many troops and civilians on both sides were killed. The conflict did not cease until July 21, when Moscow sent in troops to end it.

Although the defendants were arrested in May and June 1992, the trial was not held until April 21, 1993, almost a year later. It adjourned immediately, as most defendants had no attorneys. Originally, all defendants other than Ilascu acknowledged their guilt, but most retracted, pleading coercion. Ilascu remained unrepentant, saying that the trial was rigged, the court illegal, and the process a farce. Several international human-rights groups monitored the trial, and for a while it received major media attention throughout Europe.

All six defendants were Moldovan citizens arrested in Transdnistria. All lived on the Dnister River's east bank. Two murders were committed, but the murder weapon was never found, forensic evidence was never produced, and witness testimony was contradictory. A member of the Transdnister militia was planted among the group, a classic Soviet-style *agent provocateur* who later confessed to everything. Two years later, after his release from jail, the agent, Vladimir Garbuz, stated publicly that the trial had been rigged and the evidence against Ilascu planted. Then he sought refuge for his wife and himself in the local Russian army headquarters, asserting, "My life won't be worth anything outside." Confessions were extracted from defendants through drugs and beatings. The trial was held in a factory auditorium, with the prisoners placed in cages, as is the custom with capital punishment trials in the Baltic states. Workers were brought in to demonstrate support for the government. Constant catcalls between defendants and audience contributed to a circuslike atmosphere. At intermissions, a cheap red cloth curtain was drawn across the stage. It was poor theater, the breakaway republic's stab at a show trial.

Across the Dnister River, an hour's drive east from Chisinau, Transdnistria is a rich local agricultural region that also is the site of the most concentrated Russian industrial development in Moldova. Today, 60 percent of the country's electrical energy comes from a huge dam in Transdnister territory; many factories are here, as is commercial agricultural land. A zone one-fifth the size of Moldova, it is the country's economic center. The Transdnister region borders on Ukraine and is largely Russian-speaking, but it has sizable Moldovan enclaves as well. Transdnistria is ruled by a handful of old-line Communists who were imported to run its institutions long before independence. They are not drawn from the local Russian-speaking population and have no popular support, in part due to misadventures such as failing to change the Russian rouble when Moscow did and so flooding the country with worthless currency from elsewhere in the Russian Federalism.

This political oligarchy is propped up by a Russian military presence, the once-elite 14th Russian Army, defender of the empire's southern flank against the NATO invasion that never came. Today, the 100,000-person force has been reduced to 10,000 soldiers, but it receives rations for a considerably larger body, ensuring the good life for its troops.

Having been scheduled to withdraw on January 1, 1994, it shows no signs of leaving. Its current leaders, a politically ambitious general, Alexandr Lebed, and a colonel who has resided in the region for twenty-five years, have been openly feuding on cable television with the Transdnistrian leadership, accusing the latter of corruption and such excesses as running around the small town of Tiraspol (235,000 persons) with three bodyguards each and spending scarce money on television sets, VCRs, and stereos. (A television set was the main status symbol in the offices of several officials we visited, although the only programs most could receive were those of the local cable channel and dreary transmissions from Chisinau, Kiev, and Bucharest.)

Into this cauldron leaped Ilie Ilascu, a loud, articulate, charismatic, and unyielding advocate of reunion with Romania. Moldova's president, Mircea Snegur, Ilascu termed weak and incompetent, someone who should be immediately replaced. Ilascu viewed the Transdnistrian leader, Igor Smirnov, as corrupt and lacking in a legitimate claim to power. Whatever their differences, both leaders found Ilascu a thorn in their side; although housed in a Tiraspol jail under a death sentence, he became a leading candidate for the new Moldovan parliament on the Christian Democratic Popular Front ticket, a small but vocal pro-Romanian party. He won the election but two years later remained in jail; in his absence, his photo was placed on his parliamentary desk. Ilascu's attorney also was elected to parliament but declined to take his seat until his client was freed.

Traveling to Chisinau

Getting from Warsaw to Chisinau isn't easy. Our 8 A.M. departure is delayed while the plane changes tires. We spend six hours in the fog-enshrouded Budapest airport, where someone breaks into my suitcase and steals my indispensable Swiss army knife and an ankle weight used for postoperative leg-strengthening exercises, leaving an inexpensive Swiss watch with broken band in its place. The Air Romania flight from Budapest to Bucharest is filled with people and luggage, for few Eastern Europeans will voluntarily check their bags. The meal of cold fried meats is so unappetizing that many passengers simply hand it back untouched. The odor of body sweat is strong in the overheated plane, unfiltered Eastern European tobacco smoke stronger still. Hostesses are courteous, graciously offering plastic cups of warm orange drink and mineral water as if it is tea time in an old Empire hotel.

At Bucharest airport, a taxi driver in a leather jacket tells us that he is from the Intercontinental Hotel. I ask for identification; he points to a lit sign, "Intercontinental Rent-a-Car," and says the fare to town is one hundred dollars. Meanwhile, my Polish colleague finds a ride for ten dollars; we thank the first driver and tell him we won't require his services. The infuriated driver yells at other taxi drivers not to take us. Most fear him, but one defiantly drives us into town in a rickety grease-and-mud-spattered Russian car with no lights. At the driver's recommendation, we switch from the expensive Intercontinental Hotel to the cheaper Ambassador. As we hand the driver his fare, the chauffeur who originally accosted us at the airport stops in back of our taxi and tries to grab our driver's keys, identification papers, and money, but our driver speeds away instead. To the extent that national airports are an index of a country's order and stability, Romania has more than its share of problems.

The next morning at breakfast (a selection of cold meats), four guests and six waiters watch color-washed music videos projected with a mirage-like lens onto a wavering screen. A police film follows, the Romanian translator narrating in a monotonous voice, rising one note from time to time for dramatic effect. Nearby, an elaborate Italian coffee machine hisses steam when its handle is lowered. Boiling water then drips into a tiny cup, which the waiter carries to a nearby table, where he spoons in instant coffee.

A swarm of baggage clerks in uniforms denoting various ranks hover over our bags and load them into a taxi, which has a flat tire in the next block. Another car arrives with a repair kit, and we rattle on to Bucharest's domestic airport. Our flight to Moldova is never posted on the chalk-written blackboard; a reservation clerk nervously winds the handle of a 1930s black telephone and shouts into it, as if to the earth's center, seeking information. Since the airport is cloud-covered, we watch a pack of wild dogs, debating which dog is the leader.

Our flight to Chisinau is by way of Iasi, a sleepy Romanian border town, once the capital of Bessarabia, part of the Greater Romanian Empire. Guards mount a World War II antiaircraft gun, and a freezing soldier surveys us from a foxhole across the runway, in case our aging Russian turboprop plane should carry invaders. Again a pack of wild dogs roams about, seeking scraps. It takes an hour to clear customs; each piece of luggage is jammed into a small wooden box, where an inspector examines it through an ancient fluoroscope. Then we continue on the twenty-five-minute flight to Chisinau.

We stay at the Sebaco Hotel, a clean, modern place whose hall and lobby lights are turned off most of the time to save electricity. There is a small hotel swimming pool and sauna, costing fifty dollars an hour. "Who uses it?" I ask the receptionist. "Some of our citizens," she replies. In contrast, I obtain an excellent haircut for five dollars, including tip. I mention these figures to show the extreme differences in prices encountered. For example, lunch at the parliamentarian's club was under two dollars for three persons. I had vegetable soup with fresh dill, and a "corn mix," which would translate in English as "grits."

January 11: Pitch dark by late afternoon, Chisinau's streets and sidewalks are muddy, streetlights rare. Silent crowds of twenty or so persons gather at bus stops; sixty people are crowded into a bus holding thirty. Arms akimbo, heads pushed over other peoples' shoulders, the effect is of humanity squeezed into a garbage compactor. Since it is dark and the pavement is uneven, we walk carefully about the streets, past an art gallery lit by two fluorescent lights. Inside, numerous Socialist Realist landscapes sell for thirty dollars each.

CSCE's Moldovan mission is one of several long-duration missions set in troubled spots. Its purpose is to defuse crises and alert the fifty-three-member states to rising ethnic, political, and military tensions. Increasingly, we ask missions to undertake Rule of Law activities, such as strengthening democratic institutions or monitoring elections, but most personnel are traditional diplomats or military, to whom the democratization aspect of international relations is foreign.

On our first evening in Moldova, we dine in Chisinau's second-best hotel. (The third-best hotel's heating system broke during our stay there, and guests were moved to spare rooms in other hotels.) The acting head of mission, a Polish diplomat, Son-of-Stalin in outlook, is our host. He upbraids the waiter for opening the one-dollar bottle of local wine before he arrives, telling us, "In my opinion, they got what they deserved. I read the judge's sentence; they were terrorists and murders, I think that's pretty clear." We make a mental note not to ask him to assist us with negotiations for a new trial. Poland sends a person to staff each CSCE mission. Some are skilled diplomats, while others do little beyond collecting salaries.

Tiraspol

January 14: An hour and a half's drive eastward to the grim Russian garrison town of Tiraspol. A gray day, with light rain, a constantly chilling wind, and bone-numbing cold. A woman leans against a tree, reading a prayer book with recently purchased store spectacles, while four cows graze. Two peasant youths, with Russian fur hats and axes on their shoulders, head toward the woods, characters from Brueghel's painting of hunters in winter. The land is poor, the wintry landscape barren except for an occasional shrine over which some local tinsmith has fashioned a wondrously elaborate metal canopy bearing fish, birds, and geometric designs that would be the envy of a Victorian maker of gingerbread trim. At water's edge, the breakaway republic's military police stop us, then allow us to cross a rusting iron bridge. Over it flies a hand-sewn local flag, the old green-stripe-on-a-red-field flag of the now-defunct Moldovan Soviet Socialist Republic.

Nearby stands a Russian tank, its turret pointed skyward, a memorial to the war dead. Other monuments: an early Russian jet fighter in a park, the largest imaginable red granite statue of Lenin in flowing cape, and a red star atop an aluminum shaft to which, incongruously, an icon of the Blessed Virgin Mary is affixed. Riding around Tiraspol is like a trip behind the Iron Curtain in the 1960s.

At the Friendship Hotel, the clerk asks if we are part of an agricultural delegation, for few unofficial guests ever enter the three-story building. I am given a two-room suite smelling of fresh wallpaper paste. Nearby rooms contain rows of small beds, like factory dormitories. Bathroom water is cold and coffee-brown; a maid hastens in with a used soap bar from the next room. The bedroom is freshly papered with pink Russian flowered paper and matching plastic curtains. Empty Western perfume and cosmetic bottles, one named Nuit d'Amour, line a cabinet shelf. An empty Russian chocolate box decorates each room; mine is a ballet scene from *Romeo and Juliet*. Downstairs two hundred teenagers gather for a dance. Air in the pale blue, dimly lit hall reeks of youthful sweat and cheap perfume. I am awakened periodically by loud lovers' quarrels, plus a phone call from a melancholy woman asking if Rolfie has returned to Germany.

Breakfast is in the adjoining cafeteria, not managed by the hotel. A concierge in three layers of black sweaters has the only key between the two rooms. Slowly and authoritatively she marches, holding the large key, allowing all to savor her power. Doors are locked between the two sections because a lobby vodka bar opens at 9 A.M. and drunks will wander about the hotel, she tells us.

Breakfast cutlery is submerged in warm water; the choice is meatballs and pasta or chicken and pasta, sweet local tea or fruit compote. As in many such establishments, workers outnumber guests. The ground floor contains a door guardian, a floor guardian, a cloakroom attendant, and a dining room guardian in a blue hat with a wide yellow band, who moves between tables trying to sell fresh oranges.

Since the local water is undrinkable and the hotel has no mineral water, we stop at an unlit store on the town's outskirts, where several hundred gallon-sized jars of cloudy fruit juice are piled in green wire baskets. Bread is sold in a corner of the warehouselike building, while in another are displayed plastic dolls recently imported from Russia. The mechanical painting machine missed the facial features on some by a half-inch, making the dolls look like accident victims. More than a hundred women crowd in a line for fresh eggs; no-one buys the fruit juices. I select a gigantic bottle of strawberry-apple blend, sugary and filled with pulp. It is the only liquid we will have in the hotel for the next week.

In the evening, we walk about Tiraspol's main street. Soft rain falls, and a harsh wind blows from the east. Rzepliński takes us up to the twelfth floor of a new apartment building on the main street. Its upper floor halls are dark as underground passageways. Entrance and hall lights do not work; the main door is ripped off; drunks stagger about; someone has urinated in the elevator. Within five years the building will be uninhabitable. "How can you have any respect for individual justice or dignity," Rzeplinski observes, "when you treat people like this? This is Communism's dehumanizing side."

During the next two days, we speak with the president and secretary of state of the nonexistent republic, the chief justice of its Supreme Court, and—for seven hours—the defendant's lawyer. We are scheduled to meet with the procurator general, the country's chief legal officer, who cancels. His father has died in Moldova near the Romanian border; since there is a warrant for his arrest in Moldova, he can not attend the funeral but watches it on videotape and sends word, "I don't care if they kill Ilascu." Several months later, the procurator himself is gunned down, reportedly for investigating a local Mafia gang.

The weather is bleak, the air cold; we huddle in our rooms most of the weekend. Across the street is the four-story local KGB building, two floors of which next year will become the Supreme Court. A perky little dog sits outside the main door, ignored by people entering and leaving, including the local militia in hallmark large leather coats and carefully trimmed mustaches. Suddenly the dog wags its tail furiously; an elderly woman leads it to a small pine tree and, from a cloth sack, dumps pieces of stale bread and a jar of leftover slops, which the dog consumes as the woman walks slowly away in a different direction.

"Doom Cathedral": The Tiraspol Court

January 14: The secretary of state (the country is recognized by no-one) is a roly-poly little man who once taught Spanish Empire history at the local university and spent two years in Cuba, reportedly as a KGB agent. Like the chief justice of the Supreme Court, his office is equipped with television set and VCR. The secretary keeps a toy plastic airplane and truck beside his desk. He tells us, "We have an ability to get ourselves into problems but not to get ourselves out of them. That is why we are interested in your report and the possibility of a retrial in a neutral country or in bringing neutral experts here."

Our next stop is the Supreme Court building, two floors of a small research institute on the town's edge. Outside, on the building's wall, Russian graffiti has been painted out, but English words remain: "Doom Cathedral," "Anathema," "Paradise Lost."

The Chief Justice

Inside the research institute, we edge sideways past ten huge rolls of newsprint stored in the lobby and climb to the fourth-floor chief justice's chambers, a medium-sized office decorated with a three-dimensional colored photo of Red Square, complete with hammer-and-sickle flag flying over the Kremlin. No "new Russia" here. Olga Ivanova is a former civil judge on the Moldovan Supreme Court. A few years ago, Moldova adopted one of the harshest language policies of any former Soviet republic, requiring all government employees and officials who speak Russian to learn fluent Moldovan within five years. Many officials returned to Russia or took jobs in the breakaway republics. Ivanova comes from a military family. Her father was a Russian Army pilot; her husband, who since has left her, retired from the Russian Army and joined the Transdnistrian Battalion, the local armed force. Not a happy person, Olga rarely sees her children and says that the trial has cost her her health and given her bad dreams. At age forty-two, she says, "life is over." During the noon hour she writes poetry; over lunch she crafts a poem for the head of the Council of Europe's legal office, seated opposite her. We find her a cunning and headstrong person, not a commanding judicial intelligence. Although we sometimes work ten to twelve hours a day at the court, she is there all the time, offering us brandy, chocolates, and strong coffee.

We want to read the trial documents, but the chief justice stays in the room and continues a rambling monologue. Since Professor Rzepliński reads Russian and can follow the handwritten trial reports, I carry on the conversation. I ask how many lawyers there are in Tiraspol; she doesn't know. How many civil and criminal cases does the court try each year? She sends an aide to find out. What does she think of events in Moscow? An evasive answer. At noon the supreme court's entire staff is brought in for an unannounced discussion. Three Romanian journalists join their ranks. One, wearing a large badge urging restoration of the Romanian monarchy, kneels down and makes the Orthodox sign of the cross to emphasize a point. Court employees say they left Moldova because of the harsh language law. They have questions about the American judicial system; one asks about "Illuyshia," Alaska.

The Defense Attorney Talks

January 15: At 9 A.M., just as we leave for court, Ilascu's attorney, Ion Voznian, appears. We looked for him the previous day at his country house on Pushkin Street in a nearby village. A blue wooden dacha, one of a thousand such buildings on postage-stamp–sized plots, is his home. Inside is a large room with a concrete floor, lit by a dim bulb. Three carefully made beds are tucked against a wall, a table is set against the other wall. Several stacked crates of unpacked office furniture fill the room's center. The attorney, we learn, had gone to Chisinau to obtain medical tests on his daughter.

Of medium height, thin and trim, with an alert face and manner, Voznian has seen a lot of life. During the Communist era, he came to Tiraspol because the Chisinau law school assigned its graduates to state jobs. Voznian was named attorney for one of three large factories, but the factory already had a lawyer, so he took a job as an investigator with the state militia, where he stayed for ten years. When he left, they put his picture on the wall of Honest Militiamen and asked him to stay. Instead, Voznian joined a state lawyer's cooperative with nineteen attorneys. (There are no lawyers in private practice.) Criminal law was his specialty; there is a policeman-in-plain-clothes quality to his bearing. He said the Ilascu case brought both death threats and more clients. For seven hours we talk about the case, and the lawyer's enthusiasm never wanes. At one point we recess for additional documents, and he returns with the defense summary and apples from his garden. Although a successful attorney, he does not own a car and typed the twenty-two-page defense summation himself. At noon one day, he was told that his final presentation would be that afternoon; an extension was granted until 9 A.M. the following morning. The attorney worked all night but was unable to consult case documents. When he did, several days later, he found that page numbers had been changed, indicating that files had been tampered with after they were offered in evidence. The attorney is helpful to us in identifying court documents that had been added, or to which comments had been appended, without the knowledge of all parties, and in pointing out procedural errors. Just before we left Tiraspol, he came by our room with a small bag of his wife's homemade apple cakes.

Because the Council of Europe attaches importance to this case, the head of its thirty-person legal staff arrives in Tiraspol midway during our talks. A tired Danish barrister who spent thirty years with the council, Erik Harremoes retires next year. He is accompanied by Jiri Vogel, a Czech Eurocrat, a graduate of the elite Moscow School of International Affairs that trained up-and-coming Communist officials; now part of the Council of Europe's Political Directorate, he guides countries of the former Warsaw Pact in becoming democratic states. Suave in a Pierre Cardin blazer, today his conversation is about the comparative price of wine and vodka in various European capitals. When we speak about the difficulties of Eastern European life, it is like talking about race with a light-skinned American black who doesn't want to discuss the issue. The third Council of Europe delegate is a Dutch human rights law professor who looks like a hairy bear from a provincial zoo upon whom a full ashtray has been dumped. "I vant to read zum documents," he says earnestly; I hand him a folder, and he departs for the rest of the day.

"President" Smirnov

January 18: Our last Tiraspol meeting is with the country's self-proclaimed "president," a Lenin look-alike, in his fifth-floor office in the government's main administrative building. Originally from Central Asia, Igor Smirnov was director of a large electronics factory near Moscow before being sent south several years ago with a small handful of dedicated Communists to run party and government in this part of Moldova. His office contains a bank of heavy Russian phones, Tiraspol's only telephone answering machine, a fax machine, and, under the glass desktop, a colored card of Jesus Crowned with Thorns. Smirnov arrives late, accompanied by three bodyguards, a driver, a press secretary, and a camera crew from the local cable station. We decline to film the meeting or allow the press secretary to sit in on our talks, and we turn down requests for interviews and statements, since these are exploratory discussions. Smirnov is tall, balding, with a mustache and beard closely resembling Lenin's. Of the seventy pages of detailed notes I have of various meetings, the conversation with him is the most difficult to reconstruct, because he is a bully, parrying and thrusting in our exchange, adopting first an aggressive and then a passive manner, while chain-smoking Malibu cigarettes and glancing about the room with half-closed eyes as if playing a villain's role in a grade-B melodrama.

"Why are you here?" he asks repeatedly. "Yet you do not recognize our country."

We are here at the request of CSCE's chairman-in-office, I reply, and the secretary-general of the Council of Europe.

"Who sent you?" he keeps asking, hoping that we will say the Moldovan government.

"Over fifty nations are deeply concerned about due process of law being violated in the Ilascu case," I reply. "Public perceptions of what happened are not favorable to you. We cannot solve your wider political problems, but we can help you find a legal solution to this particular case." My proposal is this: if both sides agree, bring in an international investigating team and judges to reconsider the case, using Moldovan penal law. If the investigators do not find a case, defendants go free. If there is a trial, it will be held by an international three-judge panel in a neighboring country, all parties agreeing in advance to accept the verdict.

I try to keep the conversation on the Ilascu case, but Smirnov links it to broader political issues. "Where was the CSCE when several hundred of our young men were killed by the Moldovans in July 1992? I don't know whether to name a street after them or build a memorial. Why does the Pope of Rome write me about Ilascu when there are constant assaults on our people by the Moldovans?"

"I can understand what you say from where you sit, but perhaps you can see our position," I respond. "Basically, we can solve one problem which might contribute to reducing tensions in the larger picture."

Next I ask that Professor Rzepliński and Ilascu's lawyer see the prisoner to complete our inquiries. Smirnov says that he has reports of attempts planned on Ilascu's life; it is not possible to visit him now. "Professor Rzepliński has conducted several hundred such interviews and carries no weapon. Access to a client—in this case a prisoner in a controversial case—by an attorney is a bedrock fundament of a state governed by Rule of Law," I respond.

"All this will take time," Smirnov replies, continuing a cat-and-mouse game. The secretary of state hunches his shoulders and drops his head; everything he has agreed to just went out the window. It is clear that Smirnov will string out the case for whatever political capital he can gain. He ends the meeting. "There are some things we find attractive in your proposal and some things we find objectionable. You will have our response by Friday." He sweeps out of the room, followed by his young entourage, into the Tiraspol night. The response never comes. Smirnov declares a state of emergency the following day, suspending all legal rights and ruling by decree, squelching growing citizen discontent with his disastrous rule. He is a total fraud.

An unannounced meeting with the speaker of the Presidium of the Supreme Soviet follows, two floors below us in the government building. The ruling clique's only high-ranking member of local origin, he speaks only of the case's political aspects and asks that Russia be a guarantor of the process and that we include Russian judges. I say that we will note the proposal but that an old folk saying applies: "Too many cooks spoil the soup." We ask the speaker's secretary to make us two copies of our draft proposal; he copies them by putting the document in the speaker's fax machine and dialing his number twice.

By Tuesday our support system totally collapses. The Supreme Court's copying machine runs out of toner and CSCE's machine is rushed down from Chisinau, but the cable is sent in another car to the presidency. Our hard-working interpreter becomes ill. Instead of departing early, we leave at 8:30 P.M., encountering a two-car collision on the city's main street. Under the dim light, a crowd gathers. The dead passenger remains in one car's passenger seat, a thin gray scarf veiled over her face. Freezing spectators await the mortician. Fifteen minutes later, we reach the frontier, crossing the security zone at the region's edge, as nervous guards in Russian winter uniforms peer into our vehicle. The muddy, wet road is empty, the night landscape desolate. I am not cheered until reaching our Chisinau hotel, where two cages of birds at the bottom of the steps break into song, even if it is 10 P.M.

The Return: Romanian Interlude

January 28: Our return flight from Chisinau to Bucharest by Tarom Airlines is uneventful, except for the usual cumbersome step of unloading baggage and clearing customs at Iasi. It is so cold that guards at the anti-aircraft gun huddle together by a fire, not bothering to remove camouflage covering the ancient weapon. At Bucharest's domestic airport we are met by two cars and a suave, pipe-smoking Romanian diplomat, "Call me Joe," who spent thirty years as an Asian specialist and now has the Moldovan account as his sole concern. He gives what could have been a recorded tour as we crank into town, stressing museums and old houses while avoiding parts of the city gutted by the dictator Nicolae Ceausescu in his grotesque dream of destroying the old city and building a modern memorial to himself.

In the evening, the acting foreign minister has a working dinner for us in the ministry's guest house, attended by the Italian ambassador, representing CSCE, and the heads of the Foreign Ministry's legal and European departments. The foreign minister is short and cherubic, a former Romanian ambassador to Germany. He is confident of his views about Moldova, which formed part of greater Romania after World War I, when it was Bessarabia. Then the capital was Iasi, not Chisinau. Sometime between now and the eschateon, he begins, Moldova will return to the fold, and all will be well. (In the March elections, Moldova's pro-Romanian party lost most of its seats, and a public-opinion poll came out strongly against reunification with Romania.) The restored palace's dining room is decorated with dark, formal portraits and landscapes by deservedly obscure artists. The building is hot as a sauna; the cook and servants are attentive, serving durable local meats shrouded in cheese sauces; and the minister talks well into the second course, after which I review our discussions. We favor the Tiraspol government, he says, while the only acceptable solution is to turn the case over to the Moldovan Supreme Court now. No-one is recognizing the Tiraspol government, I reply, beyond acknowledging that six Moldovan prisoners are sitting in its jail, one with a death sentence. I add that, despite its unquestioned competence, the Moldovan Supreme Court is compromised because, sitting *en banc,* it issued several decrees condemning the proceedings. "Why not use another local court?" the minister suggests.

"Because there is no other local court. The Supreme Court sits as a court of first instance in murder cases, and there is no appeals procedure."

That morning while shaving, the minister says, he heard on Moldovan radio of our meeting with the Parliamentary Legal Committee chair. We gave no media interviews, I reply. "If I had told the Romanian media you were here, this courtyard would be filled with reporters," he notes.

As we walk toward our cars, the Moldovan desk officer engages us in "open-air conversation." He says, "Either you accept the Trans-dnistrian position or the Moldovans are not forthcoming."

"The Moldovans have not articulated a position," I reply; the acting minister of justice fell ill and could not meet with us. As for the Trans-dnistrian position, it is that the trial is over and the sentence delivered. We, however, hold that the trial must be reopened because of violations at every stage. We insist that international, neutral experts be brought in to conduct it.

As our ancient Romanian Ford rattles toward the hotel, our host becomes more vehement: "There can only be one position and that is to accept the authority of the Moldovan government in this matter," he says, arms shaking as the car hits a pothole.

"Keep saying that, and you'll continue to have six prisoners sitting in Tiraspol jail," I reply. "We are looking for a way out of an impasse that is both legal and acceptable to both sides." Rows of Romanian men fill the hotel lobby. The air is blue with smoke from unfiltered local cigarettes. Conversations are heated by small glasses of fiery local plum brandy.

In the morning, Foreign ministry officials drive us to the airport; we ask to see the marble palace Nicolae Ceaușescu had built for himself—the largest, ugliest structure of its kind in Europe, constructed at the end of a road supposed to be an eastern Champs Elysées. Its originator boasted that it could be seen from outer space. The palace now houses the local parliament and many other government offices as well. Always the spin doctor, Joe says, "Well, it's big and was built at quite a cost, but you can use it for a lot of things, eh?" Shortly after dawn, we pass a mud-covered Romanian Fiat chugging along the airport road, the car's windows covered with steam. Freshly baked rolls are piled window-high, filling the entire back seat and passenger's side.

"Look at that—modern, eh?" Joe points to the airport's marble floor under construction, as we sidestep a bucket catching water dripping from an electrical wire dangling from the ceiling.

Note: The Ilascu case will drag on for the next two years. The Tiraspol authorities make no moves to resolve the case, and Moldovans decide to settle it as part of the larger question of reintegrating the breakaway region into Moldova. Several of the convicted participants are released early. When Garbuz, the main witness against Ilascu, is released and recants his testimony, it creates a political bombshell. Still, the Tiraspol leaders will not release Ilascu. The Moldovans will not petition the Tiraspol courts, maintaining that the latter have no valid juridical authority.

A Mysterious Phone Bill

February 1: Each month our Polish telephone bill increases. It is now over a million zlotys, yet we make no international calls and only a handful of local ones, usually to order a taxi. We request a printout, but the phone company refuses, because the phone is listed in the house owner's name. He kindly seeks one for us, which takes a month. Ninety percent of the calls are to numbers unknown to us, most made in midmorning to a private number in Lodz. Our *pani* (maid) says that they are not hers; she only uses the phone to reach her husband now and then. When the embassy dials the Lodz number, the woman answering, of course, says she doesn't know anything about the calls, some of which were made when we were in Berlin. The phone company says that another party had tapped into our line. Recently the papers carried a story about a widespread scandal. Because of the demand for phone lines, telephone company employees sell lines privately to customers; billing appears on the original customer's account. Since computerized printouts are available on only a handful of lines, the scam is difficult to detect.

February 12: Perhaps the coldest day I have experienced since childhood. In the morning we visit the Jean Paul II art collection, four hundred works of European art given to the nation by a Polish couple who live in London. The Pole had been captured by Germans and Russians during World War II, escaping finally to England, where he became a wealthy chemical manufacturer. Well-intentioned but unschooled in art, the couple left the selection of these pieces to British auction houses, which took generous commissions and produced a handful of masterworks, many indifferent paintings, and some works of disputed authorship. The Polish guide is proud of showing them to us, saying, "Now we have a major Polish collection for our schoolchildren when they study the history of European art." The collection is hung attractively in a drafty old bank building with a huge, impossible-to-heat Italian rotunda. Sunlight streams directly onto several paintings.

February 10: "Fat Thursday" in Poland; everyone makes or eats doughnuts the Thursday before Lent. I walk down the main street, Nowy Swiat; several hundred people crowd in front of a building. What looks like a political demonstration is Warsaw citizens lined up in front of an old confectionery shop, Bikle's, for sugar-coated doughnuts. Since the dough-making machine has broken down, sales are rationed. After Communism's fall, several old tearooms and candy makers have reopened, giving an idea of what Warsaw must have been like during an earlier era.

To Venice

February 23: Morning flight from Warsaw to Venice via Rome. I have finally solved the Polish taxi problem by calling Wojtech, a driver whom we hired for the last two international conferences. He is prompt, pleasant, and honest. Warsaw taxi drivers are not regulated; one company has over seven hundred drivers working on commission. Wojtech belongs to a small company and does not get many calls. He owns his own cab and supports his wife and daughter. Although he does not charge for waiting, I try to be generous in tipping.

February 24: Meeting of the Venice Commission for Democracy through Law. Supreme or constitutional court judges, ambassadors, ministers of justice, and attorneys general from Europe and the awakening East congregate in the Renaissance Guild Hall of St. John the Evangelist, a huge meeting hall with marble floors and frescoed ceilings. The commission is a satellite group of the Council of Europe and is active in numerous law reform projects, such as producing commentaries on the new Russian constitution, the Latvian citizenship law, and the Georgian constitution, plus forming study groups on such topics as emergency powers or law and a market economy. We are cosponsoring a seminar with the Commission on Constitutional Courts, organized by the Romanian Court (which is anxious to advertise its successes).

The meetings are chaired by Antonio La Pergola, former chief justice of the Italian Supreme Court, a European parliamentarian who may be the next holder of a seat on the World Court. A dramatic personality, he plays well in a big hall. At each meeting, the Italian Foreign Ministry invites us to a different restaurant. Tonight we head out in a fog-enshrouded bus for an hour's drive into the interior, arriving for dinner at a place called La Columba (small bird). The restaurant must seat four hundred persons and have over two hundred citations on the wall, including pictures of the owner with various regional politicians, souvenirs of military units that dined there, and a picture of a late Pope, offering a personally inscribed blessing upon the establishment.

February 25: In the morning, we discuss the draft Georgian constitution, presented by a law professor who chairs the constitutional writing committee. Plagued with internal factions and pilloried by their large Russian neighbor, Georgians are doing the best they can in difficult circumstances. In the afternoon I walk along canals I have not explored before, a bit off the tourist route and more reflective of neighborhoods, where people are collecting vegetables, pasta, and wine for the evening meal. On the way back, I stand in front of the ruins of an eighteenth-century palace. The lower floors have boarded-up windows, but above are modern double-pane glass windows, warm lights, clean lace curtains, and the sound of flute and piano playing a Vivaldi concerto. I listen to a movement, but it is late afternoon and the chilly mist brings a bone-numbing cold, so I retire to a nearby cafe. Much of the town moves from one neighborhood place to another, sipping small cups of coffee, drinking endless aperitifs, and talking loudly with appropriate gestures.

Evening concert in a sixteenth-century church. Arrival by canal boat through the mist. Candles in each window and on each of the three ledges, a striking sight as the boat approaches from the Grand Canal, the way I suppose things were lit in Vivaldi's time. The musicians are young, skilled professionals; the program is Vivaldi, Bach, and Handel for flute, violin, cello, and harpsichord. Endless tuning of the harpsichord before the concert and at intermission, as the harpsichord quickly comes untuned in the cold and pops strings. I wear coat and gloves throughout.

February 28: A sharp exchange between Latvian and Russian delegates. Considerable tension exists between the two countries over the draft Latvian citizenship law. The document represents the collision of history with politics. Latvia, once an independent country, was forcibly incorporated into the Soviet Union on the eve of World War II. Stalin and his successors colonized it, giving its rich agricultural land to Russian settlers, packing Latvians off to Siberia, and requiring Latvians to give one in every ten apartments in Riga, the capital, to Russian military officers and their families.

The present draft Latvian citizenship law is "one person, one vote." It grants citizenship to all persons living within the country's boundaries, if they apply for it. However, only Latvian-speaking citizens can hold public office. Originally, Latvians were willing to grant citizenship to Latvian-speaking Russians. The problem is that there are sizable concentrations of ethnic Russians in several major towns; it would be easy for them to control the country if they won public office. At our meeting, the Russian delegate asks for complete participation by resident Russian citizens in Latvia's political life. The Latvian delegate answers by chronicling Russia's systematic repression of Latvia's political and cultural life during the long Russian occupation.

Adding to the situation's complexity is the ethnic Russian "resident noncitizens" who now are coming to foreign embassies for visas, presenting passports from a nonexistent state, the now-defunct U.S.S.R. About 41 percent of Latvia's population consists of Russian-speaking persons of no real country, as they never claimed citizenship in Russia and lack Latvian citizenship. Ethnic Russians maintain that they are the second generation of Russians living in Latvia and belong nowhere else. Latvians say that citizenship should be accorded to those who speak the country's language and are flexible enough to help build a new nation. They fear the presence of a Russian "Fifth Column" in their country if the automatic "Latvianization" of Russians takes place. Compounding difficulties is the strong vote among Russians in Latvia for Vladimir Zhirinovsky, the ultranationalist who won heavily in the last Russian elections. Latvians are looking at possibilities on the citizenship question, including a residence requirement of five, ten, or fifteen years. Another possibility is an annual quota of naturalized Russians for citizenship. The question then becomes who would be included on the annual list.

In Lithuania, the problem is less acute: 10.5 percent of the population of 3,720,000 inhabitants is Russian. In Estonia, 30 percent of 1,529,000 inhabitants is Russian; there noncitizens can vote in local elections, but large Russian populations in the country's North feel increasingly alienated. All over Central and Eastern Europe, there are angry minority populations who are or believe themselves to be victims of discrimination.

For many centuries, Poles and Lithuanians were united in a single state; in recent times, both were under Russian domination, and both achieved independence. Lithuanians want a state treaty with a preamble condemning the 1920 occupation of Vilnius by Polish troops. Poles say the town and surrounding countryside are largely Polish-speaking, and they refuse to accept the treaty language. Speaking of "the somber pages in the history of our two countries from which a lesson can be learned for the future," they suggest a compromise. Today, Vilnius's Polish population is about 250,000 persons, about 7 percent of Lithuania's population. Lithuanians living in Poland total only several thousand inhabitants in a country of 38,000,000 persons.

Poland's president, Lech Walesa, publicly has raised the question of the strong Russian military concentration remaining in Kaliningrad, the small enclave between Lithuania, Poland, and the Baltic Sea. Formerly the German city of Königsberg in East Prussia, Kaliningrad is part of the Russian Federation and is the strategically located home of Russia's Baltic Fleet. He asks, "What good does their presence do, at what cost, and who is threatened?" He calls for an international public discussion of the issue, for otherwise the world will ignore this question. Kaliningrad's population is about 900,000 people, 200,000 of whom are Russian military.

March 4: President Walesa's term approaches an end. His popularity is not high, but neither is that of his leading opponent, Alexander Kwasniewski, leader of the SLD post-Communist Party. Walesa, a former shipyard electrician and hero of the uprising against Communism, became a world figure for leading his country to independence, but governing a country requires different skills. A current battle is over the draft constitution. The parliament is beginning work on a draft; the president threatens to introduce his own version and put it to the people in a referendum. His opponents say this is an undemocratic, strong-arm tactic. Although there are fifty-five members of the legislative branch's constitutional commission, only a few have any legal experience. As with most new constitutions in this region, the basic unsettled issue is how to share power. Will there be a strong presidency? Or a strong parliament? Walesa does not want to be a ceremonial president. Kwasniewski, coming from a Communist background, was all for a strong parliamentary system of government until he saw the presidency within his grasp. If he wins, he wants real power. Walesa, with characteristic bluntness, says, "If the ex-Reds and Kwasniewski really take full power and Stalin remains their role model, they will lock me up." Neither side appears pressed to come up with a draft; both would like to win the 1995 presidential race first.

March 22: This evening Tigger and I head for our neighborhood place to throw his ball. The rain has stopped, the sky is winter blue, filled with high clouds. Above us a single large white goose flies, wings flapping majestically, head pointed north as if guided by a distant compass. An epiphany.

March 23: CSCE holds a week-long conference of fifty-three countries on migrant workers in Europe, a conference led by the Turks, who energetically deflect inquiries about human-rights violations against Kurds. Both German and French delegations water down discussion topics, suggesting that the presence of millions of "temporary" non-European workers presents no problems, although some have lived in the same ghettos for three generations now. The Greek delegate, representing the European community, makes an idyllic speech about how good worker conditions are now and how they are improving across Europe. That evening television news carries accounts of Turkish homes in Germany being firebombed, the inhabitants being burned to death inside.

A keynote presentation on migratory issues is by a Polish delegate. Between 1990 and 1993, the number of persons employed in the Polish labor market declined by two million, due to privatization and the more skilled use of labor. One of the saddest aspects of Polish unemployment is that young people under twenty-four years of age face a 30 percent unemployment rate—almost a million persons, the highest such number in Europe.

In the last five years, Poland has accepted many asylum seekers: war refugees, victims of ethnic purges, political refugees from Russia, young men trying to avoid military service in the former Soviet Union, and victims of ecological disasters and famines. Many of these migrations are related directly to political upheavals. In 1989 Germans escaped the German Democratic Republic, in 1990 Jews left the Soviet Union, in 1991–93 refugees from Yugoslavia moved northward to Scandinavia, in 1993–94 tens of thousands of migrant workers from Romania, Bulgaria, and the former Soviet Union went wherever they could.

Until recently, large numbers of Poles emigrated to Europe and the United States. Many were escaping Communism. In 1994, the number of Poles leaving their country declined sharply, but the number of people coming to Poland, especially from the Soviet Union, increased. Many such individuals come to Poland en route to Germany or Scandinavia, hoping for welfare payments; but these countries' restrictive entry requirements often mean that they are turned back into Poland. Some of the population influx is of criminal groups, including gangs of Russians, Armenians, Vietnamese, and Koreans.

A humorous ending to the seminar. A delegate writes that the meeting was successful because:

1. The French didn't participate.
2. The Germans have abandoned the term *gastarbeiter* for "funky helper."
3. The Greek and Turkish delegation heads were seen necking in an upstairs meeting room.

4. An accord was reached granting Frequent Flyer miles for illegal immigrants.
5. The Italian moderator (Cortese) developed laryngitis just before making his final speech.
6. The conference publication will include a full-length color calendar of the front-desk Orbis Messenger Girls.

4

Kazakhstan, Georgia, Warsaw

March 28: Polish Defense Minister Piotr Kolodzeijczyk is in Washington, where his goal is to move Poland closer to NATO membership. America is equivocating on membership for Poland, Hungary, and the Czech Republic. One of the required first steps is for NATO and the former Warsaw Pact countries to conduct joint exercises to standardize communications equipment and gain familiarity with frequently used maps, command language, and ways of operating. Despite a small military budget, the Polish military plan an ambitious program, starting first with small activities such as small joint small-unit maneuvers in Jutland or mountain exercises with a German Alpine unit.

March 30: Poland's approach to NATO membership is via "the Spanish option," essentially an evolutionary process. Poles believe that their military forces fairly quickly (within two years) can be harmonized with NATO and that, once part of NATO, Poland will have the treaty organization's fifth or sixth largest army. Poland ranks its armed forces behind NATO's most advanced members but ahead of others, such as Spain or Italy. They are proudest of an armored cavalry division, their Mountain Infantry Brigade, some paratrooper units, and several recently modernized infantry units. Where the Polish armed forces are most deficient is in large infantry units and modern technology. Polish foot soldiers are poorly armed and trained; their aircraft and communications systems are outdated. Officers need to learn English to interact with NATO counterparts. They still use Warsaw Pact operating manuals for tactical operations, and field radios cannot communicate with NATO frequencies. A whole generation of Polish military leadership was trained in Soviet command schools; a trickle of officers is studying in Western military academies presently, but discrepancies between the two systems are profound. Another problem is that the air defense system is far behind Western standards. Although Russia insisted on controlling the equipment used by Warsaw Pact members, it denied them access to advanced Soviet satellite communications systems. The central issue is how much of Poland's annual budget can be allocated to military modernization. Polish generals estimate they need 3 percent of the annual budget; at present they receive 2.4 percent, which makes it likely that harmonization with NATO forces will take a long time.

April 1, Good Friday: A warm spring day; a total transformation of the weather. Spring flowers push through the earth, furious neighborhood gardening begins. People pile leaves and brush in yards and start all-night fires; smoke filters directly into our house, but there is nothing we can do. I watch the Tunisian embassy gardener build a fire directly under the ambassador's bedroom window, then leave for the night. He seems genuinely perplexed to be greeted, upon returning next morning, with verbal salvos from the pajama-clad ambassador, gesturing emphatically from the second-floor balcony.

At noon I walk to the neighborhood Roman Catholic church; there is no service, only several people gathered at the two side altars, one with lilies and spring flowers, the other with the replica of the dead body of Christ covered with a shroud. During the Easter vigil Saturday night, the figure will be carried to the high altar. I walk by Irena's pastry shop on the way home, where a large line gathers to buy holiday baked goods. A lively discussion takes place between the woman ahead of me and the baker over which length of seed cake she will take home for Easter.

Polish Easter

April 3, Easter Day: Thundering of cannon awakes us at dawn. Since it is raining hard, I think it is a spring storm, then remember that this is a traditional Polish way of celebrating Easter. (It was from our side of the river that German guns bombarded Warsaw during World War II.) We hold an Anglican Easter service in the British Embassy's eighteenth-century ballroom. The ambassador reads a lesson, and we sing "And Did Those Feet in Ancient Times," which gives the Polish pianist difficulties, as he has only the melody part. Children bring Easter baskets to be blessed; one includes eggs, flowers, pussy willows, and a piece of dried sausage. A young couple from Philadelphia invites us to join them for brunch at the Bristol Hotel. She is a tax lawyer with Hogan and Hartson; he is an investor who has just completed privatizing the Gdynia shipyard. It is a success story; the old Communist-era shipyard, wasteful and outmoded, now is owned by the workers and an investment firm. Technology is competitive, as are prices and labor costs, they have a backlog of twenty-one ships ordered. In the evening, we eat "Alleluia cake" that Pani Anna prepared for us.

April 9: In the afternoon, we visit with Wojtech and Anna Pakowski, the Polish artists who are making a metal sculpture out of several pairs of brass Vietnamese hands I bought in Saigon in 1965. The lithe Oriental hands and arms, dating to French times, were affixed to each side of pony carts and were used to hold reins by day and lanterns by night. Anna and Wojtech just returned from Brussels, where they had a well-received show of paintings and graphics. This summer they will pack son and dog into a rickety Volkswagen van and head for Holland. A Dutch dealer who carried Wojtech's paintings has closed his Amsterdam gallery and moved to a small village, taking several of the artist's paintings with him and leaving no address. In Warsaw their huge loft combines studio and living quarters. It was entirely open until their son was born and is increasingly sectioned off; the child wants to work beside his father, who often must use sharp tools and acid, so gates have gone up.

"California Dream" in Vienna

April 11: In the morning I fly to Vienna and meet with the printer who is preparing our Russian-language compilation of human-rights accords for distribution to judges and lawyers throughout the former Soviet Union. In late afternoon, I have my only conversation in two years with CSCE's Secretary General Wilhelm Höynk, a senior career diplomat in the German foreign service. Tall and thin, he is elderly, with intense eyes and tight facial muscles. He has a surgical stare, except in those rare instances when he momentarily breaks into a grandfatherly grin. Several delegates fear that the secretary general will try to turn an administrative job into a political fiefdom. As originally conceived, the secretary general's role was that of faithful administrator to the Committee of Senior Officials, the policy-setting body operating in the intervals between annual foreign minister meetings. Now delegates fear that the organization's informal management will turn into an ossified international bureaucracy like that of the United Nations. The Italian foreign minister, the organization's present chairman-in-office, shows little interest in directing the organization, giving the secretary general a free hand. By now the Vienna secretariat has over one hundred employees, more than all the field missions combined. Under the guise of "coordination," it takes every opportunity to move with catlike stealth to extend control.

Höynk clearly is preoccupied and eager for our meeting to end. His eyes dart elsewhere, and he shifts nervously when I speak. He asks about our Rule of Law activities; I describe the Warsaw Judicial Symposium, which will, for the first time, assemble judges and prosecutors from several Eastern and Western countries to discuss common problems. "Good public relations," he comments, showing no interest in the program's substance. When I discuss our activities with Georgia and Armenia, he says, "You must coordinate closely with the Council of Europe," which we have done.

"In fact," I respond, "we have a coordination problem with your office, which is sending an Austrian constitutionalist to work in Georgia. We learned that he was going there a day before he left and a week before our own mission was to leave."

"This is exactly what I mean," he adds. His irritation is visible when I describe our Russian-language volume of basic United Nations, Council of Europe, and CSCE human-rights accords that will allow jurists throughout the former Soviet Union to have the human-rights documents at their fingertips. "Can you stop the printing?" he asks.

"No," I respond.

"This is just the sort of duplication we must avoid," he continues, saying that recently he has let a contract to a Swedish group to translate all CSCE documents into Russian and publish them.

"But these are quite different documents," I reply. "You are describing meeting reports and conference documents; we are publishing something more comprehensive than that." He stands up; the meeting is over.

(The secretary general's project to publish the CSCE documents in Russian fell through; the contractor never delivered the work. Twenty thousand copies of our compilation of basic human rights documents were published in Russian and distributed to judges, lawyers, journalists, prosecutors, and human-rights activists throughout the Russian Federation and neighboring states.)

The secretary general's mind is elsewhere as we head for the door. I leave a Polish hand-painted Easter Egg from Warsaw with him. For a moment his face lightens. "In Germany we keep our Christmas tree ornaments, sometimes for several generations," he remarks, showing me out. As I leave, I encounter a refreshing contrast, a group of American college students gathered around a guitarist, singing "We Are the World, We Are Its Children" and "California Dream."

Self-Improvement in Warsaw

April 15: Each day I wait for the evening bus, passing a pentagonal green kiosk with newspapers, magazines, and a shelf full of Harlequin romance novels, which sell in great quantities. The Cinderella-style romance stories are popular with women of all ages. Polish women work hard and have little romance in their lives; husbands are male chauvinists, often alcoholic, and sometimes violent. Harlequin novels provide a touch of otherwise missing romance. As the market for scholarly books diminishes, many established intellectuals earn extra money translating pulp fiction from English into Polish. Dale Carnegie and similar self-help books on how to be a successful public speaker, banker, etc., are popular. In a post-Communist world, where new forms of behavior must be learned, such books provide guidelines for new ways to interact with others, much as volumes like Castiglione's *The Way of a Courtier* provided rules of behavior in an earlier age. Street posters show a "successful" male executive standing in front of a late-model German car, a cellular phone in one hand and an attaché case in the other, while an admiring young woman looks on.

Free Speech and Presidential Power

April 17: Breakfast at the Marriott Hotel with Richard Schifter, of the National Security Council's Eastern Europe office. We discuss plans for the Warsaw Judicial Symposium. He agrees that building an independent judiciary throughout this region is a primary need. Comprehensive and well-written laws are of little value unless there is a judiciary to enforce them. Schifter suggests introducing individual injunctive relief against a government, especially when a citizen is denied a fundamental right, like the right to travel, or in cases where the government seizes property but does not provide indemnification. He also advises introducing class action lawsuits, something unknown in the socialist world, where presumably the constitution protected the working class, whose members in turn never would want to sue the state.

Shifter, who once headed the U.S. State Department's global human-rights programs, mentions two relevant American court cases on themes emerging democracies wrestle with. *Youngstown Sheet and Tube Co. v. Sawyer* (1952). During the Korean War, the American steel industry faced a strike. President Harry Truman nationalized the mills, only to have the U.S. Supreme Court declare the seizure illegal, thus restricting presidential power. The issue is of interest in the Central European context because it shows that, in a confrontation with the court on a war-related issue, the president backed down. In *Yates v. U.S.* (1957), abstractly advocating political violence was not outlawed, since such speech was not a call to immediate action. Both cases reflect real-life situations confronted by the emerging states of the former Soviet Union. The Yates case stands in contrast to provisions in many constitutions of this region that prohibit anti-state speech, insulting the president, or damaging the good reputation of a citizen.

A Viennese Waltz

April 19: The power struggle between Vienna and Warsaw continues, this time over personnel issues. I learn of the *Secretary General's Report on Pay and Position Levels* when I look down at a pile of the documents left on a telephone stand in the Hofburg Palace, where Audrey Glover, our new director, and I have gone in the rain to make a phone call. A talented British barrister with extensive experience with international organizations, Glover quickly grasps the document's intent—further centralization and control by the Vienna secretariat. Since the study is to be presented formally the next day, I spend the next several hours scanning it.

Of CSCE's four hundred employees, over one hundred now are located in the Vienna "support" office. The ambitious administrative director, a Swedish former defense economist who moved from a high-ranking United Nations position to CSCE, has given himself a generous budget and administrative staff of thirteen persons, the size of the entire Warsaw office. No housing or educational allowances are provided for employees, creating difficulties in places like Warsaw, where $1,000 a month is the going rate for a simple two-bedroom apartment and tuition at the International School can cost up to $10,000 a year. Finally, salaries are not indexed to inflation, which is nearly 30 percent annually in Poland. If this were a preliminary study, such lapses would be understandable, but it is presented by the secretariat as a finished product. Later, when it encounters a hornet's nest of opposition from member states, the secretariat makes a perfunctory stab at responding to employee concerns. Most disheartening, this international organization originally was conceived to be flexible, responsive, and field-based. Instead, the central staff in Vienna becomes increasingly hierarchical and sluggish in its downtown Vienna Tower of Babel.

Rule of Law in the "Wild West": Building a Judicial Culture in Central Asia

April 20: Night flight to Almaty, Kazakhstan, for a three-day intensive workshop on building a judicial culture in Central Asia. Aboard a German airbus filled with speculators headed for Eurasia's last remaining "Wild West," a passenger reviews a slide talk on "A New Telephone System for Kazakhstan," while on one side an oil worker sleeps, his right arm gangrene-colored from tattoos. The incubator-warm cabin smells of overcooked lamb (Lufthansa's stab at native cuisine) and traces of strong Asian cigarette smoke. It is as long a voyage from Frankfurt to Almaty as from Frankfurt to New York.

A multicolored route map projects on the cabin's central screen like a video game. The computer traces a wavering red line across Central Asia. Brown hills at the bottom (the Himalayas); plains at the top (Siberia); cities named Dushanbe, Samarkand, Tashkent, and Bishkek; the Tibetan Plateau, the Gobi Desert. We follow Marco Polo's silk route at thirty thousand feet.

5:30 A.M. arrival; despite Foreign Ministry help, two hours of milling about the airport. First a line to obtain visas; next a wait at passport control. A single guard behind a high wooden desk peers at passengers. A harsh light above the booth illuminates each person; opposite the desk is a recently installed oblong mirror, tilted downward. It reflects the back of each visitor's head, but why? to spot a terrorist's wig? Meanwhile, each bag individually is lugged from the bus, pushed through a small window, then carried by another porter to a line where the owner claims it and moves it to a customs inspection line, where each container is viewed through an ancient fluoroscope of the kind used by progressive shoe stores in the age of Franklin Roosevelt.

The hotel entryway belongs to Soviet-era public buildings; a vast lobby and a tiny door admit one person at a time. Enter and turn right, walk several steps, turn left through the second door, walk past uniformed security guards. This control procedure is duplicated in thousands of buildings in the former Soviet Union. This time, it's the Hotel Kazakhstan; the dual entrance-exit system prevents demonstrators from storming the lobby and guests from sneaking out unobserved.

Hotel folder English:

> You can order a long distance call with any town of the Soviet Union as well as foreign towns. Money for the telephone talk is to be paid to the Senior Chambermaid on your floor.
>
> The Senior Chambermaid on your floor will:
> —order a taxi car for you
> —take your washing to the laundry, have your shoes repaired, your clothes mended, ironed, or dry cleaned
> —take your watch, electric razor, spectacles, suitcase to the repair shop
> —wake you up at the hour you want.

Private enterprise comes to landlocked Kazakhstan, despite a decline in the economy because of dissolving Russian markets and high transportation costs. Basement rooms are freshly painted and opened as convenience stores; street-corner kiosks multiply, selling individual cigarettes or packages. ("Supreme" is a popular brand. Philip Morris, facing declining home markets, is building a $300 million plant here.) Soap from Pakistan, clothes from China, and piles of pirated audio- and videotapes with smudged black-and-white labels are piled by store windows, along with Rasputin, Petrof, and Tolstoj vodka from Germany and a Red Square brand from the United Kingdom. Just beyond the glitter, a solitary peasant woman stands between wooden crates of garlic and cucumbers, hoping for a sale.

Among the most active entrepreneurs are the two thousand members of Kazakhstan's Korean community. Shaggy Ming made his money in frozen foods in Seoul; from the hotel, he operates a casino, restaurant, bakery, fast-food joint, and multiple businesses. His establishments feature a lighted plastic sign of Shaggy's smiling, hirsute face; near it, a grandfather clock symbolizes affluence and stability. A photo mural covers one wall, showing Shaggy in signature white suit and shoes, arms linked affably with President Nursultan Nazarbaev, whose faint smile suggests the cat that swallowed the canary. I dine at Shaggy's fast-food restaurant on my first day in Almaty. The menu: hamburger and a Korean version of "English fruit cake," served on shining metal trays with a bunch of roses embossed on each tray.

On the first afternoon, we are hauled to nearby mountains by a smoke-spewing Ikarus bus, Hungary's contribution to socialist transportation. This one is indistinguishable from similar vehicles all over the former Soviet Union, except for the driver's filigreed silver tea glass holder attached to the steering column. Racheting up the hill like a cog railway train, we reach the site of the 1980 Winter Games, where the high altitude helped participants set several world records. Impressive in that decade, the stadium now needs refurbishing. Brightly colored Communist-era plastic curtains hang in offices vacated long ago. Rusted bleachers are piled behind the viewing area; someone has dumped two large iron pipe flag holders down a nearby ravine. Roadside vendors turn brochettes on wood-fired braziers. Six crows sit alert nearby, hoping for falling scraps.

Sign on a nearby building: "ReclAme at Medeo, the best guarantee of your success. Tel: 60.37.34."

The New Frontier

A National Museum historical exhibit illustrates the Wild West plow-that-broke-the-plains era of Kazakhstan's history. A 1902 iron rail, a map of the Trans-Siberian railroad, and photos of elaborately constructed railroad stations hang next to replicas of a nineteenth-century log cabin and a smaller sod house. Covering one wall are sepia daguerreotypes of dark-suited men and shawl-covered women standing awkwardly at attention, as if being interrogated by the provincial governor. The pictures could be from an American Great Plains historical society collection, except for the oriental facial features. Next to handmade wooden and metal hoes and plows are small collections of family china and a portable, hand-operated sewing machine. A local artist has painted a scene depicting a nomad camp being burned by Czarist cavalry, with cattle being driven away, men killed, and women pleading with the invaders. The themes of violence, struggle against nature, pioneers, and settlers are the stuff of hundreds of American or Russian films and paperbacks. For many Central Asians, taming the wild frontier is a theme as significant in Russian history as Marxist ideology.

The museum's most striking display never was planned as such. Beside a large white marble staircase is a dark enclave between two walls.

Tucked inside: a huge marble head of Lenin, turned sideways. Lenin, whose statue once stared eastward toward the Chinese border, now faces a stone wall. Brooms and ladders lean on strong shoulders that once bore the burdens of empire, while an abandoned red banner droops, like a shawl, over one shoulder.

Nearby is the huge presidential building, former Communist party headquarters. In front is a red stone parade-reviewing stand modeled after Lenin's tomb in Moscow. Most of the city spread out below is comprised of generic Soviet-era government buildings or apartment houses with crumbling balconies, cracked concrete walls, and warped wooden framed windows. Within a decade, the capital will move inland toward the country's center, nearer its ethnic Russian population, which threatens to hive off and become part of the Russian Federation.

The "open frontier" theme is the peg for the lead Kazakhstan conference speaker. Basically, there was lots of land, few people, and a rich nomadic culture. That all changed when the railroad came, followed by the Czar's agents and—above all—Stalin's ruthless land collectivization. A great famine followed, in the course of which possibly 37 percent of the population died and another 650,000 people migrated to China. World War II cut deeper into the population. Next came the forced settlement of 2,000,000 to 3,000,000 Russians and Ukrainians, followed by Khrushchev's "virgin lands" policy of moving urban people eastward. The Kazak people, 90 percent of the population at the century's beginning, nearly became a minority in their own land. Of 17,000,000 residents today, 43 percent are Kazaks, 37 percent Russians. The rest are Ukrainians, German-speaking people, Uzbeks, Tartars, Uyghurs, and Koreans. The dislocation and dismemberment of local societies were as severe as anything European colonists did to native populations in America or Africa.

Judicial Reform: "Books Are as Important as the Air We Breathe"

As for judicial reforms, "We need everything," a high Ministry of Justice official says. The sentiment is echoed by representatives of the five countries present at the conference. "Kazakhstan is at the stage where we are reviving our democratic values," a local jurist states. "In this region five hundred years ago, there was no despotism; nomads had a form of democracy." Not everyone would agree with this harmonious picture of powers delegated to regions, yet a long tradition of customary contract law covering encounters along the China-to-Europe silk route characterized the region's history, antedating Runnymede by centuries.

Central Asia's legal evolution is filled with hope and contradictions—clear advances, such as the wholesale acceptance of international human-rights law as part of domestic law; and obvious regressive features, such as increasingly strong presidential control. Especially among the reform-oriented younger generation, a strong desire for change is evident. News that we are publishing a Russian-language anthology of human-rights documents, including the basic European Convention and CSCE human-rights texts, elicits requests for hundreds of copies. "We need books," a jurist remarks; "They are as important to us as the air we breathe."

Several speakers say that the lack of a middle class is a major problem in Central Asian states. In Kazakhstan, the minimum wage is seven dollars per month. A handful of people at the top quickly seize economic opportunities and exploit them. At less exalted levels of society, thousands of government employees crowd into public transportation in early morning, then sit in unlit offices sipping tea and waiting for someone higher up to make decisions. Below are peasants and farmers, whose life has changed little during the last century except when their migratory patterns were brutally suppressed.

Kazakhstan has been independent for two years. Its political system favors a strong executive—currently, President Nursultan Nazarbaev, elected in a single-candidate election in 1991. In 1995 he misused a constitutional provision on referendums to extend his reign to the century's end. The president can appoint 42 deputies to Parliament; the remaining 135 are elected. Only a handful represent independent political interests. Recent elections were rigged, by all accounts, and the president's party won handily. More than 100 foreign observers watched the country's first-ever democratic parliamentary contest on March 7, 1994. Election violations were numerous; access to national television by opposition candidates was severely limited. A radio station critical of the government was silenced for ten days as a "fire hazard," and a printing press closed for a "lack of paper." A requirement that each candidate post a bond five times his or her monthly salary created problems for many. Opposition candidates' petitions were denied for allegedly containing false signatures. Some candidates gathered thousands of additional names to compensate for those struck off by pro-governmental election officials. In a stab at equality, the government decreed that all campaign posters must be the same size and format, which only confused matters further.

The national election commission's silver-haired director speaks. He is an oleaginous politician who laces a discussion of the electoral code with sugary dollops like "thanks to the insight of our president," "the wisdom of our leader," and "the foresight of our chief of state"—phrases only slightly less fawning than references in the 1930s to "the justly named Mountain Eagle" (Stalin). Such panegyrics are a sure sign of a party hack.

The elections chair's message is the Kazak equivalent of "Aw, shucks, anyone can make mistakes, but we did our best." A candidate with eighteen thousand signatures on her petition was denied registration. She accompanied the president on his February 1994 state visit to Washington; aboard one of Air Kazakhstan's four planes, she cornered the chief of state, who agreed to put her name on the ballot. She lost in one of the capital's four electoral districts to the hand-picked candidate of Almaty's mayor, by all accounts a venal politician. She complains that (1) the complex electoral code was not widely publicized or easily understood, (2) her children and campaign workers' lives were threatened, (3) phone lines were cut, and (4) her poll watchers were not allowed to observe ballot counting. As she speaks, the chair and two rows of straphangers watch, alternating melodramatic looks of irony and bemusement. She draws blood. The chair takes the floor again, raising the decibels to oratorical level. After perfunctorily denying her claims, he gushingly thanks each international organization present for supporting the president; the gesture leaves most people squirming. At the break he and his entourage depart like a herd of startled goats.

Of the conference's seventy participants, possibly ten represent human-rights groups. Many are energetic women whose faces bear the deep lines of struggle. Their organizations are poor, barely able to rent office space or pay telephone bills. Authoritarian governments play cat-and-mouse games with them, denying travel permission, stringing out the legal registration process. None can afford Hotel Kazakhstan's rate of $15 a night. (The rate for Westerners is $120 a night.)

A local human-rights attorney says, "Two positions have clearly emerged. Some say you can't defer the exercise of human rights to better days. Both Kyrgyzstan and Kazakhstan allow demonstrations, rallies, and free speech, without catastrophic results. Governments become nervous when the talk is of individual rights. They say, 'Why don't you first

deal with group rights, like improved working conditions?' It is errone-
ous to think of Central Asia as a harmonious region."

Individual vs. Group Rights

Numerous issues are probed; a clear gulf emerges between advocates of
international standards of human-rights observance and some of the re-
calcitrant "Go slow" countries like Tajikistan and Turkmenistan. These
latter argue, "You can't do it all at once; there should be priorities among
rights. Political-military security and stability come first, then economic
rights, such as the right to work and a place to live."

Laws protecting the chief of state against libel and slander are scruti-
nized. Opponents of such restrictive laws say, "This is a smoke screen to
limit free speech and political opposition." Some Central Asian countries are relaxing their protect-the-president laws. "The president can
take care of himself; it is the opposition that needs protection," one local attorney observes; but many chiefs of state use sweeping libel and
national security laws to curb any criticism of their actions.

Human-Rights Issues

A Finnish participant pleads for an end to physical abuse and torture,
especially of journalists, NGOs, and political opponents. He urges creating a fund for the victims of torture and emphasizes the need for remedies against prosecutors who allow the physical and mental abuse of
victims.

The legal status of conscientious objectors is raised. Reportedly twenty
such persons are being held in Kazakhstan jails without judicial proceedings against them, although international accords, accepted as part
of local domestic law, clearly give conscientious objectors possibilities
for alternative forms of service.

A striking feature of many constitutions is clear provisions that accord public international law precedence over domestic law, especially
on human-rights issues. While, in the United States, public international
law has had difficulty in finding a legal toehold, it is accepted as Black
Letter law in many former Communist countries. A local jurist explains,
"It is a clear way of stating our opposition to our totalitarian heritage;
also, we have not had time to write new laws of our own."

Minority Rights: Where the Soviet Union Dissolved

Many countries face language group and ethnic group problems. Should the majority groups' language be the country's official language? What status is to be assigned to Russian, the colonizer's language? What about countries with multiple ethnic groups and languages? Do the minority groups integrate into society, or retain special status on its margins? Does the dominant group systematically isolate minorities through the legal system? Are there provisions to treat the problems of long-settled minorities differently from those of new arrivals? The January 1993 constitution makes Kazakh, a Turkic language, Kazakhstan's state language, while Russian is designated the language of international communication. About half the Kazakh population speaks Russian; about 1 percent of the Russian population speaks Kazakh.

A related question concerns citizenship, especially in countries like Kazakhstan. There, at the century's beginning, 90 percent of the population was Kazakh, but today, owing to Stalin's settlement policies, Kazakhs only slightly outnumber ethnic Russians. Is it "one person, one vote," in which case the newly independent country turns governance of part of its territory over to Russians? Or can minorities vote and hold local but not national office? While some countries encourage dual citizenship, others see it as a divisive issue, because many ethnic Russians will claim dual citizenship and, when conditions in the new countries' are not to their liking, will appeal to Mother Russia for protection.

Our closing reception is in Friendship House, a modern two-story Russian building downtown. After lengthy toasts to peace, brotherhood, and neighborly cooperation with vodka or Bulgarian white wine, bulbous hot fish-and-batter hors d'oeuvres are passed. The noise level is high, the building warm; I move next door to the darkened conference room, with its large circular table. Staring at the shiny, clean tabletop, I wonder whether the room ever held anything but ritual conferences, the dreary civic liturgies of Communist society. At first I do not see the Foreign Office official standing silently beside me. In recently learned English, he reads from a placard, "On 21 December 1991 here the eleven chiefs of state came to sign the treaty dissolving the Soviet Union." The old order is not quite gone, the new one only being built. Central Asia lives in transitional times, as conducive to fundamental change as those of Marco Polo.

Easter in Tbilisi

May 1: Air Georgia is not listed on any major airline schedules. It owns a handful of old Russian planes flying to Cairo, Tel Aviv, Prague, Moscow, Vienna, and Frankfurt once a week, and daily to Moscow. The U.S. State Department recently issued a travel advisory warning travelers not to use Russian internal airlines, as they are overcrowded, are unreliable, and have poor safety records. We arrive at 10 A.M. at Vienna Airport, ready to meet Professor Herman Schwartz, an American constitutionalist flying in from Washington, and the Austrian constitutionalist whom CSCE sent to Tbilisi earlier and who is now returning to Vienna. Both planes from Washington and Tbilisi are hours late, giving us ten minutes together at 3:30 P.M., just before Air Georgia begins its five-hour return flight (like many non-registered airlines, Air Georgia's flights usually spend only a few hours on the ground before returning home). The airline manager is in my seat, announcing that it is reserved for "crew," which turns out to be four Georgian Mafia dons, their ample figures oozing out of Italian silk sport shirts, their wrinkled bodies graced with gold chains. They and we are given bottles of Georgian wine, they a fruit basket and we individual apples. Despite its length, the flight seems short, for Herman Schwartz is an energetic conversationalist who is writing a book on the constitutional courts of Central and Eastern Europe. He is also a born debater who will explore an opposing point of view simply to spark discussion.

We arrive in Tbilisi in wind and rain and are met by the CSCE mission head, a Ukrainian diplomat who speaks halting English, and a representative of the Foreign Ministry, whose car will not start. The hotel, built as an Austrian-Georgian business venture, rises like an eight-story Phoenix above the small, crowded concrete dwellings with tin roofs that surround it. A sign at the hotel entrance reads: "For the comfort and security of guests, kindly check all arms at the front desk before entering hotel." A picture of a pistol with a diagonal red line crossing through it, like a road sign, is next to a metal detector. A local business figure enters; two armed guards in matching gray business suits wait outside. Later the American embassy declares the hotel off-limits and houses official visitors elsewhere; some local people were killed at the hotel in Mafia feuds, and when the Austrian manager dismissed the locally hired guard force, they beat him badly. He left Georgia the next day.

May 2: Easter Sunday, the third for me this year: Western, Orthodox, and now another Orthodox. Bright sky and strong spring winds. We visit the old Georgian capital with its ancient cathedral. Outside, women sell candles and devotional picture cards; young men, carrying Russian rifles, stand about, smoking and talking. Lilacs are piled beside the altar, along with loaves of homemade bread. The country is poor, and people hang single Western cigarette cartons or candy-bar containers from front window shutters, indicating a few goods for sale. We visit a market where the only things for sale are a rind of fly-specked cheese, a pile of radishes, and bread. Having no change, we offer a dollar for a loaf of bread. The baker says that is too much and gives it to us free. There are few cars, owing to the high cost of gasoline. Drivers swoop along cobblestone streets like figure skaters, cutting to the left or right around other cars. Few signs of Easter are evident, mostly a few eggs dyed red. At an Easter celebration in our hotel, a circle of Mafia leaders, including some from our plane, delight in a large mushroom-shaped Easter cake which is served them. In the evening, we visit a "dollar restaurant," a place called the Diplomatic Club, a converted cellar decorated with modern Georgian art. An entire wall is devoted to pictures of the visit by former Secretary of State James Baker and his wife to Chairman Shevardnadze, and to Baker's evening at the restaurant.

May 3: In the evening, we walk about the neighborhood, along cobblestone streets. There are few people; children draw modern replicas of cave art on flat rocks with stones; malnourished dogs walk lethargically about or sleep on curbs. Standing out on the drab streets are a few solid buildings with heavy doors, many locks, and strong iron grills covering windows, reflecting the fortress mentality of most residents. Exteriors are deliberately uninviting; inside are large rooms, elaborate chandeliers, and ornate furniture, plus vine-covered verandahs where friends and families gather for long conversations, wine or coffee, and a view of the softly colored landscape. The city is built up from meandering river banks, and hills rise sharply on both sides.

We return to the hotel, which houses a handful of guests although a thousand could be accommodated easily. A call to room service about the lack of hot water produces the reply, "Let it run for ten minutes; there has been no-one in the room for several weeks." Dining choices are a forty-dollar "traditional Georgian buffet" or soup and sandwiches in the Cafe Danube. In the cafe, for a second night, we watch as a waiter carrying a tray of crockery walks into a closed door. Turkish coffee for three dollars a cup is offered in the hotel lobby by a young woman in traditional dress, but in the week we are there, we see no takers. Each evening a conservatory-trained pianist plays the lobby's Bechstein concert grand, then packs her music into a worn leather case and heads into the Georgian night, on some evenings to the sound of automatic-rifle fire in the distance.

May 4: During the week we meet with drafters of the Georgian constitution. Our venue is the Parliament building, erected by German prisoners during World War II but now being reconstructed because great sections of it were destroyed two years ago in an armed rebellion. Initially we are shown a draft constitution favored by the government and asked to comment on it, being told that it offers "a strong presidency, strong legislature, and strong judiciary." In fact, it gives the president the right to dissolve the legislature anytime he thinks doing so is in the national interest. The president also appoints judges, who, on constitutional matters, have only an advisory role. We say this is not really separation of powers but a patchwork effort that will hardly last out the year. During the next two days, a procession of constitutional drafters meets with us, including some bright young law students and members of political parties.

At noon we drive in a rattling Russian van to a village three hours from Tbilisi for a long family feast at the home of one of the constitutional commission members. Mountain streams have washed out the road in many places, and police roadblocks are set every few miles. The journey through rolling hills and vineyards leads to a border town near the Chechen frontier. Cows and goats wander across the road; gasoline is sold in rusting jerry cans and wine bottles. The market is poor, a collection of auto parts spread on a car hood and cuts of meat displayed in the open air, guarded by an elderly woman with a fly whisk. Card games and dominoes interest those not engaged in trading. Nearby fields are watered by a handmade circular water wheel held together with bailing wire, from which old tires are hung to collect water.

"Dear Toasts, Go on Forever"

We arrive at a two-story house with small garden and chicken coop. The parlor has a Russian upright piano and an elaborate glass-fronted sideboard. It is the home of a village school teacher and her husband, a retired government worker. The table is set for twelve; set upon it are six carafes of Georgian white wine and bottles of Georgian brandy. The family's old silver is polished, and at least fifteen dishes are served, followed by strings of walnuts dipped into grape jelly, while the remains of the wine-grape crop are strung out as candies. "We don't have meals like this much any more," the host remarks; such family gatherings were frequent in the days before the present troubles. Then families gathered for birthdays, anniversaries, and weddings. A feature of Georgian meals is toasts throughout the entire three or four hours—toasts to peace and friendship, to our respective countries, to families, to the war dead (all stand), to the women who prepared the meal, to love, to constitutions, and to our host's son's birthday ("and may he get married soon, move out, and start his own family"). A guitar passes from person to person, and an attractive young woman from Shevardnadze's office sings songs about Georgian history, as well as "My Bonny Lies Over the Ocean" in English. A final round of toasts is drunk from a cow's horn.

Toasts are part of a social ritual in which guests are welcomed, family members praised, differences smoothed over, and controversial topics avoided or, if mentioned, treated in a positive way. "Dear toasts, go on forever," a Russian saying goes. After a final toast urging us to "come back again next year at this time," we stand on the back porch.

"And over there is Chechnya," our host remarks casually, pointing to a row of medium-high tree-covered hills. Chechnya conjures up images of a fractious Russian-loathing people, whose spirit never was subdued by the invaders who conquered militarily. Georgia's last ruler, Zviad Gamsakhurdia, after nearly destroying the country in a bloody coup, sent his family over the hills to Chechnya, where they were warmly received. Proponents of geopolitics say that mountain people can be independent, often quarrelsome, and individualistic. That certainly is true of Chechnya's peoples, where armed bands snipe at one another, lay ambushes, and occasionally hijack Russian airplanes. At present, Chechen groups coalesce around two centers: the Moscow-supported opposition (the largest concentration of Chechens outside their homeland is in Moscow, where many of the gangs are Chechen-led) and a retired Russian general of Chechen origin, Dzhokar M. Dudayev. Until 1990, Dudayev commanded a nuclear bombing wing in Estonia, but he returned home to become the Chechen Republic's first president. (No-one as yet recognizes the country.) Small, with fine features and a Zorro-like mustache, Dudayev, a nominal Moslem, is a lover of flowers and karate and has called for a holy war against the Russian empire. His goal is to create an independent, secular Islamic state next door to Georgia. Rigid and uncompromising in his views, the question is how long Dudayev can last in such a volatile region.

The Chechen Republic has at best a million inhabitants, spread over thirteen thousand square kilometers of rich farmland and mountainous terrain. Never fully under Czarist control, in Chechen lands an uneasy peace prevailed in Communist times. When the Soviet Union broke up, the Chechens made an unsuccessful bid for independence. President Yeltsin, without consulting the legislature, sent two thousand troops into a once-autonomous republic of the Russian Federation. In response, Chechens ridiculed the troops and sent word to Moscow that they would assassinate individual Russian leaders. The country's motto is "Independence or Death," the state symbol the solitary wolf standing under the moon.

Dudayev's goal is not only an independent Chechen state but also a "Caucasian house," a confederation of neighboring states united against Russia. Georgians scoff at this, for Dudayev has supplied arms to the Abkhazian separatists, making him an enemy. (At this time I never suspected that, within a year, I would be riding through Grozny, the Chechen Republic's capital, in a Russian armored personnel carrier, exploring ways to end the conflict.)

We sit on the balcony, sipping the last of the local white wine, as our host explains Georgian sentiments toward their neighbor. The wild hills are peaceful in the late afternoon light. I look at them for a last time, then head to our van for the bumpy return to Tbilisi. Bread and the meal's remains fill my companions' arms, and a jug of wine and bottles of Georgian brandy are provided for the journey. We pass cemeteries filled with purple iris in full bloom, beautifully catching the evening light as in a Van Gogh painting.

May 6: Our final meeting is with Edouard Shevardnadze, chair of Georgia's interim government and former Soviet Foreign Minister. The American ambassador has told us that Shevardnadze works long hours, sometimes from 9 A.M. until late at night; travels with his own retainers; and trusts no-one. His translator, a young woman who speaks cultivated British English, has been out of Georgia for only one week. She asks for permission to review our presentation, so that she can be sure of the language. She was translator on Shevardnadze's Washington trip. The entourage was scheduled to spend a day in Canada as well, but Air Georgia's plane had mechanical problems, so the official party stayed on the ground at a New York airport instead.

Shevardnadze is in his sixties, vibrant and energetic; we are shown into the presidential ceremonial office, a large, spartan room with a shiny table, elaborate crystal chandelier, microphones, and mineral water. This is his sixth meeting of the day. He enters with a burst of energy, is of medium height, a bit portly, his blue eyes alternating intense concentration and explosive humor. "Let the debate begin," he remarks when we are seated. I give him a copy of our CSCE poster, with hope at the top as a blue sky, history at the bottom as a pyramid, and justice in the middle as a figure holding a scale. He studies it quickly and points to the bottom rung. "Georgia is here," he says. "We are at the beginning. We will move up if our temperament will allow it. As for constitutions, if the idea comes from abroad, Georgians will like it; if it comes from Georgia, our politicians will oppose the idea just because someone else suggested it."

I begin: we want to raise three issues. Considering the present state of Georgian politics, it is impossible to get a constitution passed, for fractious regions presently are in armed conflict with the central authority. In such circumstances, why not pass a Bill of Rights and create a constitutional court to enforce it? This can be a legacy to his country that will be advantageous politically and should have popular support. Shevardnadze says that the idea has merit and asks members of his constitutional commission to prepare a study on it. (Two weeks later, in one of his periodic radio addresses to the people, he endorses the idea.) "If we did not have the Abkhazia and Adzharia problems, I would favor adopting the whole constitution now, but these problems will take a long time to solve," he says. "We thought it would take a short time, but that is not the case. Georgia's civil and military authority does not extend to these regions at present."

On the content of a Bill of Rights, we suggest inclusion of more of the CSCE Helsinki, Copenhagen, and Moscow language on human rights, and provisions from the European Convention of 1950. The present Georgian drafts follow the traditional Soviet model of stating rights unequivocally and then modifying them through phrases like "according to interpretation by the courts" or "according to action by the legislature." We say that this leaves no clear standards by which courts can judge the law; it leaves everything to executive and legislative interpretation. Professor Schwartz adds, "Countries have a narrow moment when they can pass human-rights legislation, and it is unlikely they will have more favorable opportunities in the future."

"Personally, my attitude toward these proposals is very positive. I need time to think about it. This approach may have advantages for us in this situation," Shevardnadze responds. He adds, "A constitutional court is an absolute must, we know that today. We have a unique opportunity. You know what the situation is like in our Parliament. People who were in the street or fields yesterday are in Parliament today. Sometimes they will oppose you just to show their strength." We had watched on Georgian television as a deputy dumped mineral water on the speaker, who in turn threw an unplugged telephone at the deputy. "An advertisement for our mineral water," the chairman quips.

Next we raise the most sensitive issue of all. "The final question is power," I say. "You are caught between the present situation and your desire to leave a lasting legacy of a working constitution. The distribution of powers in the present draft does not achieve this end. There are imbalances that will leave people frustrated because their government is not responsive to them."

Professor Schwartz elaborates: "There are two specific problems. First, to override a presidential veto a three-fifths vote of the deputies is required. That is almost impossible to achieve. In the United States, President Bush vetoed forty-two bills, and Congress was unable to override forty of them. The other question is the president's prerogative to dissolve Parliament if it does not vote a budget. That is a disruptive feature. There are other ways to achieve the same end, such as making it a confidence/no confidence issue." We add, "Americans were fortunate to know, at the time they were writing their Constitution, that their first president would be George Washington; Georgians know that they have a similarly prudent leader in you. But no-one lives forever, and the crucial issue is: will the next person exercise the same discretion you do, or be as tyrannical as your predecessor?"

Shevardnadze replies:

> The distribution of powers is a delicate problem. I agree that a person can't be eternal. You are lucky people; you were able to create lasting institutions. Should we have a strong parliament or a strong president? There are debates about this. Because of Georgia's geographical and historical setting, conflicts appear over and over again. We are a multicultural society, with separatist tendencies now and possibly in the future. The Adzharia and Abkhazia issues are examples. Neither place has any possibility of being a viable entity. The Adzharians can only live because they live here. Those are laws of geography. Meanwhile, their inhabitants create obstacles and do everything they can to make it difficult for us to rule. We now see that our transitional period will not be short and that it will be affected by what goes on in Russia.

He smiles and says, "Russia will never be indifferent to Georgia. Georgia always has been a tasty morsel for Russia." He gestures as if eating a grape. "Europe always tells us that it supports us, but when it comes to action, that is a different matter. We are up against very powerful neighbors. When we asked for help from NATO, no help came." He looks mournful. "No-one has provided a single gun for us. Russia conducted the war; they armed our opponents and us. The Russian empire is like a plant that has been cut off," he continues. "But it still has deep roots. Any help you can provide, economic or constitutional, is greatly needed. This is a region of good prospects. Our present moment is a deviation in our history. The present draft constitutional text reflects our actual situation. We are looking at ways to improve it."

Professor Rzepliński asserts, "The best way to create stable politics is to build a multiparty political system."

Shevardnadze replies, "We made a mistake when we used proportional representation; it created parties with only a few members. Today we have twenty-six parties. This is temporary. We will work on party reform. I did it that way because we were just starting out." An hour has elapsed; the chairman is willing to continue but has an 8 P.M. meeting. We ask for a group picture; Shevardnadze shakes hands warmly and briskly departs. We exit; the young guards in his outer office watch a cartoon show on television, their Russian rifles stacked in a corner.

In the evening, the secretary of the Constitutional Commission, an able young law professor, Avtanil Dematrashvili, invites us, along with a member of Parliament and of the presidential staff, for a family dinner. Part of the family is Jewish, so this is a seder meal, lasting almost until midnight. Toasts continue throughout the carefully prepared meal, and no plates are removed, should a guest want to eat further. I am struck by how difficult the week must have been for many at the table; but, for an evening and a day at least, the husband and wife, wherever they might be, are king and queen of the Sabbath. In a toast I recall the biblical Celestial Banquet and how it bridges time and eternity in a moment of stability and peace. This is what we are trying to do, imperfect as our efforts might be.

Progress on the Polish Constitution

June 6: A. E. Dick Howard of the University of Virginia Law School is in Warsaw for a meeting with the Polish constitutional community, parliamentarians, judges, and law professors. Dick and I call on one of the architects of the new Polish constitution, Lech Falandysz, legal counselor to the Polish president. Falandysz, a long-time human-rights activist and criminal law specialist, says that Poles are moving closer to an acceptable draft. "If it works, it will be a bit like Poland winning a world cup in soccer," he says as coffee is served in his spacious office near the Polish Parliament.

> Our society is thirsty for a success, even a symbolic success. Even if the constitution isn't ideal, people will support it. There is the possibility of reasonable compromise between the post-Communist parties—whatever you call them—and the post-Solidarity deputies, who are no longer a monolithic bloc. If Walesa, Kwasniewski [head of the ex-Communist parliamentary faction, elected Polish president in 1995], and Glemp [the leading Roman Catholic cardinal] would ask people to vote for it, that would be enough for the constitution to pass. From the point of view of writing a document, it would not be difficult. The professional drafters could do that easily. As you know, there are two possibilities—a complete document or a step-by-step model, solving one key problem at a time. People are saying that the parties are closer and closer; it's time to have a constitution.

We ask what the crucial issues are. "Social rights," Falandysz replies without hesitation. "The separation of church and state is not a big issue; a semipresidential or a parliamentary system is not a big issue. I think it will be pretty much what we have now." As for social rights, "there probably will be two categories of rights, one justiciable in the courts and one as guidelines for the legislature." Falandysz's main concern is the legislature's instability; "for a parliamentary system to work, you need a strong stable majority in place for several years so they can build a legislative record. The parties have hidden agendas; they would all like one of their members to be president, so they would like to see strong presidential powers. As for prime ministers, who can even remember them, there were so many of them. We have a specific situation in Poland to which we must respond. We are not in a hurry; we have taken our time, and now we have a center-left Parliament, which is easier to get a constitution from than a center-right Parliament, which would be more aggressive, more clerical-oriented, more wanting to introduce a church-supported agenda."

Falandysz sees a gradual increase in the constitutional court's powers, along the lines of the German or Austrian constitutional courts. "If they try to be too ambitious, they will face setbacks," he cautions. "Polish legal thinking is closer to the French-German tradition; I am closer to the functional thinking of the Anglo-American tradition." We ask what powers will remain for local governments. "It is an exaggeration to say that we have effective local self-government, although there are some attractive parliamentary proposals. We will probably adopt a European model, with most powers reserved for the central government, especially on issues like taxes and police. We will probably not move as far as the Swiss model. Presently we are a society wrestling with several tendencies. We have experts who know Western governmental systems; they advise us on which ideas to pick. We have other people who look to Polish history and tradition for models. The Russian era made it hard for us to build a civic culture. Now people are worried about finding jobs." We ask if Poland, like many countries emerging from the Communist orbit, would give the European Convention on Civil and Political Rights and the CSCE accords precedence over domestic law. "Our intention is to write a Polish version of the European Charter, which will be more important for us than the European Charter. It is important for us to do this our way, for in some ways we are ahead of the European Convention. Our own charter is more inclusive in many ways."

He returns to the soccer metaphor as we leave. The fifty-five-member commission is now more active, and differences in the seven tabled drafts have been narrowed considerably, he says, "but it's like soccer. If everyone is in training, there is no interest, but if it is World Cup soccer, everyone feels good if you win, if you have a victory. Also, I think the post-Communist parties will push for a constitution quickly because they feel guilty. They want expiation, acceptance in European society, so they are willing to do more. On the other hand, the political right will be more cautious, more xenophobic, more desirous of seeing the Communists punished."

5

Romania, Armenia

June 8–10: There is no larger building in Europe, none gaudier in the world. The People's Palace in Bucharest can be seen from outer space. Six hundred architects worked on plans for a decade; historic sections of Romania's capital were leveled, as wide streets, like an eastern Champs Elysées, were erected. The tons of marble and forests of hardwood that went into the building all were Romanian. For years, Romanians sacrificed so that the vast palace could be built. Each household was allowed only one small light bulb per evening, and fuel supplies were desperately low.

"I try not to think about what went into the building," a young Romanian diplomat remarks. "Now the problem is what to do with it." The Supreme Court has offices and a courtroom on an upper floor; a parliamentary chamber is under construction, and several other government offices are housed there. It takes twenty minutes to walk from one side of the building to the other. When I enter the parliamentary dining room, the large metal doorknob comes off in my hand. The Romanian Constitutional Court is hosting a conference on the Role of the Constitutional Court in Promoting Democracy, but I remember the building more than the conference. The huge chandeliers create so much heat that it is necessary to turn off lights in our conference room and open windows for fresh air. Although it is June, a tape recording of Christmas carols plays at breaks, with Franck's "Panis Angelicas" being repeated several times.

On the final afternoon, Robert Badinter, who is completing a seven-year term as head of the French Constitutional Court, speaks on "Europe's Common Legal Space." Twentieth-century Europe is like Europe in the thirteenth and fourteenth centuries, he says, when scholars in Salamanca, Paris, Cracow, Berlin, and Oxford shared a common legal culture, discussed similar problems, and partook of a common vocabulary. It is a crisp performance; then I realize that I heard it, word for word, when he keynoted a conference on the Bicentennial of the American Constitution in Washington eight years ago.

The most interesting remarks come from a retiring justice on the Spanish Constitutional Court, Luis López Guerra. He answers the question: what does Spain have to share with countries of the former Soviet Union and Eastern Europe? "First, I can tell them that anything is better than civil war," he responds. "Then I can tell them how we rebuilt our government after a long period of dictatorship. Next, I can share how we dealt with regional issues, like Basque separatism and Catalonian regionalism, and how we structured a court system to anchor our national life." As much as any of the longer-established democracies, the Spanish experience has relevance for people of the former Soviet Union.

On the last day, we visit Transylvania in a ten-vehicle motorcade, including four police cars with flashing lights, an ambulance, and a backup bus, into which we pour when our aging Irannational bus blows two tires and limps off the road. In the early morning, we drive through a fertile wine-producing region, where ancient steel mills were sown like dragon's teeth—ugly, dirty, expensive, and obsolete the day they were built. We drive past shepherds with recently shorn sheep, upon whose sides numbers are painted. Past a small Allied cemetery for airmen shot down in raids on the German-held oil fields nearby. Past a large granite column with an eagle on top, next to an old Iluychen four-engine plane sitting in a corn field. Past a field of storks recently returned for summer. Past an elderly gentleman perfectly attired in 1940s tailored woolen suit and period Homburg, with lace pocket handkerchief, walking stick, and plastic bag for his morning's shopping.

Our goal is Dracula's Castle, a fourteenth-century structure sitting atop a hill overlooking two important trade routes to and from Germany. The castle's owner was authorized to collect 3-percent customs from passing caravans. The castle is perched on an irregular, jagged pinnacle. Strangely shaped rooms are piled one above the other, accessible by circular staircases built around rocks. Each room is shaped differently, as if illustrating forms in a beginning geometry class. Even in Southern California, the design would have been considered awkward.

First Annual Warsaw Judicial Symposium

June 12–22: Since arriving in Warsaw a year ago, I had wanted to organize an event bringing American, Western European, and Eastern European judges together to discuss issues helpful to the judiciary in emerging countries. Two windfalls allowed this to happen: an unexpected grant from the U.S. State Department and some year-end money squirreled away by our director, who suddenly had to allocate it within hours or lose it. The First Annual Warsaw Judicial Symposium was born. Logistical planning is a nightmare. Telephones don't work in much of the old Soviet Union, only some places have fax machines, Russian airlines are unpredictable, and their schedules are unavailable. On June 1, we had only one certified applicant, a Latvian judge. I recalled the old saw: "Suppose we gave a party and nobody came."

Suddenly applicants descend upon us like hailstones. Three Moldovan judges arrive by train and spent the night in Warsaw's thief-ridden Central Station; they are nabbed by police, who call us, saying, "We've picked up three strangers at the railway station who claim to be Supreme Court judges. Do you know anything about them?" The Armenian delegation arrives early, comes to our office with bottles of brandy, and toasts international cooperation. By the time we open for business, sixty-three judges and prosecutors from eighteen countries assemble to debate vigorously legal reform issues.

We use case studies and group discussions, relative rarities in Central and Eastern European seminars. In the evening, we alternate seating arrangements at meals, so that different groups can mix with one another. After dinner, we form two large discussion circles in the lounge. Free speech is facilitated by free beer. A Belarus prosecutor produces a dried fish, an Uzbek judge offers a pocketful of nuts from home, other delegates bring olives or raisins, and the evening discussions are launched.

Jurists share their efforts to sort out relations with the legislative and executive branches and to obtain adequate salaries, court rooms, law libraries, and other equipment. A judge makes a good monthly wage in Poland, $5 in Armenia. There are long explorations of judicial ethics and professional behavior, plus issues concerning how to conduct trials while assuring defendants' human rights. The program's goal is to support building a judicial culture in Central and Eastern Europe; no aspect of a judge's life is left unexamined.

Sessions cover basic CSCE documents, especially the 1990 Copenhagen Human Dimension Meeting Document, containing extensive provisions on the independence of the judiciary. The European Convention for Human Rights and decisions of the European Court for Human Rights are reviewed, as are provisions in constitutions of former Soviet Union countries to meld international human-rights accords with domestic law and have them take precedence over domestic law when applied to actual cases.

Some of the most spirited discussions contrast the adversarial role of judge and prosecutor in Western judicial systems with the setup in Soviet-style systems, where the judge is under the procurator. Another issue involves free political speech and criticism of public officials and policies versus laws on defamation, slander, libel, and protecting state secrets. Most Central and Eastern European constitutions protect government officials from media scrutiny through libel and state secret laws, making it difficult for journalists to report on fraud or highly questionable acts by those in high places.

The Polish Ministry of Justice Conference Center at Popowo, near Warsaw, is our conference site, with visits to constitutional and supreme courts in Warsaw and to district and local courts. The location is attractive but isolated; there are groans from participants who want to sample Warsaw's night life instead of fresh air and birdsong at dawn.

Discussion leaders are members of the Polish judiciary who share the experience of being a free country that had suffered from the darkest days of communist repression. Professor Lech Garlicki of the Polish Constitutional Tribunal and members of that body tell many stories of the courts' struggle for independence from the legislative and executive branches. The event's two stars are two articulate American federal trial judges, Michael M. Mihm, chief judge, U.S. District Court for the Central District of Illinois; and Lloyd D. George, chief judge, U.S. District Court for the District of Nevada. Judge Mihm had been a prosecutor before going on the federal bench, and Judge George had long experience as an attorney and had handled an unusual variety of complex cases through the years. They answer questions directly; are strong, articulate presences; and have an incredible range of insights to share with participants. Their frankness and good humor are unusual in official discussions and earn them many friends. In addition to the booth interpreters, we assign student interpreters to both Judge Mihm and Judge George during coffee breaks, meals, and in the evenings. One of the booth interpreters is a chain smoker, the other pins her microphone above her heart and breathes heavily throughout the conference. It is like having a stethoscope wired into the audio system; a doctor could read her vital signs by listening in briefly. If two delegates talk among themselves, she stops the conference, raps loudly on the booth window, and tells them to be quiet.

When evening discussions end, a guitar is found, and folk songs are sung around an open fire. Judge Mihm is a quasi-professional folk singer; Lowrey Wyman, active in legal reform programs in Central Asia, was trained as an opera singer. A prisoner from the nearby low-security prison provides a guitar covered with pornographic illustrations. Multicolored regional beverages appear, as do Central Asian and Transcaucasian delicacies. Tajiks cook lamb pilaf one night; Georgians and Armenians make shashlik; participants exchange souvenir pins and flags. Kazakhstan and Ukraine offer to host the next gathering.

"Do You Like Armenia?"

June 23: In the afternoon we fly from Warsaw to Paris, standing in a long line at an Air France counter for the night flight to Yerevan, Armenia. Air Armenia is an unlisted airline; we can not book places in advance, except by calling an Armenian travel agent in Paris. The affable Armenian couple who run the mom-and-pop agency step deftly, like small goats, over bundles and bags, including plywood crates with Chinese characters marked "Armenian National Museum, Yerevan." Cardboard boxes are piled high, their wide bands of tape working loose before goods are loaded. Because of its prolonged armed conflict with neighboring Azerbaijan, almost all imports into Armenia must come by air, except for a trickle of goods across the Iranian or Georgian borders.

There are no reserved seats; I ask to board the plane early, a courtesy extended to Mafia leaders and high government officials, explaining that we are "guests of your Foreign Ministry." Somehow this is translated to mean that our imposing, bearded colleague, Professor Rzepliński, is "your country's foreign minister," so we are led past one hundred high school students who have spent the year in America and are given the first two rows of the large Russian plane. Our party's third member is a federal trial judge of Armenian-American origin, Dickran Tevrizian, from Los Angeles. Together we will critique the draft Armenian constitution and related laws and hold a seminar on the judiciary in a post-Communist society.

The plane is late in leaving, and the five-hour flight brings us to Yerevan at dawn. After descending the stairs in the plane's interior to the cargo bay, we climb down more steps to the ground, where a crowd of Armenians waits for relatives to disembark. After clearing passport control, we line up at a low table where a guard with a chit book registers each foreigner, who pays one dollar to receive a newsprint receipt. At the customs control line, we are met by the head of the Foreign Ministry's Human Rights Department, a thirty-one-year-old woman who studied public international law at the Sorbonne and lived for a year in New York. Sonia Bakar's father is a prominent Istanbul lawyer, attorney to the Armenian community there, which numbers about fifty thousand. Her mother runs the Armenian school in Nice. Sonia speaks five languages and earns two dollars a month. Her two-room rented apartment costs forty dollars a month, bottled gas thirty dollars a month. From her own money, she supports an orphanage; after two years in her present job, she plans to resign and tour Africa.

We pile into two black Lada cars, the preferred official cars of the old Soviet Union, and rush through unlit streets to the Hotel Armenia, which resembles a welfare tenement. Built eight years ago, it is falling apart. My room has fading brown wallpaper, worn through at bed level where bodies have rubbed against it. The yellow carpet is unpeeled in places, showing black divots where furniture has sunk into warm tar. Black smoke stains from a space heater's unsuccessful electrical branching smudge a wall. Paint peels; water from the next floor leaks into the plaster. Brown toilet water from the room above dribbles past the bathroom mirror one morning as I shave. Early each morning, a chambermaid runs from door to door, shouting "Hot water," available only an hour a day. Since the city is without power much of the time, ingenious Armenians rig automobile batteries to Yerevan's electrical system, charging the batteries for use during the rest of the day.

Although the country declared its sovereignty in 1990 and became independent in December 1991, when the Soviet Union was dissolved, our hotel's tourist folder still reads, "Dear Guest, Welcome to Yerevan, capital of the Armenian Soviet Socialist Republic and one of the world's oldest cities. Today's Yerevan, picturesquely situated on the bank of the Razdan River in the Ararat Valley, has a bright and poetic look. Nothing has remained here to remind you of the old dusty pisé town, which

Yerevan was before the establishment of Soviet power on the ancient land of Armenia."

The final touch: "Spacious squares, avenues and streets, verdurous parks and gardens, cool jets of the fountains, and buildings built of pink tuff—this is how you will remember the Armenian capital, a city of scientists, poets, artists, writers, and students."

The chief judge of the Supreme Court, Tariel Barseghian, is a former professor of civil law. As we walk to his office, he shows us places where, during the recent hard winter, hundreds of tiles separated from the wall. Supreme Court judges are named to the bench for ten years; there are thirty-two judges, usually hearing cases individually or in groups of three, or sometimes in larger numbers if the case is important. As in many other civil-law countries, the Supreme Court is really an appeals court, or a court of first instance for particularly grave crimes. The court is proud of a recent reform—paying the two lay assessors who sit with a judge the same salary as the judge. Lay assessors are a feature of the Communist judicial system, the argument being that justice should be meted out by the people. In reality, they usually defer to the professional judge, and some countries of the former Soviet Union wisely have abolished them as a relic of the previous totalitarian era.

If any litigant is not satisfied with the verdict, the case is appealed to a three-judge panel; if it is appealed further, a nine-judge panel hears it. Should the chief judge or the prosecutor still disagree, the case is reconsidered in plenary session of the entire court. The Armenian judiciary is considering adding an additional appeals court before the case reaches the Supreme Court. That's lots of judges.

Last year the court heard 500 civil cases, 21 as a court of first instance, the rest as an appeals court. About a third of the cases were reversed, new decisions were handed down in almost as many cases, and 5 percent were returned to lower courts for reconsideration. In criminal cases, the court was a court of first instance in 215 cases, double what the court might consider in ordinary times, "because of the harsh economic situation we now face." It was an appeals court in another 456 cases.

We speak of the need for an independent judiciary. "I'm doing all I can to make our judiciary independent," the chief judge says, "but it won't be easy. We depend on the Ministry of Finance for funds, and on the prosecutor for nominations. I will consider myself happy if our courts have one-fourth the independence of your courts." He says the country does not as yet have a constitutional court, although one is in the works.

Personally, he believes that a constitutional chamber of the Supreme Court will be fully adequate for Armenia's needs.

Like many countries of the former Soviet Union, Armenia not only accepts basic human-rights accords of the United Nations, the Council of Europe, and the Conference on Security and Cooperation in Europe, but gives them precedence over domestic law, should there be a conflict of laws. However, Armenian judges, like counterparts elsewhere in the former Soviet Union, have no copies of the relevant treaties and very few law books of any kind.

Armenians are a lot like the Irish; this is reflected in political discourse, often impassioned, dramatic, and inconclusive, ending with toasts to "peace and friendship," to family members, and "to your dead."

Our week in Yerevan coincides with intense constitutional debates, and both sides—those favoring a strong presidential system and those favoring a strong parliament—invite us to endorse their positions. Our response is that both systems have merit and that the choice is entirely a local one; however, for either to work, there must be an independent judiciary and a clear separation of powers with appropriate checks and balances.

There are three hundred lawyers in the country, and the bar association, although nominally under the control of the Ministry of Justice, is virtually independent. A massive effort is under way to revise Soviet-era codes to make them conform to modern democratic legal norms. The draft Law on Citizenship and several other proposed laws are given to us to review. The cavernous offices of the former Communist party headquarters, now the parliamentary building, is our meeting place. Halls are long and dark, windows heavily curtained, offices filled with party-commissioned art, usually heavy autumnal landscapes. The whole atmosphere conspires against humor or open conversation. In one such meeting, a deputy outlines the need for material assistance, such as information processing machinery. Outside, his secretary sits at one of the ministry's few word processors, playing a card game on the colored computer screen.

June 25: That weekend, we race along almost empty roads in Russian cars, speeding recklessly ahead, then braking suddenly at potholes or washed-out roads. We pass long bread lines. The price of bread is controlled by the state and each citizen given a monthly ration, obtainable through coupons. Bread also is sold in private markets for cash; most

Supreme Court judges join the bread lines, exchanging paper coupons for food.

Armenia is surrounded by unreliable (Georgia) or unfriendly (Iran, Turkey, Azerbaijan, plus the disputed enclave of Nagorno-Karabakh) neighbors. The country is blockaded, and almost all imports are flown in, adding greatly to their cost, although trade with Iran is increasing. Armenian diplomats find Iranian counterparts pragmatic and sensible, interested in expanding economic cooperation and having no ideological axes to grind. Gas and gasoline are piped from Russia through Georgia, but, because of Georgia's turmoil, the pipeline is blown up periodically. No gasoline stations line the roads, although the archeological remains of several were visible outside Yerevan. Mafia-controlled gasoline trucks are everywhere, the price per liter chalked on the rear. When we attempt to pay with a 1977 twenty-dollar bill, the proprietor returns it, saying that only American currency printed after 1985 is still in use. Many people rely upon horses for transportation, keeping cars and trucks garaged until better times. Few people and little farming are visible; children crowd the road, desperately pointing bouquets of flowers at our car, hoping for a sale. A crumbling shop offers "Cold Bear."

June 26: In the morning, an air show marks the Armenian Air Force's second anniversary. It is a wet, windy morning, and the Air Force's five helicopters fly over in formation. One bobs and weaves and others trail orange smoke, while the lead airship displays the national flag. Next, two groups of four parachutists drop above the airfield, circling slowly to polite applause. Colored smoke trails from smoke grenades attached to their feet. First one, then four 1960s MIGS stream over the small airfield from behind a hill; the display ends as the rain increases. Several troop units march past; not all their combat boots are of the same color.

The Church of Holy Etchmiadzin

The mother church of the Armenian Orthodox Church is our next destination, a structure dating from the fourth century A.D., to which various brownstone porches and anterooms were added through the centuries. On our way we stop at another church, one of three such historic buildings in the region south of Yerevan. It is dark inside the small, squarish building, where a priest conducts baptisms one after another, spending only a few minutes on each, although the families have dressed carefully in their best clothes for an important event. In a melodramatic gesture, he shows participants how to put their rouble offering on a small silver tray covered with an embroidered lace handkerchief. Quickly he tucks the money under his threadbare cassock, shiny at the edges from body grease. Nothing in his shifty eyes or casual manner suggests spirituality. Outside two youths sell sacrificial pigeons on the church porch. The main church of Holy Etchmiadzin, "the place where the only-begotten descended," was founded circa 285 A.D., when St. Gregory had a vision of Christ descending with a gold hammer in hand, instructing the saint to build a church at that place. A ram is staked at the church gate, ready for sacrifice. The cruelest example of such sacrifice we see is at another ancient church. A band of young men carry two young roosters by their wing tips, one youth per wing, obviously hurting the creatures. When we protest, they hold the animals upside down; the creatures struggle to keep their heads upright. The last scene is of the youths jabbing the animals, taunting them, in front of the church; the indifferent priest stands nearby, talking with villagers who smoke and drink wine.

At the main church, a monk, whom one of our number tips generously, breaks into schoolbook English and begins a tour. He shows us, first, remnants of a pagan temple underneath the church, then what he says is the actual spear used by a Roman soldier to pierce Christ's side. "I have studied the evidence and am convinced it is authentic," he continues without blinking. Next he produces a hunk of wood supposedly from Noah's Ark, grounded on nearby Mt. Ararat; plus assorted saints' bones and a late-nineteenth-century silver container resembling a Victorian punch bowl. This bowl holds forty-five pounds of oil and is unveiled once a year for making a batch of chrism, holy oil used in baptisms or to anoint the sick. During Holy Week, a secret combination of dried flowers and herbs is dumped into the container, chrism from the previous year is poured in, and the mix is stirred with a slender silver hand with a pointed finger containing a fragment from a saint's bone. Outside several churches, the faithful hang cloth strips from trees and make intercessions. For good measure, some toss pebbles in a nearby hole; if the stone stays in the hole, the prayer will be answered. "These people are like African shamans," a colleague observes of the clergy. My impression of religious life in Armenia: it is ancient, authoritarian, and out of contact with the world in which it functions.

At breakfast, a staff of nine serves seven guests. I am given "pancakes," deep-fried crepes. When we visit a local market, I buy plastic buckets of apricots, tomatoes, and strawberries. Fruit and vegetables are piled high, soon to rot, for there is no possibility of exporting them.

In the evening, we walk along a dark, lumpily paved street to the town's second hotel for dinner. (The remaining hotel houses refugees from the Azerbaijan conflict.) Our translator has a flashlight, as do many people, given the total absence of streetlights. We enter a cavernous, semi-circular hall; twelve guests hunch at tables that can accommodate two hundred. The waiter sets a generous portion of expensive caviar before us, but we tell him that we will order from the menu instead. As in every restaurant we visit, sonic boom music is provided by three persons manipulating a keyboard, synthesizer, and electric violin. The first half-hour set ends with a medley weaving together dance-beat versions of Grieg's *Piano Concerto* and Tchaikovsky's *1812 Overture*.

The basement restaurant we visit the following evening is guarded by a young man with a Kalashnikov rifle across his knees. A young woman dances sensuous Oriental numbers; her partner has a pistol strapped to his back. One song is entitled "Open Your Window, I Want to See Your Beautiful Body."

June 26: A concert by the Armenian Philharmonic Orchestra, with Loris Tjeknavorian conducting, is held in a spacious concert hall with excellent acoustics. The eighty-person orchestra plays in shirt sleeves, dedicating the performance to Judge Tevrizian. The program includes Sergei Prokofiev's Suite from *The Love for Three Oranges* and Dmitri Shostakovich's *Concerto No. 1 for Piano and Orchestra*, with Yuri Rozum, a talented young Russian pianist; it ends with Nikolai Rimski-Korsakov's *Scheherazade*. The orchestra could play with credit in any world concert hall. It is well-rehearsed, has a good ensemble sound, and plays an ambitious concert season, Friday, Saturday, and Sunday nights at 5 P.M. Only twice has the orchestra been abroad, once to Athens and once to Vienna; in both cities, several musicians defected. Orchestral scores are on sale in the lobby, as are 33-1/3 rpm records, some with hand-lettered jackets.

June 27: In the afternoon we attend a parliamentary debate on the draft constitution, but it turns out to be on the electoral code instead, since neither faction has the necessary votes to push their constitutional draft through. Two key electoral code issues concern candidates' eligibility to run for president. A proposal that only persons born in Armenia can run would eliminate the present president, who was born in Turkey; a provision requiring local residency during the last ten years would eliminate the former foreign minister, a popular figure (an American citizen who until recently was a successful Los Angeles attorney).

The meeting room, the motion picture theater in the former Communist party headquarters, has space-age features but also resembles a 1960s Russian television studio. Huge cameras with gun-mount tripods wheel about like World War II relics. On stage, a state-of-the-art electronic screen, with green letters and numbers like the most advanced soccer scoreboard, registers votes and lists information. The ancient wooden desk on the speaker's dais contains three word processors, behind which clerks type; when the speaker pushes a control button, it releases electronic impulses like a 1950s pinball machine hitting the jackpot. Deputies line up to talk for a half-hour each; dress favors black shirts with thin gray ties and matching gray shoes.

June 28: The author of the government's draft constitution invites us to dinner on two consecutive evenings. Vlademir Hosvannian is vice prosecutor of the republic; his associate is the Yerevan city prosecutor, Michael Baderian. Our first dinner is at a Mafia-run restaurant with excellent fresh-vegetable hors d'oeuvres followed by shashlik—meat and vegetables on skewers. The second dinner is at the Brandy Factory, the country's leading state-owned industry, which produces cognacs for export primarily to Russia and Ukraine, although the brand is increasingly popular in Southern California, where 250,000 Armenians live. The factory is in an Italian-style complex of brick buildings constructed in 1872. Our tour is delayed for an hour because there is no electricity. "If I had steady electricity, production would go up by 300 percent," the manager tells us. We are given a glass of hundred-year-old cognac in the "degustation room," a dark, wood-paneled room with an old Armenian carpet on the wall, together with a photo of a nineteenth-century general who defeated the Turks. Thinking that the evening is over, I say my good-byes, only to be told that we are invited to the tower room, four stories above the factory, for a nightcap. The room has a commanding view of the city and countryside. Few buildings are lit in Yerevan, but the moon is full and the view spectacular, suggesting the ruins of an ancient Mediterranean city. Two women Foreign Ministry staffers play Armenian folk tunes on the upright piano; one plays what my high school music teacher would call "a concert piece," punctuated by a strong right thumb glissando, accenting the piece's mood. Until this point, the prosecutor has parried our questions on the draft constitution; now he feels that it is time to talk.

What role will Russia have in the emerging constitutional drafts, we ask. None, our host replies. "Historically, Russia has always been our protector, against the Turks in the nineteenth century and now in our dispute with Nagorno-Karabakh. Russia always will assert hegemony in this region, which need not be bad if Russia and the West are at peace. We are a small country, and Russian power comes and goes in cycles; right now we are between cycles."

"What do you think of our constitution?" he asks. A silent, sullen waiter approaches with cognac glasses. "Much hard work has gone into the draft, but many questions remain," I open. The drafter says that the central dispute is between proponents of two drafts, one favoring a strong president, the other a strong parliament. "The President is like my brother," the prosecutor explains, making a Slavic embrace, as if the president were there to receive it. To demonstrate a point about how effective is the balance between legislative and executive bodies, he locks two forks together by their prongs, inserting a match stick in their midst, and balances the forks on a cognac bottle's rim. This illustrates the new constitution's balance. The construction crashes to the table.

Next we turn to separation of powers, checks and balances, separation of church and state, free media and human rights. Our host at first says, "No problem." He explores each issue with us, confidently stating his position, asking inquisitively, "What do you think about that?" Hosvannian takes in the arguments elliptically, sometimes asking questions, reluctant to admit problems. The prosecutor raises several crucial political issues, such as the economic blockade and the Nagorno-Karabakh dispute. Our response is, "Not all sensitive political issues of the moment are constitutional questions." Judge Tevrizian adds, "Let your constitution be like a machine into which issues can come and go, depending on circumstances; it should provide the basic structure of government around which other issues can be defined in various law codes."

Some constitutional deliberations are measured and rational; this is like a Saturday night Irish pub brawl. Intense discussions alternate with toasts, participants lean across the table, gesturing at one another, then shaking hands or embracing. Our table collapses, and cognac glasses roll across the floor. I ask the Foreign Office representative to play an ancient Armenian air, which produces a last round of embraces. "My brother, my friend," says the prosecutor, giving me a full-body press and bear hug, smelling warmly of garlic and cigarettes.

It is midnight. As we slowly descend the stairs, lights are extinguished throughout the factory, and people leave for home. They stayed on duty in case we decided to visit their sections. There are no lights at all along the stone walkways and steps, owing to the energy blackout, and I thread my way precariously.

"How do you like Armenia?" the prosecutor asks yet again, my response being rewarded with a final hug. Black Lada cars, waiting in the distance, quickly flash their lights like semaphores so that we can find them, and we speed through darkened streets to the hotel.

Human Rights and the Judiciary

Sixty members of the Supreme Court, Parliament, media, and human-rights organizations gather at Yerevan State University for our seminar. Electricity is rare, so each conference room is equipped with a grandfather clock which chimes the quarter-hours. At least ten such clocks throughout the building punctuate the discussion with lovely sounds at regular intervals, each chime differing a bit from the others. Judge Tevrizian speaks on judicial ethics, Professor Rzepliński on the jurisprudence of the European Court. I discuss separation of powers and checks and balances. Our chair is Deputy Foreign Minister Jerair Libaridian. He and I were doctoral candidates in history at the University of California at Los Angeles at the same time, but we had not met before.

On separation of powers, I contrast Abraham Lincoln's view that government is "of the people, by the people, and for the people," with Mussolini's opinion in the *Fascist Encyclopedia:* "Everything comes from the state, nothing must oppose the state, nothing be outside the state. The individual does not exist except as part of the state, and individual needs are subservient to the state." Then, from Hitler's *National Socialist Manual,* "You are nothing, the racial community is everything." "The most important question your constitution writers can face is the origin of political power—does it come from the individual or from the state? The answer to that question will determine the shape of your constitution," I conclude, moving on to discuss how abuse of power is prevented by the separation of powers enforced by an independent judiciary.

The level of discussion is high. The questions jurists ask reflect actual situations: How are judges protected against physical violence and intimidation? Can you think of examples of judges being persecuted for making unpopular decisions? Since an earthquake destroyed courts in an outlying region, court must be held in a small wooden house. Sometimes the judge sits across from a violent criminal; the judge's fear cannot be hidden. What can be done in such circumstances?

Can you still have democracy and many political parties? What international accords protect a free press and how can we learn about them? Can a judge be a member of a political party? When are cameras permitted in the courtroom? Are there rules of conduct for attorneys as well as judges? Under what circumstances can a judge be disqualified from hearing a trial? When can a judge be impeached? What is your personal and professional opinion of capital punishment?

At the seminar's end, I head down the dark stairway; three Supreme Court judges who have just returned from our Warsaw Judicial Symposium meet us. "Let's go someplace where we can sit at a table and talk about our memories of Warsaw," they say. The afternoon is free, we head for Lake Sevrn, a vast, crystal-clear inland lake surrounded by high snow-capped mountains. We climb winding steps to two ancient brown stone churches, dark as cellars on the interior. Tiny lancet windows high on the walls provide shafts of brilliant sunlight. Faded, sweat-stained vestments lie near the altar; the altar cloth, covered by gobs of wax from dripping candles, has been in place for much of recent history. Outside, a pilgrim's bench overlooks the lake; we sit there, shading ourselves from the brilliant afternoon sun, then descend to the lakeside for a lunch of freshly grilled trout and vegetables, plus ten toasts, one from each person at the table.

We speed back to Yerevan and the long wait for our plane's 4:30 A.M. departure, followed by a landing for fuel in a Bulgarian coastal resort. The Bulgarian airport staff treat us like prisoners of war, driving the bus to an unopened building and ordering passengers to dismount. We are left in the smoke-filled, airless waiting room for over two hours. When Professor Rzepliński and I move outside the door to a bench, a Medea-like captain of the guard and two associate furies order us back inside, using the rubber-covered antennae of their portable radios as prods. We are entitled to information on our plane's departure and to nonsmoking waiting space, we tell her. "Don't worry," I add, "you are an independent country now. Be nice and tourists will want to come here." The three guardians of post-Communist provincial airport security are furious. The leader pushes a large red-painted fingernail onto a telephone button and screams into the mouthpiece, threatening the wrath of Bulgaria's security forces upon us. Then she stalks off, because the phone is broken. We are left to sit in the cool morning breeze.

6

Belarus, Central Asia

July 9: Afternoon flight from Warsaw to Minsk, Belarus, to observe the presidential runoff election between a longtime Communist stalwart, Vyacheslav Kebich, and a thirty-nine-year-old collective farm manager, Alexander Lukashenko. Running as an anticorruption populist, Lukashenko came from nowhere and won 48 percent of the vote in the June 23 presidential elections—almost enough to give him a winning majority. Kebich, who has held every important position in the Belarus Communist party for years, gained only 17 percent of the vote in the June 23 election and drops to 14 percent in this election, which Lukashenko wins handily.

Minsk is a grim concrete apartment building town of 2,000,000 people, spread out endlessly along a rolling wheatlands landscape resembling a midwestern American state. Designated a Hero City of the Soviet Union, it was destroyed by Germans in World War II, when one out of four Belarussians were killed. Local partisans killed an additional 80,000 remaining survivors to settle internal political scores. It is a blood-drenched land; in 1988, Belarussians learned that Stalin, in one of his purges, ordered the massacre of 250,000 persons at Kurapaty Woods near Minsk. The land is flat, agricultural terrain for the most part, with some electronics plants, for the local people are quick learners, among the most educated people in the former Soviet states. The country depends totally upon Russia for raw materials and markets. Nothing in that equation will change in the foreseeable future, although, with the slow start of privatization, local people look to neighboring Poland for technology and nearby Lithuania for access to the sea.

Things have not gone well for Belarus. Russia's decision to sell energy supplies at world market prices resulted in Belarus's debts of $350 million for oil and $100 million for natural gas by June 1993. There was a seesawing of threatened cutoffs of supplies, cutoffs, partial payments, and more cutoffs, further hindering operation of the country's outdated industrial plants. In foreign policy, the country hoped to win aid and acceptance from the West by signing the Strategic Arms Reduction Treaty and by early removal of eighty-two long-range mobile nuclear missiles, ahead of the seven-year date agreed upon. As a fillip, the country made sizable cuts in conventional weapons as well. None of these steps resulted in any tangible rewards for Belarus. The country's chaotic economy and lack of economic progress scared off potential investors and international financial institutions. Russia treats its smaller neighbor as a vassal state. Belarus is too small, too unsettled, and too distant to attract Western interest. After a brief flirtation with the West, Belarus increasingly returns to Mother Russia's embrace.

"No Concert; This Is Minsk, Watch the Beautiful Sunset"

The Italian ambassador's driver should be meeting me at the airport forty kilometers from town, but he left early, so I negotiate a price with a rickety Russian taxi, cutting the fare in half. Not knowing a hotel, I wrongly follow the driver's counsel and go to the Planet Hotel, its shabby decor built around a Russian space-shot theme about how the conquest of space results in peace and friendship among peoples. "I'm here to watch your elections; are there any other observers?" I ask at the check-in desk. "You are the first and the last," a weary clerk replies. "For our elections, nobody," she adds, "We are not ready for democracy."

Although free and fair elections are routine in most Western countries, they are new to most of Central and Eastern Europe, and Western countries and international organizations send several observers to watch for fraud or ballot-stuffing. CSCE's Warsaw office originally was established as an Office of Free Elections to provide such observers. My visit is sponsored by the Italian embassy, because this year the Italian foreign minister is CSCE's chairman-in-office, responsible for conduct of its affairs. Calls to the Italian, French, and American embassies produce no replies; it is late Saturday afternoon. The clerk phones another hotel for the numbers of Swiss and British journalists staying there, but they are absent. I ask if there is an evening concert. "No concert. This is Minsk; watch the beautiful sunset," is the reply. Although she is helpful in making phone calls, the clerk confiscates my passport, saying I can not have it until after 8 A.M. the next morning, when the woman registering passports will return. "I need the passport now. You are no longer a Communist country. The KGB will not trouble you," I reply, receiving a nervous "Oh, yeah," smile in return.

A walk about town in the late afternoon leads to a meandering swamp with gardens and trees on its banks, the main feature of this part of town. A black dog swims briefly after a stick; brown ducks paddle through dark green weeds toward an island in the middle. Families stroll by the water, young lovers sit under trees. At an apartment house, eight young men stand on a balcony, passing a rifle with a telescopic sight from hand to hand. Most strollers are inexpensively but neatly dressed. Many young women stroll slowly up and down the walk together, hair neatly combed and lipstick and makeup applied with care. Most have only one good dress for outings, but clothes are carefully ironed and behavior correct, as in a Spanish *paseo*. Some young people pair off and sit at sidewalk cafes, endlessly sipping single small cups of coffee and smoking.

I enter the Hotel Belarus, known locally as the Belaroach, where the Italian Embassy occupies a wing. Although guests register on the ground floor, they collect passports and keys and pay bills at a second-floor "service center," a bedroom from which the furniture has been removed. The downstairs lobby is filled with youths playing electronic games; in a nearby bar, hunks of cold chicken rest on plates under a spotlight, surrounded by cans of beer and bottles of vodka with unfamiliar names. Saturday afternoon regulars sit in dark corners smoking and drinking. Outside, a wedding party gathers in a small sunlit courtyard. Near the long abandoned bandstand, an eight-person bridal party sips lukewarm Russian champagne and talks excitedly. There is no cloth for the rust-colored metal table, and the waiter long since has departed. It is a one-drink wedding reception; participants talk long after the bottle is emptied. The bride's dress and the groom's tuxedo are of heavy, shiny cloth, the sort used to line curtains.

I have never seen so many employees doing nothing as in hotels in the former Soviet Union. Three people sit at the reception desk, one at the second-floor service center. A woman attendant on each floor collects keys, while two uniformed guards stand outside the door, other guards sit within, and additional employees spend much of the day sleeping in chairs.

As I wait in front of the hotel, a BMW arrives. Like most modern Western cars, its front and back insignias have been stolen. The Italian ambassador says that thieves visit the drivers, saying that they have "found" the ornaments. I greet the driver, who I think might be the one who missed me at the airport, but instead he is a vender of Russian military hats, caviar, Russian army watches, and medals. "Do you need anything else?" he asks, visibly disappointed by my failure to buy something.

"No," I respond.

"Do you have any friends?" he asks.

"Yes, but not here," I reply. He packs his two cloth bags and heads off to another hotel.

It is Saturday night. The second round of presidential elections takes place the following morning, and I have yet to complete a phone call. World Cup soccer is showing on the lobby television set, and I join two police guards and the night clerk. The evening ends with a shower (the shower is a single pipe extending from the wall, the bathroom floor the drain). At 3 A.M., the hotel parking lot dog begins a bark-off with a dog passing on the next hill. At dawn I move from the Planet to the Belarus Hotel, and things take an upturn. A call to the American Embassy connects me with the duty officer, who also is in charge of election monitoring for Minsk city. We ride to several polling sites, mostly schools and social centers, where voter turnout is low. A cloudless Sunday means that people gather in parks or at country dachas; most will vote on their way back to town. By 8 P.M., voter turnout rises to 70 percent of the registered voters. The voting procedure is simple: the voter presents a government registration card, is given a ballot, enters one of two cloth-covered booths, marks her or his ballot, and deposits it in a sealed wooden box. Representatives of the country's four main political parties are free to watch the entire proceeding and then stay for vote counting at 10 P.M. Not many countries of the former Soviet Union have such open procedures.

After visiting several voting places, we head for the diplomatic compound. The Italian ambassador, silver-haired and in his late fifties, occupies the dacha of the former head of the Secret Police. It is one of a dozen old wooden houses set in the spacious tree-covered compound, surrounded by a high fence, and protected by guards. It could be the setting for a Chekhov play. The house has a long living–dining room and two smaller sunrooms on the north and south. The ambassador gives us tea and a political briefing, saying basically that Belarus depends totally on neighboring Russia; that the country is increasingly corrupt, with gangs from Moscow and elsewhere invading Minsk; and that Lukashenko is running on a reform ticket, promising to throw out at least seventy corrupt politicians. Belarus is one of four Russian republics with nuclear weapons, and disposing of such weapons remains a key problem. Additionally, nuclear scientists and technicians are unemployed and are being courted by potential employers from Libya, Iran, and Iraq. The Western program to find them alternative employment is, like so many aid programs, stillborn. We talked about Chernobyl ("wormwood" in Russian), the faulty nuclear reactor in neighboring Ukraine, from which clouds of radioactive waste blew over Belarus's best farmland in 1986. Despite the risk, the land is still farmed, and people live on it; often they are sent to other countries for rest cures.

Afterward, the ambassador shows me his locally acquired art collection of perhaps fifty oil paintings by Minsk artists; a few are of museum quality. We are joined by his wife, a tall, buxom young Belarus woman in flaming orange lipstick, slit skirt, and loosely-laced halter from which ample breasts protrude. She had been his interpreter, carefully studying English for several years in a Minsk school, waiting for her big opportunity. Her elderly husband, standing there in T-shirt and shorts, is politically shrewd but disorganized. He calls several drivers and translators for us, none of whom materialize, for he uses a portable phone whose receiver is not plugged into the wall.

In the evening we drive to the Central Elections Commission. A sign board lists a press center, a center for nongovernmental organizations, and, on the fourth floor, the Central Elections Commission. Only the fourth floor is lit. We pass the communications center, where four young people and a guard stare intently at a computer screen. Thinking that it contains incoming election results, we look; they are playing "Hangman." Nearby is the office of the Central Elections chair, an energetic, efficient law professor who organized twelve hundred persons around the country to conduct the elections, tabulate results, respond to complaints, and announce results. The only criticism the international community has, we say at a roundtable discussion the following day, is that there are possibilities for fraud because political party representatives are not present for the final crucial count at election headquarters. But this is easily correctable; as elections go, this one has been capably and honestly conducted.

At the same time as the Belarus election is held, there are presidential elections in its much larger neighbor, Ukraine. In both cases, new persons come to power in an anticorruption campaign; in both instances, the winners have called for closer cooperation with Russia. The Ukrainian winner, Leonid Kuchma, is faced with the problem of an East-West split. The country's western part looks toward Western Europe, while the eastern part, which includes eleven million expatriate Russians, seeks closer union with Russia. Ukraine has a turbulent history. Its western lands were not claimed by Russia until 1944 and the final months of World War II; the strategically rich Crimea, historically not part of Ukraine, was given to it by Khrushchev in 1954. In December 1991, Russia, Ukraine, and Belarus voted to dismantle the old Soviet Union and create a Commonwealth of Independent States, with these three Slavic states as its core members.

Return to Central Asia

August 27: Arrival at Almaty Airport in Kazakhstan at midnight Warsaw time, 5 A.M. local time. Three hours to obtain an airport visa, have passports stamped, pick up luggage, and clear customs. One clerk for each of these four functions, serving two hundred passengers from the German airbus. Lufthansa is the only Western airline servicing the Central Asian capital, and the thrice-weekly airbus is filled each way. Our Foreign Ministry driver is a no-show, so we pile into a rickety but clean Lada taxi with a Russian driver who uses the twenty-minute predawn ride to criticize Kazakhstan since its independence from Russia. As we look among the various drivers waiting outside the airport, this one, an elderly, heavy-set Russian, probably retired military, is obsequious and polite. However, once we enter his cab, all that changes. The small red vehicle shakes both from hitting potholes and from his anger. "No one works any more," he says. "These people will come crawling back to Russia as soon as Russia is strong again. Vladimir Zhirinovsky was born here . . . he should be given unlimited powers . . . those who oppose him should be shot." Like many Russians in Central Asia, the unhappy driver will return to Russia if he can afford it. He represents nostalgia for a lost order, a sentiment shared by millions of other Russians in Central Asia.

An Angry *Homo Sovieticus*

The Russian stance toward the lands of its former empire differs little from that expressed by the taxi driver: "They'll come crawling back." In

Tajikistan and Azerbaijan, Russia supports forces favorable to Russian interests. In Georgia, Shevardnadze's bid for independence confronts the reality of having to ask for Russian military support to maintain peace. Russia also sees itself as protecting millions of ethnic Russians scattered throughout the old empire, from Latvia to Kazakhstan. Russians in the new republics of what used to be the Soviet Union would like to return to the Russian homeland, but that is unlikely. Many are retired or are near retirement, living in homes they have owned for years. Housing is difficult to find in Russia; at last report, more than nine million persons were looking for apartments there.

No nationalistic population is potentially more volatile than the twenty-five million ethnic Russians living beyond the former Soviet Union's border. For many, life was privileged, with access to the best jobs, apartments, medical care, schools, and stores. Their status resembles that of the British in India or the French in Senegal. Two difficult choices emerge: to stay and watch the visible shrinking of income and status, as has happened to expatriate communities in Africa, or to return to Russia as strangers in a chaotic land with high unemployment and nonexistent housing.

While the Soviet Union is gone from the map, Stalin's carefully drawn internal state borders divide ethnic groups in two, as in Georgia and Tajikistan; in other places, large ethnic groups live as perpetual minorities, cut in two by arbitrarily drawn frontiers. The problem of assimilating minorities into mainstream political life will plague this region for generations.

At the hotel in Almaty we are met by our Foreign Ministry contact, a young diplomat dressed in blue jeans, who apologizes for the no-show driver. The young diplomat has just been assigned to the Kazakhstan embassy in Washington, D.C., which has a staff of twenty-one persons. When I describe the Russian taxi driver's conversation, he replies, "I am pessimistic. Russia is getting harder and harder to deal with. The eastern third of our country is occupied by Russians. They want to break off and become part of Russia."

Bishkek in August

August 28: The drive from Almaty to Bishkek, Kyrgyzstan's capital, is three hours by car across flat farmland; the flat landscape resembles Kansas but with high mountains. Piles of melons and baskets of raspberries are for sale along the roadside, as are plums, sold by the plastic pailful. We pass a truck filled with travelers and two horses, then move past loads of lumber and Russian trucks loaded with cotton bales, packed so heavily that each truck leaves a trail of floating cotton fluff. We also pass a roadside shop called "Bubble Gum" and partially destroyed concrete bus stops, where passengers built fires in the corner on cold winter days. Roadside repair places allow drivers to mend small Ladas or Moskvich cars, which often rattle apart on the bumpy roads. Every few kilometers is the turret-like concrete-and-steel entrance to a bomb shelter; Kazakhstan is one of the few non-Russian republics with supplies of nuclear arms.

Bishkek is small and unspectacular, a dusty concrete-and-steel Russian garrison outpost filled with four- to eight-story apartment houses crumbling and patched together, falling apart by the time they are built. At what once was the town's edge but now is a suburb stands a Russian power plant, a vast mausoleum to archaic technology; three nonfunctional smokestacks tower over it.

Our affable, confident chauffeur, Victor, is at least a major in the Secret Police, for no ordinary driver could order pedestrians over to ask directions and then dismiss them so abruptly after they provide information. A dusty haze envelops the sprawling town. This is late summer; days are hot. Meat is fetid, as there is no refrigeration. Flies explore piles of overripe vegetables. Since it is Sunday afternoon, we visit the two-story National Museum. Near the entryway, a small Chinese tractor, the remains of an earlier exhibit, is parked. The museum contains a carpet display from Almaty, oils and watercolors by local artists, a room of plastic reproductions of Greek sculpture, a replica of a nomad's tent with the ground under it covered with rugs and piles of embroidered pillows, signs of wealth stacked behind the family chief's seat. My favorite room is filled with Soviet realistic works with titles like "The Nomad's Son Joins the Army," "Electrification Comes to a Rural Village," and "Building the Lenin Tunnel," as well as portraits of local officers who fought in the Russian army. The artists were skilled painters; their message was pure propaganda—the victory of socialism over capitalism. One painting, "My Collective Farm," shows the political commissar's car, a truck, a council of elders listening to a speaker, children dancing, and government workers gathered in a tent listening to a hand-turned period phonograph playing a political message.

The "Colombia of Central Asia"?

Ominous news in the *Kyrgyztan Chronicle*. The Bishkek Regional Court has closed the Parliament-sponsored newspaper, *Svobodnye Gory (Free*

Mountains) for "deliberately discrediting state bodies and the legitimate state power in the person of the president." Also, the Osh regional court returned a not-guilty verdict against several persons, including a militia captain, accused of smuggling fifty-two kilograms of heroin. The paper concludes, "Against the background of the Afghan opium traffic that goes through Osh, the case in Osh court is alarming. It shows a real threat of closing up the judicial bodies and rule by the narcomafia. If Kyrgyzstan goes this way, it may turn into the Colombia of Central Asia in the future."

Many narcotics traders are very young or very old. The young have no jobs and are dealers, out to make quick money, while the aged are on fixed pensions, live in poverty, and grow opium poppies, often hidden among swamp grass, so that government helicopters cannot spot them easily from the air.

In the evening, I meet with Conrad Huber and Elizabeth Teague from the Office of the High Commissioner on National Minorities in the Hague; they plan a seminar on responses to interethnic conflict. From my room's balcony, we watch the sun go down over the city. A strong breeze from the Central Asian desert fills the air with powdery dust, tinting the sprawling city a chalky color. At dinner in the Hotel Dustik (Friendship), a clever waiter tricks us. Although Elizabeth speaks excellent Russian, the fresh fish we were promised is two cans of rubbery-tasting canned Russian fish in oil. Generous portions of red and white caviar, which we did not order, are added, doubling the bill. Bowls of watery Chinese noodle soup comprise the first course, to which chunks of inedible meat are added. A bat darts about the circular room; suddenly the three of us leap up from the table, opening all the windows we can, hoping that it will escape from the Dustik Hotel's dining room.

The next day I meet with American Ambassador Edward Hurwitz, who is leaving after two years. He says that until now he has called the country "the Switzerland of Central Asia," but he is concerned about the government's increasing authoritarianism, including the recent closing of the two newspapers. *Svobodnye Gory* he describes as an old-time Communist rag, "low quality stuff, anti-president, not pro-democracy nor for human rights." The second paper, *Politica,* a weekly supplement to a popular daily, *Jella,* is outspoken in its reform-minded criticism of the government. It was closed for not being properly registered, a device often employed by authoritarian governments and one that easily can be used to shut down virtually any opponent. The state's indictment was sweeping: "The paper also spreads materials which violate the norms of civil and national ethics, [and it] deliberately insults the leaders of foreign states and their national symbols. All of these things damage the interests of the state, its unity and stability." The most frequently cited example of the paper's transgressions was offered by the Chinese prime minister during a recent state visit; the paper ran an article entitled "Here He Comes, Looking at China's Next Colony."

August 29: The Ministry of Foreign Affairs conference room is furnished with an imported dining room table and chairs, buffet, and credenza. An unplugged bedroom lamp sits atop the buffet. With the International Organizations staff, we discuss possible seminar subjects. Next we meet with Minister of Justice Kachyke Esenkanov, who proposes a conference on "How do you have free yet responsible media?" He says that the May 5 constitution contains an article supporting free media, but since it was adopted, the government has closed two newspapers. "We do not know the limits of what one can do in criticizing the president; there is no clear statement of how to close down the media, or what constitutes a responsible media. We are preparing draft legislation on political parties, nongovernmental organizations, and mass media. The drafts aren't optimal ones; you can study them and give us your remarks. It would be good if your experts would discuss these issues with our journalists, politicians, and jurists. We also are preparing a criminal code and a criminal procedures code; they should be ready in a month. In these drafts we foresee a new approach to a criminal justice system. We want your comments on them as well."

The deputy chair of the Supreme Court, Larisa Gutnichenko, who was a participant in our Warsaw Judicial Symposium, says:

> This summer we had our first congress of judges. Now all our court bodies are independent from the Ministry of Justice; now we have self-management. A council of judges was appointed, with thirty-one members, two from each oblast [district], plus one each from the military, supreme, constitutional, and administrative law courts. The council will create new legislation about court structures, the status of judges, and the further unification of all courts into one judicial system. I was in Kentucky and Mississippi in the United States and came back with a clear idea of what can be done. Equality between prosecutor and defense is important; our preliminary decision is to introduce the concept in several regions. One problem is that we may not have enough lawyers; under our Soviet heri-

tage, the idea of an independent lawyer was unknown, and everything was done by the state. Recently our Supreme Court decided
to cease being a court of first instance and be an appeals court.
The tradition was that a citizen could appeal to either a district
court or to us, or a district court could send a case directly to us,
which meant that there was no possibility of a step-by-step appeals process.

She says that Kyrgyzstan is one of the few countries of the former
Soviet Union to limit the procurator's power, giving control of the judicial system to judges instead. She adds, "I'm of the same opinion as the
minister, that the law on mass media is far from being perfect. We have
discussed the law for two years; the opinions of jurists were not taken
into consideration, and the law is not clear. We need a much clearer document, that is why we must consider the experiences of other countries.
"I would like you to pay attention to our draft civil law code. Many
of its provisions are not favorable to a country with a market economy.
The problem is it contains 376 articles; many people worked on different sections of it without being aware of what one another were doing."

"The Clerk Does Not Have a Working Pen"

Later, Chief Justice Cholpon Bayekova of the Constitutional Court adds:

Much of our material is from the 1960s and 1970s. We have no
computers, no fax machines, no modern law books. Having such
technical problems, we cannot function as a modern judicial system. Payment is important. Judges receive less than the average
civil service salary; a local judge makes less than a local police officer.
In such a situation, we cannot expect our judges to lead a proper
life. There are lots of judges, especially young ones, who rent rooms
or flats, who don't own their own homes. Sometimes, if a building
owner knows the tenant is a judge, they will be asked to move out.
All of this is expensive, and our budget is not even increased for
inflation. Judges must use public transportation. Sometimes a judicial proceeding must stop because the clerk does not have a working pen. Also, there are no adequate pensions for judges; women
must retire at 55, men at 60, yet they will spend their final years in
poverty.
We are still working under Soviet-era law; for example, crimi-

nal defendants are put in cages; all the judicial practice of the past favored the state. Take Article 80: the death penalty was presupposed for economic crimes, yet personal robbery brought a ten-year sentence. We heard so many lies we did not know what the truth was.

September 1: Return by car to Almaty. It is Saturday afternoon, time for weddings, with cars racing up and down the town's main street, horns tooting, people hanging out of windows. Red and white streamers and large imitation wedding rings are tied to the roof of each wedding car.

Today we planned to meet with the minister of justice, but he was called to Parliament, so instead we visit the National Gallery, a spacious, well-laid-out museum with few visitors. It has rooms full of early European and nineteenth-century Russian works, plus several landscapes and still-lifes by local artists and a room of Central Asian fabrics.

In the afternoon, we meet with Dr. Leonid Stonov, representing the Union of Councils, an American Jewish human-rights organization; and Eugenii Zhovtis, his associate with the Kazakhstan-American Bureau of Human Rights. They describe how the government uses a system of registration to control the activities of nongovernmental organizations (NGOs) and professional groups. "The system of registration is very complicated; it is a way of controlling people. For example, a political party cannot register unless three thousand people sign their names and are verified. That is why we have only three legal parties registered at present. The organization also must present its program and constitution in two languages; this takes a long time, and people are apathetic. Parties are small; five to seven hundred active members is a good number for most. The procedure for NGO registration is simpler, but the government will try to control an organization's activities by comparing its constitution with what it actually does. The Ministry of Justice tries to control NGOs; we blocked it in parliament, but the battle goes on."

There is an elaborate system of social controls. For example, the 1991 Supreme Soviet Law on the Rights of Association says that, ten days before an organization plans a demonstration, it must apply for a permit. Most such requests are denied for "unsuitability of the action in the present situation."

Most NGOs say that the local human-rights climate is "Not Iraq, Uzbekistan, Turkmenistan." There are no political prisoners and no direct pressure on the media or human-rights groups, but the vagueness of regulations, the government's omnipresence, and the lack of a tradition of political independence means that most groups practice self-censorship. If not, newspapers find that they are denied newsprint or that printing costs are increased sharply.

September 2: A meeting with the deputy chair of the Constitutional Court, Professor Igor Rogov, a specialist in criminalistics (the study of criminal behavior), who says that many questions remain unanswered about both the court's role and its working conditions. Kazakhstan's Constitutional Court has a clear function to control the acts of executive and legislative branches, and of other courts.

> We had unpleasant times in 1992; some people thought we had too much power and wanted to reduce our role, but the deputies supported us. Now the Parliament is discussing constitutional amendments. Our main problem is to sort out our function in relation to other courts. On constitutional issues, many courts similar to ours are required to give advice to Parliament before a law is passed, but we give it afterwards. Still, the question of citizen access to our judicial system is unsolved. Some citizens apply directly to us, but others go through other courts, like the High Court of Arbitration. Our tradition is the Soviet tradition; when I was professor of law, I sometimes read what a sentence was before the case was tried. We knew about American justice from books and films, but not until I went there did I see a judge's power. Even prisoners are treated differently. Here we put prisoners in a cage; in the U.S. a prisoner sits with their lawyer, not in a cage.

September 3: In the evening I buy two small local landscapes. The woman selling them is the Russian equivalent of the woman-in-the-floppy-hat from cartoons from the *New Yorker*. Six policemen move through the art dealers outside Hotel Kazakhstan, ordering them to pack up. Why would the police repress merchants when there is so little trade? When the police see us, they leave the dealers alone. "Will you be here tomorrow?" the woman asks. "I will bring you an apple." She pays my Polish colleague, Irek Stępiński, a supreme compliment: "You are more difficult to bargain with than the Koreans."

September 3: On our final evening in Almaty, we walk along the hotel's promenade, as crowds of well-dressed young people pour into a concert hall easily holding five thousand people. A local rock band, Free Style, plays. A local bank and construction company, eager to promote business, sponsors the concert. The music is hypnotic, the light show carefully synchronized with the singer. At least thirty young women and many children parade onto the stage following numbers, presenting the singer with bouquets of roses. A "New Kazak," a wealthy businessman, bid eighty dollars for the group's latest record album.

A sleepless night, punctuated by the barking of at least three different dog packs and an occasional car racing by with its tape deck turned on full blast, playing metallic rock music. My room's refrigerator kicks on, sounding like a Russian plane about to take off; later it shuts off automatically, with a metallic jolt, after which the machine shakes four times and succumbs into silence.

As we leave for the airport at 5:30 A.M., sixty young employees of Shaggy's Casino—croupiers, cashiers, bar girls, and guards—stand in the night air, chatting like recently awakened birds, waiting for a rickety bus to take them home.

7

Albania, Ukraine, Tajikistan

September 8: This week an Albanian Court hands down its decision in an espionage and possession-of-firearms case against five Albanian citizens of Greek origin. They are found guilty and given six- to eight-year sentences. The trial has attracted world media attention and observers from international legal groups. The Greek government has conducted a shrill anti-Albanian campaign, expelled thirty thousand Albanian workers illegally resident in Greece, appealed to NATO and the United Nations to intervene, dropped leaflets on Albanian villages, and issued condemnatory statements. At the request of the High Commissioner on National Minorities, we have sent a trial observer, Professor Andrej Rzepliński from Warsaw University, with whom I had investigated a human-rights trial in Moldova. Rzepliński had been to Albania twice before to train police officers in human-rights standards and had monitored over two hundred trials in Poland in the dark days of Communist repression.

The courtroom was small, like a schoolroom, and crowded. The country had purged its Communist-era judges; new prosecutors and judges were in their late twenties or early thirties. Neither they nor the defense attorneys knew international human-rights norms nor how trials are conducted. The indictment was an emotionally charged but factually vague document; although aimed at the five Albanians of Greek origin, it could have applied equally to hundreds of other such persons. Ostensibly a criminal charge, it was a broad-gauged political message to the Albanian-Greek community to "cool it."

Originally, the defendants were charged with treason, but this charge was dropped after pressure from the Greek community in the United States was conveyed to the Albanians, whose prosecutor announced he could not support the Stalin-era criminal charges. Part of the problem was that the Albanian criminal code is undergoing revision, but no one is sure at what stage which laws apply. Although the espionage and arms-possession charges remained, the only viable citation was illegal possession of firearms. However, almost all Albanian men are hunters and keep old fowling pieces in their huts. The prosecution harangued defendants but rarely referred to the indictment. The defense attorneys were powerless. There is no tradition of an independent bar in Albania, and the defense attorneys rarely objected to anything said by the prosecution or the judge. In fact, the entire defense summation for the five accused took only half a day. Procedural errors made this proceeding a case study in how not to run a trial. Defendants were arrested without warrants and were denied counsel. In one place, the inexperienced judge instructed the defense to begin questioning a prosecution witness before the prosecution had conducted its own examination of the witness.

My hope has been that monitoring this trial, and one I was working on in Turkey, would establish our office as an independent trial-monitoring agency in human-rights cases. Such a role is clearly within the mandate of the "Office of Democratic Institutions and Human Rights." Human-rights trials are always controversial, and if we assume this mandate, it must be done prudently and professionally. But, as Professor Rzepliński left the courtroom, he gives an interview to an Albanian radio journalist, who asks if it was a fair trial. "I suppose the Albanians think so," he says. This is translated by the world press as "CSCE Observer says Greeks Get Fair Trial." The Greek Foreign Ministry protests before Rzepliński returns to Warsaw. At a stopover in Vienna, he releases to the Helsinki Foundation, a human-rights organization of which he is a member, the draft report that he is preparing for us, allowing them to distribute it publicly before we see it. For good measure, he phones a Warsaw daily and gives it an interview about the trial.

I follow his return from city to city by protests from Greeks or Albanians and see our potential trial-monitoring role disintegrate before it ever is established. Rzepliński shows me the report after returning to

Warsaw. It is a set of working notes and impressionistic comments. Its English is spotty, its arguments presented only sketchily. I spend the next few days defusing the situation. By then the trial is over, and the defendants are in jail. The publicity Rzepliński impulsively generated obscures his perceptive insights into the case. It is a rigged trial violating criminal procedure and international human rights norms. But that fact is buried in the mounting Albanian-Greek conflict. The Albanian ambassador in Warsaw releases a crude but clever press release, quoting a conversation with Rzepliński, who said it was a fair trial and that our office apologized for the report being leaked to the press. I rework parts of the report, but only sitting down with the author for a few days and producing a new document would suffice. In the end, I write a brief summary of its contents for CSCE's chairman-in-office, the Italian foreign minister, who shelves it as "non-official study," thus burying it.

Meanwhile, tiny Albania, a country with a bloody judicial heritage, tries to limit our human-rights monitoring activity, arguing that our office exceeded its mandate and should only monitor trials when the CSCE Permanent Committee requests it, and then only with the host country's approval. The ploy is obvious. A trial will be over before a request is forthcoming from Vienna; and host countries, especially totalitarian ones, rarely will allow human-rights trial monitors. Other countries, like Turkey, defensive about their human-rights records, side with the Albanians. The question is tabled for the forthcoming Budapest Review Conference, where it dies. Meanwhile, CSCE's secretary general says we should avoid anything controversial and that activity like this is another justification for moving our office to Vienna under his direct control.

Rzepliński, director of a leading Polish human-rights organization, has torpedoed our human-rights monitoring effort before it is launched. Given the difficulties he has created, I could not use him on another mission and in fact never see him again. He gives an interview to a Greek newspaper, telling them that, to avoid compromising his role as a human-rights activist, he would not accept additional trial-monitoring requests from CSCE. There are to be none to refuse.

Warsaw Autumn

September 27: An evening walk with Tigger. Days grow shorter, leaves fall, the autumn cold sets in. Two young lovers are locked in a passionate embrace in the small park near us, their tiny poodle nearby. Suddenly I hear a death howl from their dog but can see nothing because of a concrete parapet. The couple disengages quickly, adjusting clothes. Tigger trots busily in my direction. Visions of a dying or mutilated poodle flash before me; I try to compose a sentence of condolences in Polish, when the small dog patters busily toward us. Meanwhile, Tigger inspects a pile of fallen leaves, and the couple walks soberly away, the fleeting evening moment lost forever.

A Changing Neighborhood

October 7: The greatest change in our neighborhood during the past year has been the amount of new construction. Zoning laws do not exist in Warsaw, and entire new floors are built onto frail structures, walls moved out, new roofs added. Plumbers, carpenters, and electricians often moonlight, so work takes place most evenings and weekends. On a walk, Tigger and I watch four workmen walking precariously along a rooftop undergoing reconstruction. Further down the road is an old house with new prefabricated windows and doors with double-thick glass and carefully cut wood instead of the crude construction of Communist times. Several houses have added newer, brighter kitchens; others have modern brick driveways and sidewalks and carefully landscaped gardens, one with an old statue of a cherub set among geraniums. Rusting, noisy Russian cars are being replaced gradually by German, American, and Japanese models. Next to our bus stop, on a tiny sliver of land, an entrepreneur has opened a fruit and vegetable shop, sandwiched between another shop selling beer and soft drinks, and a parking lot. The new shop is built of prefabricated steel and offers quality imported fruits and vegetables, including six different types of American or English catsup. Passengers descending from homeward busses line up for their evening purchases.

Within a week of its opening, the shop is spray painted with graffiti. About the same time, a restaurant a block away is fire-bombed. In the absence of a strong police force, protection rackets are everywhere. Purged for its strong ties to the former Communist government, the police force is rebuilding slowly, often with young officers from the country. "Warsaw is like Chicago in the 1920s," a Pole tells me; his daughter's bicycle was just stolen, and last year his car was taken from the parking space in front of his house. This summer, at the height of the tourist season, most major shops in historic Old Town closed for three days to protest the lack of police protection against extortioners; then, for several months, police vans were everywhere.

Ukraine in Transition

October 12: Morning flight to Kiev, Ukraine's capital. The Soviet-era airport is fog-encased, but the sun breaks through; surrealistic images multiply. Several wild dogs curl up asleep at the airport's entrance, although it is 9 A.M. Others wait for scraps outside an airport workers' outdoor buffet—slim pickings. The town road is long and flat, but birch trees with golden leaves line both sides. Contrasts. A black-clad woman with straw hand-broom and four goats sweeps up leaves under a billboard advertising the latest Japanese car. Lumbering Russian trucks, props from a Soviet realist film, inch through the fog, passed by late-model Mercedeses and BMWs. Young men with new leather jackets and cellular phones drive these cars, passing old men in cloth jackets on barely working bicycles. Blocks of fourteen-story apartment buildings rise canyonlike on each side of the road, badlands mesas in the morning sun.

Our destination: the Ukrainian parliament building and a conference on elections sponsored by our office and the International Foundation for Electoral Systems, which helps countries conduct elections and modernize their electoral systems. Perhaps forty persons attend, mostly members of the parliamentary staff. The invited deputies responsible for actually writing the law are no-shows, as they are engaged elsewhere in mortal combat with the president. Parliament says that his actions are unconstitutional; the president replies that it is a renegade body lacking legitimacy. Ukraine has no constitutional court to decide the issue.

The morning session chronicles vague electoral laws and no courts to enforce them and election officials intimidating voters by entering balloting places with them. Several cases are reported of militia bringing portable ballot boxes to housebound voters and telling voters which candidate to select. "Dead soul" voters, "tombstone voters" as they would be called in America, are numerous. Complaints about government employees using their state offices, telephones, and transportation to support official candidates are widespread. Numerous obstacles prevent opposition candidates and parties from registering.

The country is large, fifty-two million people; its economy is a shambles, its precedents for dealing with democratic political systems nonexistent, and its politicians headstrong. The old Communist and Socialist parties retain the structures and numbers of earlier days but have no new ideas. Likewise, the broad-based democratic opposition, the Rukh (movement in Ukrainian), was effective in the final days of Communist rule but has disintegrated, its handful of leaders having been co-opted into the government.

There are unresolved issues about the Black Sea Fleet, the flotilla of aging rust-bottom ships claimed by Russia and Ukraine. The present proposal is for both parties to divide the ships, then Russia will purchase Ukraine's share. A dispute over shore assets and choice sea-front land is another issue. One proposal is for Russia to lease the land; Russia wants a ninety-nine-year lease, but Ukraine offers twenty-five years.

The thorny Crimea question is partly an economic issue. Ian Brzezinski, in Kiev as adviser to the Parliament, says of the Crimea, "It used to be the Palm Springs of the Soviet Union and now it is the Coney Island of Ukraine." Once a choice retirement site for Russians and a tourist center, in recent years its political and economic problems have reduced it to shabbiness.

Russian Interests

Russia regards Ukraine with lasting geopolitical interest; Ukraine is Russia's soft underbelly. Consider a map with Moscow in the center. Russia is vulnerable, as it has been for centuries, with soft western and southern borders. Russia wants to keep Ukraine divided, weak, and off-balance, and thus retain control. The basic decision before Ukraine is which way to head, toward Europe or toward Russia. The region's history reflects classic Euroslav and Russoslav orientations. Russia will work vigorously against Ukraine's entry into NATO or the European Union. As long as Ukraine's orientation is undecided, Europe's eastern frontiers will be unclear. The present indecisiveness could lead to an economic Curzon line, the proposed 1920 line dividing Poland and Germany. It could also divide Europe into a Europe of haves and have-nots, rich northerners and poor southerners.

October 14: In the afternoon, at a European Media Institute Forum, we discuss media laws. Its Ukrainian representative is Elena Chernyaskaya, an attractive and purposeful young woman who has just completed a doctorate in English at Oxford, writing on the novels of Salman Rushdie. Her mother was lead dancer in the Kiev ballet and now teaches dance. Her father is a safety inspector with the Ministry of Labor; Elena is the only child. The family lives in a large apartment near the opera. Elena, who is of Armenian-Russian-Ukrainian-German ancestry, wants to establish her own import-export business, but privatization has yet to take hold in Ukraine. At least ten offices must approve any permit. Bribes are expected, and foreign currency must be exchanged immediately into local currency. One day last year she arrived home early and met a worker who said he was there to repair the telephone, and could he borrow a ladder? He installed a small box to the line connecting the apartment's telephone line with the exterior. When asked if all the building's phones would be improved in such a manner, he replied, no, just theirs. KGB headquarters is around the corner, and the family, since signing two petitions in the 1970s, has been under periodic surveillance.

In the mist we walk past the great gate of Kiev, a squat brick pile which would make the entrance to a nineteenth-century British railway station look as impressive as Stonehenge. Nearby is the opera house. Tonight's performance is an early Tchaikovsky opera, with a conductor from Slovenia who says he will take the company there in a month, if warfare in the former Yugoslavia does not deter their travel. Waiting in front of the opera, I watch the faces of people arriving for the spectacle. Their looks are intense, their gait determined and hopeful. Life in Kiev is hard, but here, for an evening, is escape to a fairy tale world where a blind princess is rescued by a prince from a distant land, and her sight restored.

The opera's stage setting looks as if it has been constructed by a high school carpentry class. Several long burlap runners are attached to bamboo turrets and spray-painted gold; four red wagon wheels are stuck around its edges.

The opera house, beautiful but badly in need of refurbishing, was built at the nineteenth century's end, with a deep stage and space for a large orchestra. Ms. Chernyaskaya says that Kiev, like Russia and many countries of the Commonwealth of Independent States, experienced an exodus of Jewish musicians and doctors, resulting in a deterioration of cultural and medical life. The opera has two excellent singers, a young tenor and a mezzo-soprano, a statuesque thirty-two-year-old woman with an exceptionally lovely voice. At intermission we chat with the cast backstage. The young mezzo, a student of Ms. Chernyaskaya's cousin, is like a "second daughter" to the family. She has had difficulty making a career breakthrough, despite her exceptional voice. Although she was picked for advancement by the company's aging director, her career prospects ended when she refused to sleep with him. Later she signed a contract with the St. Petersburg Opera, a prestigious company, but for political reasons the director reneged. The young singer had no telephone in her apartment but went to the Chernyaskayas' to call the director and plead with him to reconsider. When he refused, she fell paralyzed, there at the telephone, and did not recover for several weeks.

Our interpreter is named Ninel, *Lenin* spelled backwards. During the 1920s and 1930s, many parents, caught in revolutionary euphoria, named their children Oktyabrina (October Revolution), Lenina or Stalina, or sometimes Revmiru (World Revolution). Another name is Traktora (tractor). Today, Ninel is still used. People think it is a diminutive, the Slavic equivalent of "Nellie."

The Hotel Rus, where we are staying, is hosting Ukraine's first annual Tourism Fair, a gathering to which travel agents from all over the world are invited. Only a handful come, from countries that might be expected to send tourists to Ukraine, or that Ukrainians might be able to afford to visit: Albania, Bulgaria, Croatia, Egypt, Israel, Poland, Russia, Spain. Young entrepreneurs with expectant looks sit behind tables no one visits. Pitiful Intourist hotel posters show aging busses, crumbling airports, and hospitable villagers in costumes.

Our rooms are on the "hard-currency floor," where foreigners are usually housed in hotels of the former Soviet Union. Outside the elevator, a young prostitute in a heavily patterned brown dress sits with a large book and a bottle of Pepsi-Cola and two glasses.

The Budapest Annual CSCE Meeting

November 20: For several weeks, the Conference on Security and Co-operation in Europe (CSCE) has been holding its annual review meeting in Budapest. More than fifty-three nations and over one hundred private nongovernmental groups attend sessions from which the future design of the organization's activity will emerge. A front-burner item is the role of the secretary general. The incumbent, the senior career ambassador of the German foreign service, has made his agenda clear. He would like to be a political czar, able to pronounce on international issues, negotiate difficult questions, and send missions into conflict spots in the fifty-three nations belonging to CSCE. Additionally, he would like to move our autonomous Warsaw office to Vienna under his own direct supervision. Since he is supposedly an international civil servant, he cannot take a visible lead in promoting this agenda, but the German delegation raises it instead. As might be expected, there is considerable resistance. The secretary general is skilled in his presentations, never once advancing his own desire for more power, always presenting the consolidation of power as a matter of coordinating policy or making the best use of resources.

The Russians call his number. At the Budapest review meeting, the Russian delegate, V. V. Shustov, says, "Many of the Secretariat's proposals are directed towards duplicating the CSCE's executive hierarchy with the same negative features that Member States have been so actively combating in other international organizations, especially the UN.

"We are appalled to note that the CSCE Secretariat is already showing signs of those types of cankers which, if they are not cut away in time, could—possibly even in the immediate future—metastasize throughout the entire body of the CSCE executive organ, turning it into yet another expensive and ineffective bureaucratic mechanism concerned with nothing but its own welfare—a mechanism which, as they say in the UN, is 'overstaffed, overpaid, and underworked.'" Shustov points to a proposal to classify the post of secretary general at the level of the undersecretary general of the United Nations, noting, "The unwritten laws of bureaucracy are such that if we give our secretary general the grade of USG, then all the other posts below that grade are bound to creep upward, pulled up and supported by this maximum grade."

When I left Washington for Warsaw, Max Kampelman, who for several pivotal years headed the American delegation to CSCE, said that his two greatest concerns for the organization were that it would build a large bureaucracy with power concentrated in Vienna; and that the administrative head, the secretary general, would try to become the organization's political leader, instead of leaving that responsibility with the chairman-in-office, which rotates each year. Both of Kampelman's observations were prescient.

Having visited several OSCE field missions, seen the Vienna headquarters in action, and witnessed the Warsaw office in operation, I have concluded that the organization turns in a spotty performance. It has a broad, well-crafted mandate, carefully worked out by leading world diplomats over the last twenty years. And, unlike such behemoths as the United Nations or the Council of Europe, it can respond with speed and flexibility to crisis situations. But a lofty mandate means little unless mission leadership has the means to carry it out on the ground in various countries. OSCE field missions lack such means and staff members are uneven in skills and motivation; some are able professionals, while others resemble characters from a Joseph Conrad or Graham Greene novel, silently passing time in cities like Tbilisi or Dushanbe, holding sporadic meetings with local leaders, and infrequently trying to influence the political conditions they were sent to repair. Meanwhile, the Vienna staff grows in numbers; and, increasingly, the ossified management resembles that of the United Nations at a time when nations urge that outdated organization to change its management practices.

Presidential Election Time in Dushanbe, Tajikistan

October 31: At 3:45 A.M., the plane from Frankfurt sets down in Tashkent, Uzbekistan. Two hours in a visa line follow, the first hour spent waiting for the visa clerk to arrive. A small, shriveled man sits near us, holding his arm, then he passes out. He fell from the plane's steps and severely hurt his arm. The night airport duty nurse watches him, her cracked leather bag of medicaments useless. Uzbek passport control agents will not let him leave for a hospital without a visa, which takes over an hour.

Finally, we speed through the night's last hour across the Uzbekistan-Tajikistan border. Our goal: Dushanbe, Tajikistan's capital, where in six days the country will elect a president and ratify a constitution. (There are no direct flights to Dushanbe, except from Moscow.) The rented BMW weaves MIG-like around spectral, slow-moving, dust-covered Russian tractors; through small, scrawny herds of sheep; past a pile of melons, lit by a Russian military spotlight and spilling onto the road; through roadside villages into the Central Asian dawn, its rose-colored light framed by austere brown mountains.

By 7:30 we are at Khojant (Leninabad, it is still called by some), a provincial Tajik capital where we catch a plane, the final leg of our journey southward to Dushanbe. The opposition presidential candidate is at the airport, waiting for a flight to a campaign stop. Abdumalik Abdullajanev is a former prime minister, minister of bread, and ambassador to the Russian Federation. A northerner, business entrepreneur, and reformer, he was allowed to run for the presidency only after numerous embassies and international organizations protested against a single-candidate presidential election.

Before his candidacy was pronounced valid, Abdullajanev had to produce 130,000 verifiable signatures, 5 percent of Tajikistan's 2,800,000 registered voters. A large, affable man with a ready smile and handshake, he tells us that he is under strong pressure from the government not to run. He and his campaign manager chronicle electoral code violations (lack of state-provided funds, transportation, media access), check their watches, and bustle off toward the plane, joining a line of passengers waiting for an ancient Russian jet. Two days later, the evening news says that poor weather prevented their flight to another campaign stop. (It is a cloudless late autumn day when the news is announced.) According to Abdullajanev, airport authorities would not let him board the plane; he and his manager spent the night at a provincial airport.

Suddenly a lumpy red carpet is unrolled, school girls in traditional dress form two lines, and the cool morning air is shattered by an eerie fanfare of native instruments. Two twelve-foot brass horns and hand-held snare drums sound a regal "Here Comes the Khan," or "Hail the Conquering Emir." Immomali Rakhmanov, the acting head of state and leading candidate to be Tajikistan's first democratically elected president, descends from the presidential jet, confidently receives the traditional welcoming gifts of bread and flowers, and greets a line of local military and civilian leaders.

A gregarious, pudgy former collective farm manager, Rakhmanov is from the agricultural South. The preferred candidate of his Kulyabi clan, he rose steadily through Communist party ranks and in 1992 was elected head of the Majlisi Mili, the Supreme Soviet. He is acting head of state until presidential elections are organized. Rakhmanov was popular originally, and it looked as if Tajikistan's post-independence history of coups, civil war, and repression might end. But the economy continues to plummet. "Everything in the country is broken, our buses are old, we have no electricity, no bread. People are afraid to go out at night," a local writer says. Rakhmanov rules with Kulyabi clan members in such strategic ministries as the Interior and State Security Service, but the military and police forces are divided, and the government becomes increasingly isolated from the people.

The entire state apparatus in Tajikistan swings behind the incumbent at election time. Instead of assuring strict governmental neutrality in elections, the electoral code provides candidates with supposedly equal air and ground transportation, funding, media access, office space, and fifteen paid campaign workers on released time from government jobs. Thus the government controls the elections. Political parties were banned last year.

After the folk ensemble performs at the airport's entrance, the presidential motorcade sweeps toward downtown Khojant. We board a Russian Yak 40 (its interior resembles a welfare hotel or a sharecropper's bus) for the hour-long flight over the mountains to Dushanbe. The pilot opens the cockpit door with a huge metal key, the sort used to turn on water mains, and we lumber skyward past a line of abandoned Aeroflot planes, their motors and instrument panels salvaged to keep other planes flying. (Four Russian internal airlines' planes went down that week, victims of poor maintenance or the lack of adequate parts.)

No cartographer would willingly design a country like Tajikistan. Its present configuration is a result of Stalin's divide-and-conquer policies. Conquered by the czars in 1895, Soviet power was established in this outpost of empire in 1920, at the end of the civil war that followed the 1917 Russian Revolution. An almost impassable mountain chain divides the country into three distinct regions. In the South, cotton and vegetables grow on a fertile plain. The North is the industrial center of Leninabad-Khojant. Dushanbe, the political capital, is in the center, while eastward lies the inaccessible, hilly, underpopulated Goro-Badakhshan region, covering 45 percent of the country but inhabited by only 230,000 people. Tajiks say, "Northerners work, southerners farm, easterners dance."

Poorest of the former Soviet republics, Tajikistan borders on China and Afghanistan; from Bukhara and Samarkand (now in neighboring Uzbekistan), emirs and khans ruled this Islamic region for centuries, until it was forcibly incorporated in 1929 as the Tajik Soviet Socialist Republic. Today's population is 5.1 million. About 62 percent of it is Tajik, 24 percent Uzbek, and a dwindling proportion Russian. Russians and Jews leave as quickly as they can, a fact indicating the country's declining political-economic opportunities. On September 9, 1991, Tajikistan declared independence from a weakened Soviet Union. Several short-lived governments ruled briefly from the three-story former Communist party headquarters.

Small opposition groups rise and are outlawed; their leaders flee to Moscow, where Tajik and Russian Secret Police stalk them. Local arrests are common. Dushanbe's mayor was jailed in 1992 on "corruption" charges; he ordered Lenin's statue removed from the city's main square. In the absence of any governmental structure to contain political factions, civil war erupted in 1992, resulting in at least 200,000 refugees and more than 20,000 dead. Regional and clan politics were revived and feuds renewed. Islamic fundamentalism is a small but real presence; more important, the country's large, diffuse Sunni Moslem population does not support the ineffective and corrupt secular government.

The 1,360-kilometer border between Tajikistan and Afghanistan is easily crossed, allowing armed opposition groups to move about freely among the millions of ethnic Tajiks living there. However, Russia slowly is building an iron curtain of barbed-wire fences, with mines, sensors, and trip wires along the border. Russia now provides 10,000 border troops, a Danish major with the U.N. observation force tells us, plus the 13,500-member 201st Mechanized Division, and is an active conflict mediator. Tanks patrol Dushanbe streets at night; until recently, armed bands of vigilante youths roamed the capital. Young people are bored. There is nothing to do, no jobs; youthful energy channels easily into violence. "It will take Tajikistan a long time to become a democracy; look at Turkey," the deputy minister of justice remarks.

Long lines wait for bread. Obtaining the day's food is a major preoccupation for most Tajiks. "Life became terrified, especially after our Civil War," a local citizen remarks in newly-learned English. Bread costs 165 roubles when available at state shops, three times that price from roadside vendors. (One dollar equals three thousand new roubles.) Sunday neighborhood markets offer a few items of clothing strung out on clotheslines tied between trees. The minimum wait for an apartment is ten years. Few vehicles circulate because of gasoline shortages, but an occasional Russian car races by with loaves of local bread piled on the back window shelf to keep them warm.

Human rights abuses abound in such a restrictive setting. International agencies chronicle more than eighty murders or disappearances between March and October 1993. Paramilitary forces conducted programs against dissident ethnic groups in Dushanbe. Treason charges were levied against moderate opposition members, nascent political parties were banned, opposition publications were seized. By late 1994, Tajikistan was a political wasteland; such a fragile society cannot sustain such blows and prosper.

No one meets us at Dushanbe airport, so we fall in with a Gypsy cab driver who tells us he knows where the Conference on Security and Co-operation in Europe (CSCE) office is. (He is lying through his teeth.) The ancient Moskvich's floorboards are made of linoleum, its front window cracked with lines like a giant spider web. Generations of electrical wires hang from the dashboard. My fellow election watcher, a Polish professor of constitutional law, and I push the car while the driver jump-starts it. From the Hotel Dushanbe, where journalists and election watchers gather, we call the CSCE mission.

Hotel lobby sign:

> Dear Ladies and Gentlemen!
> If you are interested in the works of art and culture of Tajikistan you have to visit the firm "Eden." All types of art of our republic

will be present to you judge. We hope you will experience the upper pleasure from this exhibition.

The CSCE mission is located on Omar Kahyan Street, in the unfinished walled compound of a young medical doctor killed in the civil war. The mission was established a year ago with two mandates: to help bring the warring parties together and to work with Tajiks on building democratic institutions. The acting head of the four-person international staff is Gancho Gantchev, a Bulgarian diplomat who spent last year in rural Cambodia; his deputy is a young Pole who will do nothing to help us, sending lengthy messages, copied to the chairman-in-office and secretary general, about why he is too busy to work with the Ministry of Justice on setting up the conference. There are four local employees, one the sister of a former presidential candidate who fled to Moscow. Communication with the outside world is by portable satellite dish in the front yard, which makes possible phone and fax contact with Vienna headquarters.

The international and Tajik staffs share a noon meal, usually a vegetable stew. There are no restaurants in Dushanbe outside the two hotels, and if the lunch hour is prolonged, people must return home after dark, which is not safe. Pieces of circular local bread are served, as are small plates of nuts, dried fruit, apples, and grapes. Each afternoon, one of the employees walks through the two-story building with a shovel full of smoldering aromatic straw, to drive flies away.

We are lodged in a government guest house built in a vast orchard park not far from the town's center. Surrounded by high walls and with only one entrance, it is patrolled by armed guards in high Cossack hats and flowing coats. One building houses the Council of State's president; there are other villas for visiting heads of state, a hall for international meetings, fountains that do not work, a covered gun emplacement, tea houses set among trees, and a squarish blue wooden platform where elders in black and white embroidered caps could play cards or drink tea. After thirty hours' travel time, I fall asleep, only to be roused by the maid, who asks, "Do you require any provisions?"

November 2: Over the next four days, our meetings follow a pattern. The Tajik government wants international observers to declare the presidential election and constitutional referendum free and fair. None of the international organizations takes the bait, even when the foreign minister tells one diplomat, "confidentially, Slav to Slav," that the minister will lose his job if he does not come up with election observers. We speak of international standards for electoral activity, including free speech, multiparty participation, and an independent electoral commission. Tajikistan has signed such international accords. Additionally, Article 10 of its Constitution says, "If the republic's laws do not conform with recognized international legal documents, the norms of the international documents shall apply." A local jurist says, "We put this article in because we have no body of local law and believe that the international standards will help us."

The high-level government leaders we meet are tough politicians. Two oft-repeated phrases are "the recent well-known events" (the civil war) and "reforms must take into account the real situation in our country." "That can be wise counsel," I reply, "or an excuse to do nothing for twenty or thirty years. The real issue is power sharing. To what extent are you willing to broaden the political power base to include others? Most of your opposition is in Moscow or Afghanistan; they should be here, helping build the country. It is better to fight with ballots than bullets. Unless you allow political disputes to take place in the legislative halls, the media, or the courts, people will become bitter, either withdrawing from civic life or taking to the streets with guns and coups."

In many exchanges, we are like ships passing in the night, articulating different world views. The traditional Communist response is that labor unions and youth organizations can nominate candidates and that banned parties should come back to life and try again to register at the Ministry of Justice. A Foreign Ministry representative is upbeat: "Communism can change with the times. All of Central Asia's current presidents come from the Communist party. The local party has about 70,000 members; they do not know what to do next, but they are the country's only effective political organization."

"Your electoral code works against any real political parties forming," I reply. "Independent candidates cannot run; it is almost impossible for a candidate to obtain 130,000 validated signatures to get on the ballot." Two additional provisions eliminate potential opponents. A candidate must live in the country for ten years (Article 1), but most dissident politicians are abroad. No-one with "previous convictions" (Article 24) can run, but many potential candidates were jailed for political activity at one time or another; now their reentry into active political life is blocked.

Free media do not exist in Tajikistan, but if there were any, candidates would have to thread a legal minefield to express their views. The first obstacle is the electoral code's Article 27, "The program of a candidate must not contradict the constitution." More sweeping is Article 37, which restricts free speech under the prohibition of "discredit[ing] the honor and dignity of the candidate for the post of president" or "insult[ing] members of the electoral commission."

These provisions are almost impossible to define as legal concepts, but they wave a red flag on the horizon, warning political opponents, "Watch out, if you make trouble you will pay for it." At a time when Western courts increasingly hold that public figures are justifiably more exposed to critical media scrutiny than private individuals, Central and Eastern European press laws become more limiting, protecting heads of government from the political arena's insults, rough speech, and embarrassments.

Although CSCE asked several international experts to send detailed comments on the draft constitution to Dushanbe, the appraisals were mostly ignored. "We looked at the constitutions of Iran, Turkey, Pakistan, Uzbekistan, Germany, and the United States," the Constitutional Commission's head tells me. Separation-of-powers issues are unclear in the draft approved on November 6. Individual rights are barely mentioned, and the document carries a standard Soviet-era disclaimer that individual rights must not interfere with the state's rights or those of other social groups. The section on an independent judiciary remains the shell of a concept at present.

The Central Election Committee head is the president's agent, hand-picked to make sure everything works. An energetic, stony-faced, Moscow-trained party operative, Kadriddin Giysov, with his staff of nine, has the formidable task of organizing 64 electoral districts and 2,700 polling places for 2,800,000 voters. No neutral or opposition members sit on the commission, whose word is final in any dispute. The whole process is like sending the goat to guard the cabbage patch.

November 5: The country is apathetic. On election eve we see two crowds, one for bread, the other for a wedding. A handful of Abdullajanev posters is visible, but there are more for Rakhmanov, bearing a color photo and a brief textual paragraph. Party loyalists display the president's poster in their offices; outside, it is pasted high enough on walls to prevent its being defaced, but that puts it too high to read. Campaign activity is minimal, although shortly before the election, Rakhmanov workers distribute bread, butter, and cooking oil for a half-hour at a Dushanbe crossroads.

The government's official four-page newspaper is the sort Lenin might have designed in 1917. There is little election news. The lead story is "Dushanbe Celebrates 70th Anniversary." Television news clips are a day old; the 7:00 P.M. evening news leads with hand-held camera coverage of a new concrete building going up, beam by beam. Then a soldier appears on prime time to announce, "Comrade Rakhmanov, the army is behind you."

The *pièce de résistance* is an hour-long call-in program, rebroadcast for a second evening when it is cut by a power failure the first night. Those with access to phones feed anodyne questions to candidate Rakhmanov, who sits placidly behind a desk on a carpet-covered dais, hands folded in front of him, rattling off answers, infrequently making a point by slightly lifting his left hand.

Six bouquets of fresh flowers surround the president; behind him, two large vases of yellow chrysanthemums are perched atop pillars lit from the bottom by stage lights. The table in front of the president's desk contains a large rambling rose, its vines edging toward two vases of long-stemmed roses on the studio floor. On each side of the roses are square white silk pillows; on the pillows are television monitors with blue clocks showing how much time remains. The full camera shot: a modern-day Oriental potentate surrounded by rugs, technology, and flowers. "Although we signed many European treaties, we are an Asian country," the vice foreign minister reminds us.

There is gunfire each evening. Two days before the election, four small plastic bombs explode near the presidency: at an agricultural office across the street, an international telephone exchange, a government printing plant, and a district electoral office. I see the broken windows and blown-out wall of the elections office. Fortunately, the staff was in the next room for a meeting. Only minor injuries were inflicted by the bombs.

November 6: Sunday morning. We visit polling places in Dushanbe's four wards. They are Soviet-era in design, featuring a sealed urn draped in red cloth standing in the room's center, voting booths covered with curtains, and a long table with registrars poring over handwritten voter lists. Ballots are in Tajik or Russian (Uzbek in some places). Sometimes election workers enter booths to translate for voters. Aged voters are steered through each step. Some family heads cast their families' ballots in the red wooden urns, and neighbors vote for neighbors, a practice not unusual in Central Asia. Following Russian custom, voters draw a line through the name of the candidates they vote against, which can be confusing. Official poll watchers huddle on corner benches; usually they are trade union representatives or aging youth organization officials. Uniformed police guard doors but do not interfere. Ministry of Interior representatives, many of them young men with gold chains and black leather jackets, watch from the perimeters.

Polling stations are at local schools or government buildings. Outside, vendors sell tea and cakes. The electoral commission provides free breakfasts for voters in some places, attracting mostly pensioners from nearby apartments, for whom this is an outing. Two drummers and an accordion player perform at a polling place near the Academy of Theatrical Arts. Outside a downtown theater, also a voting site, a large crowd watches three sequin-covered dancers mime the words and gestures of several Indian popular songs. Neither food nor entertainment affects voter turnout, which runs close to 60 percent at most stations. By 4 P.M., thirty-four Dushanbe polling places report a 69 percent turnout.

Local officials offer us tea and are talking eagerly. Voter turnout is good, they say, but would be higher if the price of bread was lower. One supervisor thought that "CSCE" was the same as "BBC." My Polish colleague was prevented from leaving town initially. Army units had sealed Dushanbe's road to prevent demonstrations. A soldier escorted Professor Jarosz to army headquarters, where an on-duty State Security officer then accompanied him, assuring unhindered access to surrounding villages.

November 7: At midnight we meet to review election results at UN headquarters, a two-story building that makes a stab at traditional local architecture. The American ambassador and several embassy staff are present, as are some of the UN's military observer group, led by a Jordanian general. The International Foundation for Electoral Systems has sent a professional team as well, led by Gwen Hoffman, their regional representative who spends two years in Almaty, traveling about the region, assisting with elections. Most observers agree that the turnout was high and that polling places generally were well-organized and honestly administered. If there is electoral fraud, it will come later in the evening, when the vote count moves to an increasingly smaller circle of trusted headquarters cadre.

At one polling station, a uniformed guard dropped 193 ballots for Rakhmanov into the urn while the local committee was at supper, a poll watcher told us. When the urn was opened at 8 P.M. after the polls closed, the new ballots tumbled out *en bloc*. The presidential party's poll watcher suggested that they be burned, but the seven-person local committee decided to file an irregularities report with the Central Elections Committee. One woman member said she feared for her life.

Early morning broadcasts from Moscow say that Abdullajanev is winning; local radio reports only high voter turnout. By late morning, it is all over. Rakhmanov wins handily, 60 percent to 35 percent, although Abdullajanev's supporters had their candidate ahead at 9:00 P.M., with big majorities in several cities. By early morning, the contest is safely in the president's camp. Election Day is over in Tajikistan.

Taking the long view, there are both positive and negative aspects to the elections. There was a national election, with a stab at making it a two-candidate contest. Some differences of opinion were aired, despite the lack of free media. Charges of fraudulent vote counting could not be verified readily, but the fact that they were raised publicly shows that Tajikistan is a step removed from its past. The willingness of cabinet members to discuss improvements in the constitution and electoral code is a positive sign. Progress may be slow, but there is movement toward a modern state structure.

November 7: As ye enter, so shall ye leave. We board the 8:30 A.M. Yak crop duster for a return flight over the mountains from Dushanbe. There are only eight persons aboard, so the pilot waits an additional hour for more passengers. In Kohjant, the task is finding a taxi with Uzbekistan plates for the three-hour trip to Tashkent. The first car's motor growls briefly like a street dog robbed of its bone, then fails. A second car, used recently to transport cement, is hailed; and we head through the windy, gray landscape. The next morning, our 6:30 taxi to Tashkent airport runs out of gas. I hold a plastic spigot while the Uzbek driver pours from a jerry can.

"Where do you come from," he asks.

"Dushanbe."

"Tajikistan. Are they still fighting there?"

8

Prague, Kyrgyzstan, Kazakhstan

Back in Prague

November 23: Although I had been posted to Prague in the dark period of East-West relations, from 1975 to 1978, we had not returned to the Czech Republic in fifteen years, except for a brief conference visit in 1991. Today the airport is brightly lit, the passport control desks cheerfully constructed of multicolored metal wiring, and the guards in pleasant blue uniforms instead of grim Warsaw Pact olive drab. Several money changers' kiosks line the entrance; as a handful of brilliantly colored, carefully etched bank notes are handed me, I think, "This artist is familiar." A once-vilified dissident artist, who was jailed and denied opportunities to exhibit in his own country, has just designed a complete new line of currency for the Czech Republic. The old bills showing collective farms, aging steel and chemical factories, and Communist-era heroes have been replaced by Czech writers, historical monuments, and landscapes. I recognize a scene reproduced from an etching that we own, and I remember numerous encounters with Oldrich Kulhánek, a gentle, cherubic artist-engraver, whose work places him among contemporary Europe's master artists.

A recollection.

It is 1977, and the Vltava River runs in front of us. A castle fills the skyline, and along the hills are the centuries-old Prague buildings. My favorite spot is a chair in the sixth-floor apartment opening on the horizon. It is one of those ornate buildings that no sensible contemporary architect or builder would attempt—curved glass windows, elaborate Jugendstil stucco, brass, and woodwork. Kulhánek's studio is there, and I sometimes drop by in the late afternoon unannounced, because it is 1977 and neither Czechoslovak dissident artists nor American diplomats trust the telephones.

Once when I visited the artist, a neighborhood guardian followed me. This is the lowest level of secret police functionary, a neighborhood gawker who reports suspicious activity. Like a villager in a Brueghel painting, he shuffled after me, wearing a small-brimmed cheap felt hat. An inexpensive plastic raincoat circled him as if he were a building wrapped and tied by Christo. I knew there was little I could do, but, instead of entering 78 Englesova Nabrezi, I entered a building three doors distant. My shadow followed, and we climbed all eight flights. He was relieved and noted the name on the doorplate. Then I descended, remounted the stairs in the next building, and the next. By then the state guardian was sweating and wheezing and came only to the entryway of No. 78. I did not know that it was one of the Havel family buildings, seized in the 1948 Communist takeover. Father Vaclav Havel's two sons, Vaclav and Ivan, retain apartments in it, just below Kulhánek's.

Now, Vaclav, whom we knew as a dissident writer, is president. Kulhánek has moved to a larger suburban studio. It has no river view but good work space. He is puzzled by my work with the judiciary and says, "It is not like the United States, here the people have no respect for judges." He leafs through a folder, producing four large etchings about his 1971 political trial: *Portrait of My Weasel, Interrogation, Ruzyni Prison, Cell 321,* and *Tribunal.*

The judicial proceedings against him began in 1968, when an arts jury sent eleven of his works to an international exhibit in Japan. This was not unusual, as his work is in the permanent collection of the Library of Congress, and he has shown in the Museum of Modern Art, the Pompidou Center, and other major museums. However, as the works were unpacked in Tokyo, the embassy's political guardian found their sexual and political content disturbing. A long inquiry followed, then the 1971 trial, jail sentence, orders to liquidate the offending art, and lengthy interrogations every second weekend for two years. No wonder Czechs regard court officials as vermin.

During the pretrial proceedings, this exchange (captured for posterity in official transcripts later obtained by Kulhánek) took place between the artist and his interrogators.

> Interrogator: Look here, you needn't put on this intellectual play acting for me. This is pornography in print. Here our comrade ambassador to Japan, Kozusnik, testifies that the female comrades at the embassy were outraged by the size of the sex organs when he showed them the prints.
>
> Kulhánek: OK, I can't help it if the female comrades at the embassy don't like big sex organs.
>
> Interrogator: But the female comrades were outraged!
>
> Kulhánek: Yes, then why did the ambassador show them?
>
> Interrogator: You are not here to ask questions. Admit that you have been producing pornography.
>
> Kulhánek: No, I'll not admit that. The genitals are not excessively big.
>
> Interrogator: They are. The female comrades said so.

The Ministry of Interior pursued Kulhánek with testimony by an obscure "expert" from a provincial city and the party-controlled Artists' Union. It is hard to find overt political content in Kulhánek's work, but the interrogators pressed the case that he had "reviled the representatives of a friendly state," i.e., the Soviet Union.

> Interrogator: Why has the child in the bottom right corner a hole in his head in the shape of a five-point star?
>
> Kulhánek: OK, that is not true, the hole is not in the shape of a five-point star.
>
> Interrogator: We know it is! Admit it. If Stalin were here now, I should not be talking to you like this. The working class would make short work of you. Look here, we know everything, we know very well what you are thinking. Admit it, and you will be left in peace and I too. Do you think I enjoy this? I know absolutely nothing about art.

A skillful prosecution builds a case from multiple sources. Here, the Ministry zeros in on the artist's foreign influences.

> Interrogator: Who is Hieronymus Bosch? Who is Hugo van der Goes? Who is Hans Memling? Inform us of their addresses, when

and where you met them, their profession, and the names of their employers. Denying will not help you. We know everything. One after the other, in turn. Who is Hieronymus Bosch? When and where did you meet him?

Kulhánek: Hieronymus Bosch was a Dutch painter. He was born in 1450, and I became acquainted with his work in Bruges.

Interrogator: That will do! I should like his address and the name of his employer.

The trial was held in 1971. The defendant had an elderly, well-respected human-rights lawyer who could do nothing but insist that procedural points be observed. A complication arose: The Czechoslovak president declared an amnesty on the provisions under which Kulhánek was charged, so he was released from prison. Still, the three-judge panel let stand the order to liquidate the seized works. Usually this means burning books or paintings in the Ministry of Justice courtyard.

The story's ending could have been scripted by Franz Kafka. Policemen seized the eleven prints, unaware that they came from plates which could produce a press run of several hundred copies. A few years later, Kulhánek encountered the chief judge by chance and asked him how the works were liquidated. "Oh, we divided them among ourselves," the jurist replied.

In the Old Neighborhood

We walk around town: our old apartment is on Namesti Miru (Square of Peace) in the Vinohrady (King's Vineyards) district. On the ground floor, a chrome and marble bank with halogen spotlights has replaced a dark, high-ceilinged neighborhood restaurant, the scene of many of Jiri Balczar's works. Balczar was a well-known painter-printmaker who died during the 1968 Russian invasion. His widow lived just a few blocks away from our apartment, and we sometimes visited her.

Zdenek Mylenasz, a leading dissident economist and former high government official, lived in the same building and, since he signed Charter 77, a large Tatra police car always was stationed at the front door to tail him and intimidate him. The grim neighborhood stores that housed district Communist party headquarters, trade unions, youth organizations, and government stores have been replaced by fashionable boutiques carrying the latest Italian fashions or by fast-food places. At the entryway, where secret police used to photograph guests coming to our apartment in the mid-1970s, is a brightly lit travel agency offering inexpensive fares to Cairo, Mauritius, and Canada. In the earlier period, the only places Czechs could visit were Bulgaria, Cuba, or other Communist countries. Travel to the West was almost impossible; if a person was allowed to travel, a spouse or child had to remain behind, for fear of defections.

The American Embassy, where I was cultural counselor (1975–78) during the early days of Charter 77, is our next stop. The small but active library we carefully built is now an empty room in which a Star Wars Marine Guard Post looms. In the mid-1970s, Czech police sometimes came from their cabin across the street and searched borrowers' bags or took visitors to the nearby station for questioning. In the garden, which extends high on a hill overlooking Prague, we staged concerts, such as a bluegrass group, Hickory Wind, which the government would not allow to play in town, because the music was decadent; besides, young people might like it. After my departure in 1978, a local radio program said that I was a spy who asked people to put information in dirty socks and throw it over the embassy wall.

We call my former secretary, who has left the embassy, the last person of our era with whom we have contact. Her husband, a former champion skier, has a job between meets with a huge government construction company. After retiring from professional skiing, he worked his way up in the company. With privatization, the massive state enterprise was divided into sixteen smaller companies and sold off to multinational corporations. Radim was made director of a company restoring building exteriors, something always in demand in the Czech Republic. Zuzana, his wife, now stays home with her two daughters, is partner in a downtown exercise salon, and goes on winter holidays with the family to France, Austria, and Switzerland.

Most striking of all, the Russian tanks, monuments, and lighted street signs all have been carted away. One of the largest statues of Stalin in Eastern Europe once stood high on a bank overlooking the river. With Stalin's fall from power, it was pulled down and the pedestal left blank for decades. Now a starkly modern piece of metal sculpture stands there, its beaconlike prong moving slowly back and forth across the skyline.

The Hotel Europa, a 1905 Art Nouveau monument on Wenceslas Square, is our hotel. The period mosaic floors, intricate iron grillwork, and carved wooden doors remain, as does some of the stained glass. The hotel stands opposite the balcony from which Vaclav Havel spoke to a crowd of 800,000 at the climax of the 1979 Velvet Revolution. There are memorials to Jan Palach, a young student who burned himself to death in the square as a protest against Communism, and to a handful of others who stood up against the iron-fisted regime and paid for it with their lives.

In the evening, we attend a chamber music concert in the Clementium Hall of Mirrors. Prague has been called "Europe's conservatory," and a local chamber music ensemble plays a superb program of Mozart and Dvořák. The enterprising ticket seller, who came out on the street in pursuit of us, offers us student rates since the concert is already under way. The next day we walk around the castle grounds and visit the Alchemist's Lane, now a series of small shops. In a closet-sized record store, I find treasures, inexpensive CDs of historic recordings of Czech composers by Václav Tallich and the Czech Philharmonic, piano works by Jan Panenka and Ivan Moravec, and violin pieces by Josef Suk. A reality of the new central Europe is the demise of most government-subsidized record companies. With them have gone the historic archives of companies like Supraphon and Melodia; they have been replaced by Sony's *Dvořák's Best Hits* or *Wedding Favorites*.

Dissident Artist Friends Revisited

Zdeněk Beran and his companion of thirty-three years, Zdenka Schirlová, are our hosts the next two evenings. In 1975, Zdenek was a banned artist; when I first visited his studio, he was working on drawings for the ceiling frieze of a Bratislava pub. An architect friend had shared a commission with him. Other artists made their livings as commercial artists or illustrators of childrens' books (not using their real names). The best a non-approved artist could hope for at that time was a twenty-fifth anniversary showing in a provincial gallery. Denied membership in the powerful party-controlled Artists' Union, they were denied access as well to art supplies from abroad, travel to other countries, choice commissions, and gallery shows. I got to know many of the artists through Jindřich Chalupecky, a well-known art critic, who likewise was banned from publishing. "Dissident" is not an exact word for most such artists; few had any political involvement, and many were shy, retiring personalities. Their crime was their refusal to turn out works in the Soviet Realist mold, exemplifying the glory of *Homo Sovieticus*, "Socialist Man," as it was known in Warsaw Pact propaganda tracts, at work "building socialist society."

Today Zdeněk is vice-rector of the 2,200-student Art Faculty, as is Hugo Demartini, another artist who lived near us. Hugo, 67, married a thirty-year-old second wife and has a year-old child. Zdeněk has a photo of some of the former dissidents in an academic procession, merry spirits and lively minds looking as solemn-faced as ancestral portraits on a dimly lit castle wall. Their academic dress was designed by the rector, a gifted Slovak graphic artist who never designed robes before. The conical yellow hats could have been props for *The Wizard of Oz* and the billowing black and red robes the garb of palace retainers in *Kismet*. But those who were on the outside for decades are now insiders, tenured full professors at prestigious academies, subjects of one-person showings at home and abroad or successful in their private studios. None of this was anticipated in the mid-1970s when we met clandestinely, sometimes setting next month's meeting in advance or using different public phones to call Czech friends. I remember the strong smell of creosote from the dark wooden phone booth near our apartment, where I would call dissident friends, inviting them to see a Milos Forman film which had been lent to the embassy but which the government would not show publicly.

Beran's art has changed subtly through the last two decades. Always a brilliant technician, he has employed both humor and surrealism in his work from his earliest years. "Surrealism is realism," he used to say, reminding us that Czechs consider Franz Kafka a humorist, among other things.

The first work by Zdeněk that I saw was called *The Rehabilitation Hospital of Dr. X.* It consisted of two rooms that Zdenek retained in a decrepit slum, filled with hospital beds; distorted bits of medical equipment wired together to produce a puzzling, frightening new image; recreated hunks of human bodies encased in plaster, wrapped in bandages, sprayed with blood-red paint. The hospital was, of course, Czech society, the patients its citizens, and rehabilitation the political restructuring of society.

Later he produced a comparable series called *Suitcases,* in which wires and ballast grew like grass or seaweed from small containers. The suitcases contained all that is frightening in dreams and reality. Zdenek, however, is quick to laugh. Our children called him "The Teddy Bear Man" and Zdenka "The Easter Egg Lady" in the days when we used code names for friends to make the government electronic eavesdroppers at least earn their money. "Yes, I'm an optimist," he remarks, his face beaming as we leave the brightly lit, overheated studio for the dark spiral staircase leading to the ground.

Warsaw Trains

November 28: The number of Warsaw train station robberies increases. Recently a gang of Russian Mafiosi with clubs and hand-held radios beat up Russian traders on a train arriving from Moscow. The passengers called repeatedly for help; when none came, they pulled the train's emergency cord. By the time station police arrived, the robbers had left, so police arrested the robbery victims. The incident caused the Russian prime minister to cancel his Warsaw visit and the commandant of police at Dworzec-Srodmiescie Station to be reassigned.

A week later, another robbery was reported. This time it was the Zairian ambassador to Poland. The African envoy spends nights among the station's homeless. Having been evicted from various hotels and apartments for nonpayment of rent, he spends days in a tiny apartment without telephone, in space provided by the Polish Foreign Ministry, feeding himself at diplomatic receptions. His own country will neither pay the mission's bills nor provide its representative with money to return home. Interventions by the Polish embassy in Kinshasa have been fruitless; the ambassador has sold the mission's car and furnishings to stay alive.

December in Central Asia

December 1: Return to Central Asia for two democratization seminars, one in Kyrgyzstan, one in Kazakhstan.

Kazakhstan attracts international attention because it is a nuclear weapons power and because of its large oil reserves. On November 20, an expert Western scientific mission secretly spirited six hundred kilograms of top-grade enriched uranium, enough for thirty-six bombs, out of a desolate storage site at Ust-Kamengorsk in northern Kazakhstan. Part of the haste was to keep the lightly guarded stockpile out of Iranian or Iraqi hands and away from other potential buyers. The incident belonged in a *Mission Impossible* television script: a twenty-hour flight in lumbering supply planes to an obscure Central Asian airfield and thirty-one persons working secretly for six weeks in an isolated metallurgical plant, filling fourteen hundred steel cans with radioactive ore.

The uranium had been brought to Kazakhstan by Russia in the 1970s, with the intention of making it into fuel rods for Soviet ships. When the Soviet Union collapsed, however, enriched uranium became a liability. Independent Kazakhstan declared itself a nuclear-free country. It was costly to guard the uranium, which was sold to the United States for under $100 million. After waiting several days for weather to clear, the U.S. Air Force flew the cargo directly to Dover, Delaware, and then trucked it overland to a final resting place in Oak Ridge, Tennessee.

December 2: That evening in Almaty, we attend a concert with our interpreter and her boyfriend. She is a delicate, fine-boned young woman; like many Kazakhs, she is of Chinese-Russian lineage. Gudmila is an interpreter and television announcer, and she is studying to be an eye surgeon. When she finishes her internship in two years, she will earn twenty dollars a month as a government doctor. (There are no private practitioners in Kazakhstan yet; none can afford the startup costs.) Since her grandfather was a high party official, the family has a spacious apartment, to be coveted more than gold in the former Soviet Union. Her boyfriend, an attractive young Kazakh of Russian origin, is local representative of an American electronics firm. Presently local tax, banking, investment, and other commercial laws are holdovers from the Soviet era, so Western investment is not extensive.

The concert is held in an acoustically balanced eight-hundred-seat concert hall built in the 1930s. It has elaborate stucco work, parquet floor, and walls decorated with five kinds of local marble. The season's concerts are listed on a bulletin board—an ambitious series covering much of the classical symphonic repertoire. This evening's program is Brahms's *First Symphony* and Beethoven's *Violin Concerto*. A young Kazakh woman violinist gives a dazzling interpretation of the latter piece. The sixty-person orchestra, thirty of whom are women, could play convincingly anywhere. The musicians are products of an excellent local conservatory; their ensemble sound has been honed closely during weeks, if not months, of rehearsal time together. There are sixty musicians and one hundred people in the audience. The ticket price is only ninety cents. Why are audiences so small? Gudmila says, "Our people are tired. They work all week and must put their money toward bread. Besides, it is not safe to go out on the streets at night anymore."

December 6: Hotel Dustik (Friendship) in Bishkek, Kyrgyzstan. We are on the ninth floor, one of two hard-currency floors. The elevator panel has buttons for fifteen floors, but the building has only nine stories. Merchant traders from Korea, Pakistan, Iran, Turkey, and Arab-speaking countries steer suitcases or plastic bags of merchandise through the lobby. Almost all imports are by cargo plane, although a few Iranian or Turkish trucks are parked across from the hotel. The merchants in the lobby represent a deep truth about Central Asia: it is an Asian not a Russian region, despite Western perspectives to the contrary. The merchants waiting at the hotel check-in line with plastic valises on rollers are successors to traders who for centuries slowly traversed the region by pack animal. In this context, the Russian-Soviet incursion resembles a violent earthquake measured in geologic time. Today the historic trade and cultural routes resume, by train, road, and airplane, radiating southward toward Tehran, Ankara, New Delhi, Seoul, and the cites of China more so than toward Moscow and the other cites of the Russian Federation.

As we descend from our rooms, the *dezhurnaya,* the floor warden in a Russian-style hotel, calls downstairs, "Stop them, they are leaving without paying!" (The hotel has required us to pay at the entrance upon arrival.) We take the elevator. She races downstairs to head us off. When she emerges from the stairs screaming, the other employees laugh. These guardians are formidable presences; there is one for each floor of most hotels of the former Soviet Union, which means many thousands of women. They collect keys on each floor, arrange outside telephone calls (paid for on the spot), provide tea and wake up calls, sometimes sell snacks and beverages, and serve as police informants.

Four other persons gather by our floor's elevator most days. Two do laundry, the rest drink tea.

From CSCE to OSCE: A Distinction Without a Difference

It is evening, and a cold wind rattles the hotel window; outside, a "Casino" light flashes on and off over the entrance of a government building, part of which is leased to gamblers. The BBC evening telecast to Asia carries a brief report from the Budapest CSCE ministerial conference, attended by Presidents Clinton and Yeltsin. Clinton looks like he is at a college reunion; Yeltsin's cheeks are puffy and his movements are mechanical, like a soldier in *The Nutcracker.* Here I learn that CSCE's name has been changed to OSCE, a distinction without a difference. The "conference" becomes an "organization." In the lexicon of international associations, this should mean that a temporary body has become a permanent international organization with legal personality of its own, like the United Nations. However, the United States, which proposed the name change, refuses to give OSCE status as a permanent international organization with the right to lead its own organizational life, conduct its affairs autonomously, and issue diplomatic documentation to its employees. The name change is the Clinton administration's offering at Budapest, plus a promise OSCE will play a more substantial future role in promoting peace and stability and reducing armed conflict. For its part, Russia supports a stronger OSCE, seeing it as a possible foil to NATO. I had not known of the proposed name change before it happened and had ordered a complete line of stationery with the old office logo, as well as conference banners, signs, and calling cards.

Ad in the *Kyrgyzstan Chronicle:*

> Ladies and Gentlemen:
> Are you used to working in comfort?
> Do you like good pens? What about solid files?
> Is it possible to schedule your working day without a time planner? If you realize it, then stationary of the firm HERLITZ (Germany) is for you.

Our Kyrgyzstan seminar is on free media and free association; late the first morning I learn that, on the following day, we will discuss the country's new mass media law and its law on associations, which have just been given to us in Russian. Our capable translator, Irena, begins work on the document that evening. She and I spend the next morning correcting the translation. Since the hotel is crowded and smoky, we sit in a quiet, sunlit room in the nearby National Museum. The elderly attendants of the unheated building are wrapped, like patients in a home for the aged, in layers of woolen shawls or blankets. Tubercular coughs echo faintly from elsewhere in the building. My glasses steam over when I breathe. A few parts of the draft law are unintelligible in Russian or English; I make a stab at kneading the phrases into sentences, then walk between the works of Socialist Realism to restore circulation. By noon, the translation is in serviceable shape.

The three members of our panel have arrived: Judges Michael M. Mihm of the United States, Luis López Guerra of Spain, and Lech L. Garlicki of Poland's constitutional tribunal. The minister of justice presides over our gathering in the unheated former Lenin Museum. Upstairs are painted plaster scenes from Lenin's life, arranged like shop windows at Christmas but covered with several months' accumulation of desert dust. Lenin at the Finland station, Lenin at his desk, Lenin inspiring the Politburo—all covered with a thick coating of gray dust, stranger still because most of the light bulbs have been turned off or stolen.

A locally constructed plywood dais with nails hanging out the edges is where we sit. Just as the conference begins, Judge Mihm walks enthusiastically to the podium, tearing his trousers a substantial rip on a nail. "Life is humbling," he remarks in passing us. He returns to the hotel for his other pair of trousers to complete the seminar.

Kyrghyzstan is Central Asia's most democratic country, but its proposed new media law is like many documents in the Soviet tradition, in boldly proclaiming the right in Article One, then limiting it gradually throughout the rest of the document. We ask: how can you mix hate speech, state secrets, incitement to war, and anti-Semitism with "invasion of privacy" and "insulting a person's honor and dignity"? If the law's language is vague or uncertain, it will be impossible for judges to interpret it.

The conference brings together judges, Ministry of Justice officials, and editors of two publications banned earlier in the year, *Svobodnye Gory (Free Mountains)*, which was closed for alleged anti-Semitism and false reporting, and *Politica*, a weekly that embarrassed the government in an article on the Chinese prime minister's visit. At the coffee break, editors of the two banned publications and the minister of justice have an animated discussion. A side benefit of such seminars is providing opportunities for journalists and justice ministry officials to encounter one another, often for the first time; such meetings do not happen otherwise in such societies.

Americans are fortunate to enjoy a standard of free speech unequaled elsewhere in the world. In the Soviet tradition, law favors the state and the ruling class, not the individual or individual publications. Control devices are subtle but omnipresent, including prosecution for "antistate activity"; expulsion from the Union of Journalists, meaning no opportunities for steady work; registration of each publication with the government, which can be denied; and, in many countries, denying access to the government printing press, the only printing press in town, "for lack of ink or paper," if the journal's content is unfavorable to the government. Three journalists from nearby Tajikistan make the sixteen-hour trip by plane and car through snow-swept plains. Tajikistan has only one independent newspaper, a bloodless commercial sheet. Twenty-four journalists were killed there in recent years, a world's record.

Having a free afternoon, we visit an art gallery and, when we finish, return to the locked Volga car of the Ministry of Justice, with the driver nowhere to be found. Finally the driver appears, opens the car, and walks away. I leave my thumb on the horn, he hastens back, and we move on to the market, filled with vendors of fresh meat, root vegetables, winter clothing from China and Taiwan, and pirated copies of Russian and Western popular tapes. The car is heavy, the gasoline octane low. Each time the driver turns a corner, the engine develops *delirium tremens* and flames out, but we return safely to the hotel.

December 10: Return to Almaty through snow-filled fields and fog. Solitary riders on horseback watch flocks of snow-clotted sheep along the Kyrgyzstan-Kazakhstan main road. At long intervals, entrances to bomb shelters open like gopher burrows along the roadside, reminders of Kazakhstan's nuclear weapons. Snow covers the town; tree branches are magical, suggesting a Russian children's opera; but the dark streets are treacherous because of poor street lighting and drivers not turning on car lights in the city at night. At the central market, we buy fresh spices, shelled walnuts, dried fruits, and pistachio nuts. After carefully wrapping our purchases in newspaper cones, packaging that has not changed in half a century, the vendor reaches under a white apron and layers of sweaters for a cellular phone to call home. A row of Korean women sell shredded vegetable salads, handing us chopsticks with free samples. Carnation vendors place small wooden frames around their flowers, cover them with plastic outside and carpeting on top, put candles inside, and stand in the cold, hoping to sell a few flowers. The hotel food is inedible. We buy bread, cheese, and Chinese beer for our evening meal, lining up with homeward-bound customers, counting on Lech Garlicki's Russian to complete our purchases. (A sign says that war veterans, hero workers, and the elderly should go to the head of the line.)

Stopping at a brightly lit shop, we see fish pâté imported from Germany, dried soups from Israel, canned pickles from Iran, and noodles from Korea. Americans think of Central Asia as isolated, but it is a true commercial crossroads. It is cold everywhere; natural-gas suppliers in Uzbekistan demand payment for the year's past purchases, but Kazakhstan has no money, so gas supplies are cut off, as is electricity in some parts of town. We sit in our winter clothes in my room, making sandwiches and drinking green bottles of Chinese beer. It is so cold that the small blue and gold Kazakhstan flag on my table flutters constantly from the Arctic wind seeping through the warped wooden window sills. I sleep under heavy blankets and keep the two electric lights on for warmth, plus periodically running hot water in the bathtub. Even the Siberian husky guarding the parking lot is subdued by the weather.

Luis López Guerra, vice president of the Spanish Constitutional Court, tells Warsaw Judicial Symposium participants about Spain's judicial transformation in the post-Franco era.

[157]

Judge Cynthia Holcomb Hall, chair of the U.S. federal judiciary's International Judicial Relations Committee, and Judge Lloyd D. George, committee member, prepare for a mock trial at the Warsaw Judicial Symposium.

The author with a local guard near Grozny in the Chechen Republic.

[158]

KGB headquarters in Tiraspol, capital of the breakaway Dnister Soviet Socialist Republic. Two floors of the building will house the republic's supreme court.

The author with Stephan Topal, president of the Gagauz Republic, inside Moldova. The hand-made flag features a lone wolf, symbol of independence.

Judge Larisa Gutnichenko, *center,* and the author, *right,* at the supreme court in Biskek, Kyrgyzstan. The metal cage, *far right,* is used in some criminal cases, usually for capital crimes.

Larisa Gutnichenko and Michael M. Mihm, chief judge, U.S. District Court for Central Illinois, at a Ministry of Justice–ODIHR seminar on free speech and free association in Bisek, Kyrgyzstan.

Edouard Shevardnadze discusses drafts of Georgia's new constitution with the OSCE-ODIHR delegation.

Above and left: elderly Russian refugees, evacuated from Grozny during Russian army bombardments of the city in February 1995.

Luis López Guerra and the author outside the Russian Federation Ministry of Foreign Affairs in Moscow shortly before visiting the war-torn Chechen Republic.

A convoy of Russian Federation Special Forces troops accompany the OSCE mission to the Chechen Republic in February 1995.

Fighter pilot and folklorist Russian general K. M. Tsagolov and the author review a map of the Chechen Republic.

A local citizen in Prokhladlily town hall and the author.

The author trades stories with Russian refugee children housed in a former tourist spa in Vladikavkz, North Ossetia.

9

Latvia, Estonia, Moscow

January 8, 1995: Riga, Latvia. Cloud-covered and cold, a steady, icy wind from the Baltic; brisk walkers turn sideways to lessen its impact. I set out on a Sunday afternoon walk. Contrasts against the slate-gray skyline: distinctive Orthodox, Protestant, and Roman Catholic church towers; early Hanseatic dockside buildings. Later, more elaborate nineteenth-century three- and four-story structures with carefully detailed window and door trimmings, strong German 1930s architecture, grim Soviet 1950s structures like those found in all corners of the Russian empire. The skyline tells the small country's recent history: a prosperous historic port city, subject to long Russian occupation.

By now it is snowing lightly; I walk past brightly lit jewelry or clothing shops, past attractive coffee shops and small restaurants where young couples talk and smoke in front of single cups of coffee or half-filled beer glasses. On each clean and starched tablecloth sit lighted candles; the paneled woodwork is decorated with Christmas trimmings. In a cavernous Lutheran church, rebuilt to its original Gothic lines since its destruction in World War II, three young musicians play Vivaldi and Corelli with great skill. The imaginative pastor has clustered about one hundred chairs in the center of the huge nave, facing a modern stone sculpture and a few pieces of nineteenth-century wooden liturgical furniture.

Around the boat-long nave is an art exhibit by local painters and sculptors. Everyone, except the musicians, wears coats; at intermission, the musicians bundle up as well.

Baltic people are skilled in their use of light. Except for the newly opened McDonald's hamburger restaurant, buildings are not brightly lit. Overhead lighting rarely is used, and usually there is a single desk lamp in an office, which contains an indomitable green plant as well. Shop windows may be lit with small spotlights, a fan keeps the glass from clouding. Restaurants are carefully illuminated, usually with candles and small wall lamps or electric lights behind a row of wine bottles casting an amber glow over part of the room. Light is diffuse, opaque, carefully planned. Possibly this subdued illumination reflects a desire to save on the electric bill, but more likely it responds to the long gray winter days, telling the darkness, "I do not have the means to light everything, but I can create a lighted space around me." When we meet with the procurator in charge of Mafia and organized crime investigations, he lights a cranberry-colored candle on his office's coffee table before our meeting. The Hotel Ridzene, where we stay, is softly and carefully lit; a large bullet hole on the glass stairwell is marked with a brass plaque "20.01.91," the date of Russia's violent efforts to suppress Latvia's drive toward independence.

Our contacts at the Foreign Ministry and Ministry of Justice are mostly young women working on law degrees, balancing work and child care. The person who takes us to a morning meeting is replaced by another for an afternoon gathering, since the first escort is by then studying for an afternoon exam. Latvia is in better shape than many countries of the former Soviet sphere. "Our basic laws are written, and most of them are not bad," an official tells us. "Our problem is in implementing them. We do not have trained workers, and people on one floor of a ministry are not used to talking to people on another. That is our Soviet heritage. Our first priority is to train the police. They are corrupt, they do not know how to investigate, they need everything."

The head of Latvia's Supreme Court says:

> Our problem is not our laws but our poor means. Our judges do not have armored cars, they have cheap cars that often do not run. Our witnesses often recant their testimony—they are afraid. The struggle against the Mafia is quixotic. There are not many countries that follow Don Quixote, but we are one of them.
>
> For example, our citizenship law is not bad, but our government

is guilty of moving slowly in implementing it. According to the law, before we give Russians citizenship, we must give it to thirty or forty thousand Latvians who have returned here from the former Soviet Union. Russians can live a good life here; even if they can't vote or hold public office they can own private property. We must adopt a law on the position of noncitizens that settles their status. Until recently, the Russians pushed us about human rights, but since the Chechen invasion, they say nothing.

A Cathedral-like Court

January 11: Overland ride from Tallinn to Tarku, Estonia. Although we do not leave Tallinn until 9:30 A.M., it is still dark; later a few hours of sunlight filters through gray clouds. The long drive to Estonia's second city and home of its Supreme Court is across flat, frozen land, through scrawny pine forests dotted with groves of white birch trees. Road signs warn of reindeer crossings, but we see only a cold farm dog, ears back, eager to return home. The landscape is punctuated by small farms at long intervals, single one story wooden houses with tiny windows and slanted roofs with ladders tied to chimneys. Rectangular stone barns, greenhouses, and a few outbuildings are surrounded by the frozen remains of large gardens. Slate gray or dark green colors prevail, the brightest color being an occasional mustard yellow for a house or barn wall. A dry wind slowly, steadily blows snow across fields, sometimes scenting the air with the thin smell of pine wood fires burning in fireplaces.

Estonia's Supreme Court is one of the Baltic states' most impressive judicial establishments. As we enter, seventeen robed judges process past us down the darkened hall toward their courtroom, which resembles a starkly modern Lutheran cathedral. Carved seats for the three presiding judges suggest bishops' thrones; tables and chairs are from IKEA, the Swedish furniture firm whose simple, inexpensive, linear designs are widely used in places where Communist-era furnishings are discarded. Like Protestant clerics, the judges wear loose black robes with lace bibs and, over their left shoulders, a sky-blue stole with the court's insignia in gold. Rait Marutse, chair of the National Court, participated in our Warsaw Judicial Symposium. Stocky, blond, and energetic, he leads Estonia's post-Communist-era judicial reforms. His work includes construction of an impressive judicial training center for the country's 160 judges (the number eventually will rise to 250). As new laws are passed, judges are brought to Tarku for an explanation of them. Unlike neighboring Russia, the country maintained an independent bar, which now includes 2,500 lawyers.

The procurator's power has been reduced and this office placed under the Ministry of Justice. However, the court system is not problem-free. The Supreme Court is independent; it occupies a tastefully refurbished old hospital. Judge Marutse has his eye on a second small dermatological hospital next door for administrative offices. All lower and district courts report directly to the Ministry of Justice, which sets salary scales, controls appointments and administration, and thus controls the courts. Estonia is carving out its definition of separation of powers among its three branches of government, and the courts are working hard to establish their own independence. We arrive quickly at program possibilities: the court has handed down sixteen constitutional opinions to date but would like them reviewed by international jurists, as it has no experience in constitutional law.

The small Baltic states are fiercely independent of one another. The Baltics as a political unit exists only on maps. A local joke illustrates the point: In 1991, shortly after independence, each Baltic government decided to remove the Lenin statue in its main square. In Lithuania, an angry crowd, fueled by fiery oratory, tore down the statue and denounced the Communist era. In Latvia, a committee of scientific experts, led by an engineer, one night appeared with a truck and a crane and carted Lenin off. In Estonia, the new government decided that Lenin's statue must go, but no-one remembered its size; when it was much larger than expected, Estonians called Finland by cellular phone, and a Helsinki firm contracted to pull the statue down, after which massed choirs sang folk songs.

The great problem the Baltic states face in regard to NATO is they cannot protect themselves against Russia, and no-one else will defend them. The drive from the Russian border across the three countries is only a few uninterrupted hours over level land. Additionally, the removal of Russian troops will not mean the end of Russian influence. The spread of criminal groups in the three northern states is largely due to Russian gangs. An example is the transshipment through Estonia of increasing amounts of Russian export metals and armaments, with payments being made to Estonian officials at all levels. (Estonia produces no metals of its own.)

The three countries have different cultural-historical ties. Estonia is close to Scandinavia, although only nominally Protestant. Lithuania is devoutly Roman Catholic, seeing itself as an outpost of European Catholic culture, somewhat like Spain. Latvia is Thomas Mann country, strongly Protestant and deeply rooted in the German Hanseatic port heritage.

Populations are ethnic cauldrons. In Lithuania the dominant mix is 80 percent Lithuanian, with a large Polish minority. In Latvia, barely 50 percent of the population is Latvian, and two-thirds of the remainder are ethnic Russians, with higher concentrations in principal towns. In Estonia, there is a roughly 60-30 Estonian-Russian split.

The New Moscow

January 15: Night flight to Moscow, where armed soldiers and armored personnel carriers ring the airport, a partial response to the Chechen conflict. Hotel prices now rival those of London or New York, but the Foreign Ministry made reservations for us at a centrally located government hotel, the Arbat. It is barely occupied. Formerly a hotel for high party officials coming to Moscow, it still uses "Hotel October" china, commemorating the Russian Revolution. At lunch we are attended by a dining-room manager and assistant in pink suits, two head waiters in green suits, and four other waiters: eight staff, eight guests.

I have not spent time in Moscow since 1977. It is still a city of massive, closed, guarded buildings with purposeful, driven people plodding through ankle-deep snow and slush in a huge city that barely works. Historic buildings suggest a Pushkin poem, other buildings a 1940s espionage film. There are changes, too. At one end of the Arbat is a store with piles of prewashed jeans, at the other is an Italian restaurant; and every variety of Western goods is available in between. A frozen Father Christmas with Polaroid camera waits for children outside a newly opened store selling fur coats and hats in a remodeled building entrance; melting snow seeps through the hastily built ceiling and drips from electrical wires. At a two-story supermarket, at least twenty people line up for bread; no-one buys the small twenty-five-dollar tins of caviar. Irish products are featured this week, and nearby is a large display of state-of-the-art stereo sets. Outside, women bundled in cloth coats and peasant scarves stand in front of rolls of toilet paper, cans of meat, and piles of plastic shopping bags. People on the subway are better dressed than before, and the media are freer, with graphic footage on the nightly news of the Chechen war and funerals of young Russian soldiers. Television carries Duma debates urging a cessation of hostilities and the prime minister's speech calling for a cease-fire. (Two days later, when the Chechen presidential palace falls, he calls Chechen's leader a "bandit" and follows Yeltsin's hard line on no negotiations.)

Foreign Ministry employees are younger, more Western-looking than traditional party figures, and many offices are being painted or are under construction. Clearly this is a country in transition. Modest salaries are eaten by inflation, and the government has difficulty recruiting young people for diplomatic work. The military, interior ministry, and judiciary have higher priority than ordinary citizens for salaries, apartments, telephones. A Moscow judge's salary is about $250 a month, plus housing and utilities; a diplomat's would be much less. The Duma turned down a bill increasing pensioners' benefits from $8 to $12 a month because it would break the bank.

January 16: A long conversation with the interim president of the Constitutional Court, which is not yet functioning because its nineteenth member has not yet been named. (A nominee is proposed by the president the next day and promptly rejected by Parliament's upper house.) Nicholi Vitruk, acting president, is at once ebullient and cautious, mindful that his predecessor, Vladimir Zorkin, was an outspoken politician and that this cost him his job. Court members are nominated for twelve-year terms by the president and confirmed by the upper legislative house; but the court has yet to open for business, for it cannot function until all members are in place. A backlog of sixty cases awaits it, as individuals can petition the Russian courts on constitutional issues and the cases can make their way up from lower courts to the constitutional court.

In the afternoon, we meet with a consortium of human-rights organizations. A hundred mothers of young men shipped off to the Chechen conflict line the unlit halls, bundled in soggy old cloth coats, waiting endlessly for meetings with human-rights case workers concerning how they can find information on their children's whereabouts. The poorly financed but idealistic human-rights activists of the Moscow Research Center for Human Rights, the successors to Yuri Orlov and Andrei Sakharov, deal with prisoners' rights, assistance to veterans, the disabled, orphans, the homeless, gypsies, ethic minorities, and countering political extremism. One activist concludes our conversation, "There are different wars in this country. We do not know who fights whom. We do not know the legal basis of the army's invasion of Chechnya, or, for that matter, of Dudayev's election. One thing is clear to me: if we cease our work, things will be worse."

A Fast-Track Lawyer

January 17: Sergey A. Pashin's card lists him as "Head of the Department for Judicial Reform, State Legal Administration of the President of the Russian Federation, Doctor of Law, Honored Lawyer of the Russian Federation." He strides purposefully into the room, exuding a rising young politician's confidence. Dressed in a well-fitting Western suit and tie, he is, *mutatis mutandis,* the Moscow equivalent of a White House yuppie. The nine telephones on his credenza, the most I've seen anywhere, are a sign of power. "President Yeltsin asked me . . . said to me" studs our conversation, while a devoted staff member listens as if attending a concert by an Honored Soloist. I ask how law reform is going. Pashin replies, "There was a time, a few years ago, when we were passing a great number of laws, and the approval of foreign experts was sought. Times have changed, the political mood has changed. Basically we have good laws. Our problem is putting them into action, training our judges and police. We need material, we need to move the laws from the books to the people." I heard this sentiment two weeks ago in Estonia, too.

Introducing the jury system in nine regions around Moscow is an important change in the Russian legal system, and the government wants to extend it elsewhere, finances allowing. The change is revolutionary, for the norm in Russian justice for decades has been the judge and two lay assessors. The jury system, and with it the rise of the judge as an independent force in society, entails a subtle transformation to an adversarial system rather than leaving power with the prosecutor's office, sometimes called "the fourth branch of government of the socialist state." The prosecutor combines in a single person the conflicting roles of investigator, prosecutor, and court overseer.

A new criminal code is making its way through the Duma, as is a criminal procedure code. Draft laws on reorganization of the judicial system and on the status of lawyers are in the works. A Supreme Council of the Judiciary will supervise judges' work and will be allowed to remove incompetent or corrupt judges, conduct examinations for advancement, and evaluate judicial nominees' skills, a beginning step toward establishing professionalism in the national judiciary. Russia has thirty thousand lawyers, but until now most of these worked for the government.

"Another issue is human rights. There are those who want to hold any defendant for thirty days without charges. Considering the state of our jails, this is torture," he continues. "We should put our money into training programs and sending our judges to other countries for training. We also need publications, bench books for judges, articles on judicial administration and the judges' role, news of what other courts are doing."

The president's administrative office is a bit like the Old Executive Office Building in Washington, with wise senior counselors looking as if the weight of history is on their shoulders, and intense young people striding down the halls purposefully, carrying folders as if they are the czar's jewels. Let's hope it all works.

Note: Within a year Pashin resigns to become a Moscow district judge. His administration was always controversial. While he had Yeltsin's backing, Pashin pushed for reforms with the ruthless energy of a political czar, but when Yeltsin wavered and his health failed, Pashin's opponents came out of the woodwork and his work was stymied.

Moscow Nights

January 18: The Bolshoi's 1,500th performance of *Swan Lake,* seen from the Foreign Ministry's box. Outside, at least fifty warmly-bundled-up women line up like a Greek chorus, selling fur boots or fashionable Italian sweaters. A phalanx of burly young men in ski jackets greets us at the door, politely asking if we want tickets for this or tomorrow's performance of *Tosca.* Extremely efficient, they carry theater seating plans and race between two men who hold the tickets and a guard, for the sums are large. We are pleased with two thirty-dollar balcony seats which cost the vendors less than a dollar when the tickets first went on sale several weeks earlier. The performance, crowded with foreigners, is lackluster, but with excellent soloists. I count seventy musicians in the pit orchestra and thirty-two dancers in the *corps de ballet.* At intermission, we join lines as two servers sell small caviar sandwiches and glasses of Russian champagne. A retired engineer hands out programs and tells us, "Everything at the Bolshoi is old—the pipes, the wiring, it all needs repairs. We need a new movable stage and a place to store scenery, which must be carted by truck now from the edge of town." Each floor has its own coat-check stand; the operation is touching but hopelessly inefficient. The question is: how will Russian cultural institutions survive without strong state subsidies?

We return home by Moscow's efficient subway system, although the stations are poorly marked. Plastic tokens now cost twenty cents each. Some stations are lavishly decorated with mosaics and revolutionary art; I stand between bronze statues of an aviator in 1920s costume and a grenade-lobbing partisan with a pistol in one hand. There is no graffiti, and an endless army of women with straw hand-brooms keep the subway clean. It is bitterly cold when we emerge at the Arbat exit; in front of a restaurant, a well-groomed white horse stands, its owner begging diners to be photographed with it.

Chechen Interlude

January 19: The battle for Grozny's presidential building is over; now the guerrilla chapter of the winter war begins. Russian television footage, especially from an independent station, is more graphic than CNN or BBC, and there are interviews with opposing politicians and young soldiers' mothers. OSCE has been asked to send a fact-finding mission to Chencyna, and I try to assess the climate for its success or failure. The advantages of such a mission are that it will lend visible support to human-rights advocates and those who want a transition to a peaceful society, and that its findings can be used as a basis to restore peace and build political institutions. Moscow human-rights activists urge us to go, pointing out that there is a sharp division in Russian politics between the human-rights community and the hard-liners, and our failure to visit Grozny would be interpreted as a victory for the latter.

A Foreign Ministry member tells me that the Russian government held a large meeting to decide what to do about the OSCE resolution to send a mission to Chencyna. Most persons attending, including those representing the military, were for stonewalling or telling the mission to stay out. The Chechen affair is an internal Russian matter. A minority in the Foreign Ministry argue that Russia has signed the OSCE accords and that this entails international responsibilities it should honor. The result is to allow the mission, but Russian policy is split, as power is divided; the Foreign Ministry is conciliatory, the president and the army take a hard line. Russia drives with one foot on the accelerator, the other on the brake. From any viewpoint, the war is a disaster, dividing the country, weakening it economically, and failing to send a convincing lesson to other potentially rebellious republics. The Chechens' claim they were forcibly incorporated into Russia, and will now fight on from mountains and ravines. Russia faces another protracted war, as in Afghanistan. The issue could have been settled short of war, by negotiation, or if Russia refused that, by Russian economic pressure, shutting off commerce, etc. Russia's present strategy is to reinstate the country's deposed Supreme Soviet as the legitimate government, with a prominent Chechen, Salambek Khadzhiyev, head of the large petrochemical industry, as temporary head of government until elections are held.(Khadzhiyev later resigns, accusing the Russian Federation of obstructing the return of civilian government to the Chechen Republic.)

Traffic Circulation as Political Metaphor

January 20: The American Embassy in Moscow faces a main traffic artery, with six lanes of cars and trucks flowing endlessly in each direction. There is no easy way for a car going one way to turn in the other direction, so at the hill's top, possibly ten cars wait for a slight traffic break, then peel like a wing of fighter planes into the other lane. This is repeated in the reverse direction at the hill's bottom. I watch a brilliant ball of flame burn for several minutes at an intersection as I leave the embassy. It is a short-circuit in the electric lines powering city busses. Two busses now are stuck crossways in the middle of twelve lanes. Sparks shower on Ladas, Volgas, and Moskvichs nosing their way through the burning wire, which soon falls, stopping traffic in the middle lanes. Still, a few small cars edge under the drooping wires. Within minutes, police in gray imitation fur collars and white plastic belts appear; one officer urges traffic forward, yelling at drivers, while the second slows them down. At first the bus driver tries to lock passengers in, but heavily clad arms and legs push through doors; one is soon wedged open, and the driver then opens the others. Cars do not allow bus passengers to cross the road, but passengers form a wedge and move slowly into traffic, making cars halt until pedestrians reach the ice-covered sidewalk. Watching vehicles flow is like watching microorganisms moving about under a microscope; cars move slowly toward openings, trucks edge where they can. A large Mafia car full of tough young men with big sheepskin coats and short haircuts pushes defiantly ahead. A diplomatic sedan with the Czech Republic's flag attracts other smaller cars, like a school of minnows following a leader, waiting for a place to turn. No-one yields to any other driver, everyone is on the verge of bumping someone else, gently but surely nosing into another car's space. Moscow drivers have the same determination as the city's pedestrians; those who do not protect their space will lose it.

I'm freezing and try to find a ride back to the hotel. It is a Russian custom to stop a car and ask for a ride. I wonder where Russia is headed and think of a closing image in Gogol's *Dead Souls,* of a troika racing blindly toward the unknown. The observation of a human-rights activist comes to mind: "No-one knows where Russia is headed. When you think about our past, it is brilliant that we have come this far, but no-one knows what the future holds, even the immediate future. There are forces, even organized forces, actively opposing reforms. We are not a democratic society yet, and our traditions are not democratic. We are trying to change, but we are not there yet."

A Resignation at the Presidency

February 9: President Lech Walesa of Poland has accepted the resignation of the Polish presidency's legal-constitutional advisor, Lech Falandysz. A long-simmering feud exists between the urbane, introspective Falandysz, a brilliant constitutional and human-rights lawyer, and the blustery, ham-handed head of the Presidential Chancery, Mieczyslaw Wachowski. Wachowski is a former Gdansk taxi driver and presidential confidant, gatekeeper of the presidential palace, with whom Falandysz could not work. Falandysz submitted his resignation several weeks ago, but it was not accepted. He, more than anyone else, steered the presidential draft of a proposed constitution through shark-filled waters during the last two years.

According to a newspaper account, the final exchange took place when Walesa telephoned his constitutional counselor:

> Walesa: Well, what is going on, Mr. Minister?
> Falandysz: I would like to leave.
> Walesa: That is too bad; I am very sorry.
> Falandysz: So am I.
> Walesa: Perhaps we shall meet again some time.
> Falandysz: Perhaps.
> Walesa: Good luck to you.

A member of the Presidential Chancery told a radio interviewer, "I am a colonel, Wachowski is a general, and Walesa is a marshal. Falandysz was a sergeant, so he had to obey orders." He adds, taking a final shot at the president's counsel, "Legal ploys were good as long as they were effective. Once no longer effective, they became detrimental." A newspaper account said of the presidential chief-of-staff, "Wachowski is absolutely loyal, he lets Walesa humiliate him, take advantage of him, and call him names. He finds no chore humiliating and will do anything Walesa requires."

10

Chechen Republic, Moscow, Vienna

February 22: On short notice, I leave for Moscow and the Chechen Republic as part of a five-person expert mission for the OSCE chairman-in-office, the Hungarian foreign minister, to survey problems in the flow of humanitarian aid, human-rights violations, prospects for establishing civil governance, and setting up elections. Our mission head is Lorenzo Amberg, a Swiss linguist-and-translator-turned-diplomat, who speaks perfect Russian but lacks political sensibilities, generally figuring out what the Russians are doing to him a day after they do it. Another member is Pierre Filatoff, a French diplomat, a balding, bespeckled Russian linguist who, in Moscow and in combat conditions, wears a wide-lapeled dark suit, giving him the air of a head waiter at a Brighton hotel. Judge Luis López Guerra, vice president of the Spanish Constitutional Court, and I complete the delegation, along with Alan Parfait, a young British diplomat who speaks Russian. Our mandate is vague, Russian officials are hostile to our coming, and Amberg is a weak leader, never calling a planning meeting of the whole mission and giving in to Russian bullying, often without an awareness of how skillfully the Russians pressure him.

The Swiss Embassy makes our arrangements, renting a van and a driver, who resembles the hit man in a Clint Eastwood film, to meet Judge Guerra and me at the airport. The driver appears about 50 percent of the time during the next week, sometimes rattling up to the Arbat Hotel after we leave, other times showing up unannounced at the Swiss Embassy.

During our first evening in Moscow, we meet with Sergi Kovalev, Russia's human-rights commissioner, formerly a leading human-rights dissident activist who later will be nominated for a Nobel Peace Prize. Kovalev's approach to friend and foe is "in your face." He is loud, a chain-smoker, and pops out of his clothes. Someone who has seen the intransigence of Russian bureaucracy and the constantly broken promises of officialdom, his modus operandi is to flail in all directions simultaneously. "You Western visitors are sometimes so polite it exceeds the limits," he tells us; "you allow the Russian bureaucrats to wind you around their fingers. You should be talking with the Ministry of Foreign Affairs, putting forth your plan."

"But we are guests of your government," Amberg replies.

"You are not guests, you are an official international mission; tell them what you will be doing," Kovalev responds. "Otherwise they will show you prisoners in tuxedos. Ask for meetings with the Ministry of Interior, with Special Forces. Their troops are cleansing special areas of the city, it would be useful to investigate that as an international human-rights matter."

Amberg replies, "It is not possible for us to make a serious investigation in a few days, but the fact we are here represents a modest success."

"What concretely should we ask?" we inquire of Kovalev.

"You should ask about the special units rounding up people. Ask to meet detainees one-on-one. The International Committee of the Red Cross has a mandate to meet with prisoners; they say they are not being allowed to meet with prisoners. The Russians should start negotiations with the other side; there should be a cease-fire agreement and a humanitarian corridor and monitors for the cease-fire. That is how things are done around the world."

Kovalev says that the Russian Federation has declared Dudayev a National Criminal and will not negotiate with him. The military situation behind Chechen lines is complicated; it includes Dudayev's personal guard, disgruntled partisans who hate the Russians, freebooting adventurers, and clans feuding with one another for centuries.

Kovalev continues. At the conflict's start, the Russians used fresh recruits, young men who had just joined the military, many with almost no training. Some seized by the Chechens say that they do not know how to use their weapons. Other soldiers say, "We don't know why we're here." Completely different troops have been used in the assault on the city, with Marines flown in from the Far East and Special Forces. Then come the Ministry of Interior troops, whose task is to cleanse sections of the city already taken. They enter cellars where citizens take refuge, make interrogations, and find Dudayev supporters. Most reports of cruelty and marauding concern these troops. Some wear black ski masks over their faces, with only slits for eyes and mouth, but the people know who the special troops are because their uniforms are different from regular soldiers' uniforms." He shows us a ball-bearing bomb, with a thick metal casing about the size of a baseball, filled with tiny metal balls which explode and hurl through the air; he says it is one of several such bombs Russian troops rain on Chechen villages.

I ask Kovalev about Boris Yeltsin. He replies, "I think he wanted to be a democrat, but he wasn't able to do it." I ask who pushed the "Go" button for the December offensive—Yeltsin or Grachev? Kovalev isn't sure. "Rumors say Grachev spoke for a long time against it; people even thought he was a coward. He is a mean man, a stupid man, a duplicitous man, but the word I have is he opposed it. Whoever in the National Security Council believed that it would be a bloodless, lightning-fast operation should be sacked immediately. The Security Council has had three leaders in a short time, all with different backgrounds; each left many of his advisors behind, so the Security Council is multicolored politically."

Note: A month later I read news reports from Moscow. Parliament has dismissed Kovalev as human-rights commissioner. This is no surprise. While he is idealistic and well-intentioned, he attacks almost everyone with whom he speaks. His abrasive personality probably cost him the job, but how could he be otherwise after having been persecuted most of his adult life?

February 23: Breakfast with Western ambassadors. The Swiss ambassador, who just arrived a few weeks ago, is host; I drop a steamy Swiss sausage, which bounces like a basketball under the dining room table. Thomas Pickering, the American ambassador, calm, confident, and incisive in his political remarks, sits next to me. Before coming to Moscow, Pickering headed missions in Nigeria, El Salvador, and Israel, and to the United Nations. He glances at the list of people we will meet and gives me a perceptive sentence about each that is useful in our encounters. Pickering, who has a strong interest in resolving the Chechen crisis, has received persistent reports that humanitarian aid is not being allowed

into the Chechen Republic from Ingushetia and Dagestan, small autonomous republics on each side of the war-torn region. An additional problem is the thirty thousand Russian refugees trapped in Chechen-held parts
of the conflict zone—people who have lost everything and need to be
removed to safe places.

Pickering says, "You should get together with Fred Cuny. He was
sent here by the Soros Foundation to solve the aid distribution bottle-
neck. He is a big man like you with lots of ideas." I try to contact Cuny,
who has left Moscow for Chechnya. Later I plan to call him from Warsaw, but there are press reports that he is missing in Chechnya under
suspicious circumstances. For several months the embassy contacts both
sides without results; then, in August, Cuny's family holds a Moscow
news conference saying that, on April 4, Cuny and two Russian doctors
with him were stopped by Chechen guerrillas near a village. Dudayev
went to the village to congratulate the soldiers. Cuny and the Russians
with whom he was traveling reportedly were executed on April 14 after
the Chechen intelligence chief interrogated them. Cuny's family blames
the Russians as well, saying that Russian intelligence agents in the region spread stories that Cuny was anti-Chechen, information that easily
would have reached the insurgents. The bitter irony is that Cuny was an
internationally respected humanitarian aid leader, with previous work
in Somalia and Bosnia. He could have brought quantities of badly needed
food and medicine to the devastated region, but he was vilified by both
the Russians and Dudayev, the crazed Chechen leader. In the kingdom of
darkness, the children of light are its first martyrs.

February 23: The Russian Federation Ministry of Foreign Affairs occupies one of the Stalinist gingerbread-palace towers ringing central Moscow. A wire net extends over the building's front to catch falling ice; a
subway entrance opens on the building but long has been closed for repairs. Inside we watch a delegation of retired Foreign Office employees
place a wreath in front of plaques commemorating other members purged
in the years from the 1930s to the 1950s. A large book contains names
of members who died in such purges. I touch the book and stand silently
by it for a moment.

A milky-faced young man with blond crewcut leads us to the seventh
floor. We inch down a dark hallway to a reception room with huge table,
garish chandeliers, and museum-quality landscapes on each wall. Our
host is Deputy Minister of Foreign Affairs N. N. Afanasyevskiy, whose
pallid complexion and grimy shirt suggest the "Before" subject in a de-

tergent ad. A vintage Brezhnev-era politician, he tries to restrict the mission's political role—a point our chairman does not catch until after the meeting. Afanasyevskiy opens, "Since we understand you are here to work, I suggest you get down to work." He says that our itinerary, which turns out to be a carbon copy of the earlier mission's, will be available that afternoon at the Ministry of Nationalities.

I catch his ploy; we are shoved off to a minor ministry where the plan will be a surprise and they will claim no responsibility for it. I ask, "If we need to change the program, who do we see?"

Afanasyevskiy fields the question flawlessly, saying that it is difficult to change the program because several ministries are involved and because of the military situation. I ask to visit Nazaran, not knowing Nazaran's importance and simply picking it from a list of cities jotted down from a pocket atlas. Those on the Russian side of the table shoot knowing looks at each other. Afanasyevskiy says, "I personally thought you were interested in surveying problems in the Chechen Republic, but for some reason your attention is on Nazaran. I'll pass on your request, but there are military problems." I do not know that Nazaran, bordering the Chechen Republic in the neighboring republic of Ingushetia, is a center of anti-Russian sentiment. The wife of its head of state is a sister of the rebel Chechen leader, Dzhokar Dudayev, and it is the site of many Chechen-Russian talks. Also, approximately 100,000 of the region's 400,000 refugees are huddled there in crowded conditions, and it is a major center for Ministry of Interior detainee interrogations as well.

Afanasyevskiy is as unpleasant in the finale as in the opener, "We have a great interest in cooperation; I emphasize cooperation. There are certain outside figures who take on the role of judge and jury without taking time to understand the complexity of this situation" (a thinly veiled reference to the Council of Europe, which has just iced Russia's membership application for the duration). Then he says, "We see this as testing the possibilities of an organization like the OSCE, and our accepting you reflects the seriousness with which Russia treats the OSCE."

In contrast to Afanasyevskiy, Viaceslav I. Bakhmin, head of the ministry's International Humanitarian and Human Rights section, urges us to visit Nazaran, look for filtration camps, and avoid a Potemken Village tour. His contrasting performance reflects the various viewpoints existing within the ministry. Unlike the old days, talking with Russian officials today is like analyzing a complex geological mass; what you find may be totally different, depending where you dig.

We speed by rickety van through Moscow, along crowded roads with potholes deep enough to have been left by land mines. The United Nations, International Red Cross, and other ministries tell us that humanitarian aid is held up at borders and in customs sheds, and that refugees are denied papers allowing them prompt access to medical care, lodging, and food. "It's like Lebanon," an experienced case worker remarks. A humanitarian aid group has offices on the same floor as Air Afghanistan and Air Angola. Entering both offices, I ask for a timetable. The surprised Air Angola representative tells me, "We have only two flights a month, and you don't need a timetable." The Air Afghanistan agent, clicking his worry beads, volunteers, "We have not flown in a year, and I have no timetable to give you," puzzled as to why anyone would visit his office.

February 23: In contrast to Foreign Ministry stonewalling techniques, Minister of Justice Valentin A. Kovalev is fully open. He heads a commission with a long name, Temporary Commission for the Observance of Constitutional Rights and Civil Freedoms. Judge Guerra and I ask him to explain the legal basis for the Chechen invasion. "We acknowledge that it should have been a police action," he begins, "but in that setting it was not possible because Dudayev had bombers, rocket launchers, and heavy artillery. Under those conditions the use of the army was necessary," although neither a state of emergency nor a war was declared. "The president has prohibited the bombing of civilian areas and civilian targets. You will see for yourself. Now all the shooting is at military targets known to our troops. Our goal is to restore the vital infrastructure of our society. Here is where we ask your assistance. The military situation is improving; the main task is to bring out the sick and wounded." I raise the question of movement about the region different from that in the official program. "We will look favorably on your requests," the minister says, "except for questions of your safety. Sniper fire cannot be excluded; provocative acts cannot be ruled out."

The low point of our Moscow visit comes next: a meeting with the deputy minister for national and regional political affairs, a party hack named I. S. Ivanov. The ministry is located in a decrepit building far from Moscow's center. As we wait outside the minister's conference room, I stare at a poster of a woman in a 1940s dress sitting in a wooden chair at a table in a field that needs mowing badly. "Furniture from the USSR—Beauty and Elegance" is the caption. Under the poster is a cowhorn painted to resemble a dolphin. Our host does not have the promised program, only some notes, and quickly says that our stay is the Foreign

Ministry's responsibility. He clutches a pencil nervously and lists details, the exact same schedule laid on for the earlier Gyarmati mission. We respond that our mandate is to visit the Chechen "region" for several days. We want to talk to some Chechens. "Then why don't you also visit Saudi Arabia, Jordan, and Pakistan?" He adds, "There are Chechens there." For good measure, "I'm a doctor of science and I know as well as you do that you cannot do everything at one time. We don't rule out the possibility of eventual longer-term visits to these regions as well."

We race by van to different parts of Moscow to meet with humanitarian aid and human-rights representatives. James Bissett, a burly, outspoken Canadian ambassador, heads the Moscow office of the International Organization for Migrations. The Russians effectively have closed the borders with Dagestan and Ingushetia, he notes; and Russian policy encourages ethnic Russians to move from long-held lands in the Chechen Republic to parts of European Russia. If they have relatives or friends in Russia, refugees are provided with tickets to stay with them. Unlike some humanitarian aid groups, IOM moves with relative freedom about the war zone; many of its aid distribution drivers use their vehicles to carry wounded Russian troops back from combat regions. Bissett estimates that, of 400,000 war refugees to date, 112,000 are clustered in Ingushetia, another 100,000 in Dagestan; and the numbers are increasing gradually in both places. There are also an estimated 147,000 displaced persons, almost all ethnic Russians who fled following the Russian attack on Grozny; many are sheltered by friends or relatives. More than 1,200 persons are housed in rented railroad cars in Nazaran. IOM recently started a bakery to feed refugees, but bakers work extra shifts for profit and to buy the bakery themselves, in an attempt to introduce free enterprise in the North Caucasus.

Oleg P. Orlov of the human-rights organization, Memorial, gives us a fragmentation bomb, of the sort he says Russians are dropping indiscriminately in Chechnya. I tell him of the government's strong opposition to our visiting Nazaran. He says there are three reasons: the large concentration of refugees and persons released from filtration camps, Nazaran's easy access to villages on both sides of the border, and because it will be easy for us to meet freely with the opposition, something the Russian Federation does not want to happen.

Thierry Meyrat, head of delegation, International Committee of the Red Cross, is one of several Swiss members of old Geneva families who, after college, spend time with the International Committee of the Red Cross. In addition to distributing refugee aid, ICRC's fifty-five-person expatriate staff seeks access to detainees in detention centers with names like "The Tin Factory," "The Milk Factory," and "The Automobile Factory," and in other Grozny jails or detention centers.

That evening we talk with a Chechen banker, part of the thirty-thousand-member Moscow diaspora. Khumit Atnevich Paskoushev, president of the Kourben Investment Bank, wears a thick gold bracelet and a large gold watch with three smaller clocks set on the watch face. Heavy metal doors protect his office, and guards eye us suspiciously when they are not watching television. The bank president's personal guard wears cowboy boots and a purple sports coat. Paskoushev says, "I'm not a politician, but when it became clear that our small nation was being destroyed and Russia's scorched-earth policy was being introduced, I wanted to do something. The number of refugees goes up; our people are being forced into rural areas. I have evidence of targeted bombings of rural areas in Chechnya." He shows us pictures of a furnace-stoker's bombed house; the man, his wife, and eleven children are what the Russians call "an illegal military formation." Pashkoushev continues, "I told the prime minister what happened; he gave me his word that bombings in that region would cease. Two days later, bombing stopped. He gave me his plane, and I visited the commanders in the region; they assured me they would avoid hitting the village. Then I took two loads of flour in my car; when I got there the Chechen authorities wouldn't let the aid through. I left the flour with them."

Meeting with the Duma

February 24: At noon we meet six Duma members in a dark, drab hotel that houses parliamentary offices. They are members of the Commission to Investigate Circumstances of the Chechen Crisis. We are shown into a crowded, reconverted bedroom as deputies hurriedly enter, followed by reporters and camera crews. A microphone with a cover like a turkey feather duster is placed in front of me, lights go on, and a reporter asks, "Who are you? Why are you here?"

Each of the six deputies provides a sound byte. The Zhirinovsky deputy verbally attacks someone across the table as a hypocrite.

A chunky Communist woman deputy from Siberia states, "This is a public matter. We don't want members of the government suppressing it. Mothers in my district told me they would close the Trans-Siberian railroad unless their sons are brought home."

After they make brief speeches and are filmed for television, most deputies leave. One, a Moscow Communist, says that he just opened an exclusive night club and invites us to join him there on our return. As we head for the hotel restaurant and a place to hang our coats, a deputy says in halting French:

Vous parlez français?

Oui, monsieur.

Déshabillez-vous.

Do you speak French?

Yes.

Take off your clothes.

To Chechnya

February 25: At dawn we drive by rickety van to a military airport out-side Moscow. I am still half asleep when we encounter Maj. Gen. Boris S. Tretyakov of the Joint Chiefs of Staff's international treaty division. I stand in another section of the VIP lounge, looking for a cup of coffee or tea, as he begins a loud speech. At first I pay scant attention, thinking it is standard welcoming remarks, but, instead, he asks our chairman if we are an official mission or just a visiting delegation. If we are an official mission, he says, he is obliged to show us what we want to see; but if we are a delegation, we are guests of the Russian Federation, which will set our agenda. Amberg is nonplused by this ploy and mumbles a reply.

I tell the general that we are an official mission; if we are denied ac-cess to the conflict region, he can live with the consequences. Interna-tional organizations and the world press will say, "Same old Russia, what do you expect?" Tretyakov enjoys performing and tells us how many international missions he participated in as an observer and that he is part of a special office tracking Russia's participation in international treaties. I repeat our mandate. "It would be very dangerous to extend your visit," the general replies. "The Russian Army cannot assure your safety beyond the points we have suggested" (a carbon copy of the pre-vious mission's itinerary).

Joining us is the Russian side's highest-ranking member, Abdulakh K. Mikitaev, deputy from the North Caucasus, member of the Commis-sion on Citizenship Matters of the President of the Russian Federation, and chair of the Temporary Observation Commission of Constitutional Rights and Liberties of People. He is an affable smoothie who could have been Humphrey Bogart's sidekick in *Casablanca*. I ask him: does one constitution in the region stand out from others as being a useful model for the Chechen Republic? Mikitaev says that there is not much difference in regional constitutions and that Russia is negotiating new or updated treaties with the largely ethnic-based republics, preventing any of them from seeking independence. Governance in Chechnya is complicated by the presence of possibly forty clans, of which six to eight are major ones, often feuding with one another in Mafia-style vendettas. Basically, foreign relations and defense matters will remain under control of the Russian Federation, but each republic will be free to conduct economic and commercial relations with other countries. Some have even opened commercial missions in Germany and various Arab world capitals.

Finally, we load into the Tupolev VIP plane. Up front are two compartments seating six persons each around conference tables; behind is another section of approximately twenty seats, already filled with military and civilian passengers. A colonel says that our destination is Besian, a Russian base in Chechnya, but a few minutes into the two-hour flight he tells us that, "owing to meteorological conditions," the destination is changed to nearby Mozdok. (At dinner that night, a Russian general says that the Besian airport was closed for the day because helicopter gunships flew repeated raids from it on Chechen positions.)

At noon we arrive at Mozdok's military airfield. About one hundred helicopter gunships line the field, many of them armed and ready to take off on raids. (The new Russian war strategy, after considerable loss of human life in taking Grozny, is to pulverize suspected insurgent villages with patterned artillery bombardments and air and helicopter raids, leveling the whole region and causing the enemy to withdraw.) The drive by kidney-shaking bus from airport to headquarters evokes memories of Vietnam, with mud everywhere, temporary air fields, ammunition piled high, helicopters waiting to take off and bomb the local landscape into the Stone Age, and thousands of young men sitting around, smoking and waiting. A difference is that the American troops usually had films to watch or places to drink or play cards; Russian troops just sit for days on end. Outside the base are several big trucks wrecked by young drivers who lost control on the narrow roads.

In Mozdok we meet Vice Minister of Nationalities Gen. K. M. Tsagolov, an affable, blustery former fighter pilot, a Ph.D. turned military-civil administrator, someone who might be cast in a music hall production as "Caucasian Mountain Chief." He is deft at making toasts, impeccable as a host, and, I suspect, wise about the human dynamics of his home region, possessing knowledge the Russian Federation authorities will never use. We are taken to the flag mess for lunch with many of the people from the plane's back section. I wonder if they are members of the counterintelligence unit sent to track down Dudayev?

"The Military Did Not Start This War, and the Military Cannot End It"

The most impressive figure at our lunch is Col. Gen. L. P. Shepshov, chief of staff of the Federal Forces in the Region of the Conflict, who says:

> Who is to say who is right and wrong? I don't want to impose my opinions on anyone. We are convinced what we are doing is for a just cause and for the Chechen people, but not everything went as planned. The situation here is unique. We've seen the blood, the death, the humiliation of people who have experienced this war. Our military efforts alone have exhausted themselves, the opposition is so strong. We are a lot more convinced the time has come to resolve political questions by peaceful means. We are fighting criminals: 1,100 persons were let out of Chechen jails when the conflict began. We proposed the following conditions: self-defense units with small arms. Elect local officials, name people you trust, we will not interfere with this process. As a minimum, we will not negotiate with Dudayev. He is a National Criminal. For others there is an amnesty. You cannot have two armies in Russia. There are a number of mercenaries from Iran, Turkey, wherever; we would let them fly back to their countries. We cannot continue to allow a whole nation to suffer. The best people are usually those at the front lines. The military did not start this war, and the military cannot end it.

"Prisoners in Tuxedos": The Interrogation Train

In the afternoon we are taken to the same filtration center the previous mission was shown, where Kovalev said we would be shown "prisoners in tuxedos." (Outside, a group of soldiers' mothers gather; they heard that Kovalev is coming to the region and want to complain that he is biased toward the Dudayev government. Gen. Tretyakov, who accompanies us, hears them out patiently; he tells us that his own son is stationed in a military unit in Chechnya, but he cannot find him and has had no contact with him. Before we enter the filtration camp, the general reminds us, "This is run by the Ministry of Interior, not the Army."

The camp consists of several faded green railway cars set on a desolate siding with rusted tracks. It rolled into town in December, when the conflict intensified, and presently holds fourteen detainees. (Russians refuse to use the word *prisoner*, arguing that this is an internal conflict, hence the captives are *detainees*.) The interrogation cars are called "Stolypin trains," named after the czarist prime minister (1906–11) who invented them. After an uprising, he sent mobile cars and investigators to the region as part of the effort to put down the rebellion. I do not think the cars have changed much since czarist times. We pass crowded small cabins with scant possessions, a toothbrush, drinking glass, and playing cards. These are guards' cabins, followed by small, stark interrogation rooms; further down are iron cages, strong enough to transport circus animals. Four such cages are bunched at the car's end. Cells are small and dark; the car is without light, heat, or ventilation. Since the camp opened, 240 persons have been run through it, the commandant tells us.

Each cell has six wooden bunks without mattresses. A bandaged prisoner lies immobile on a cell's top bunk. Another has a badly battered face and tells us he was beaten by guards. It hurts when he breathes, and he coughs blood. A third says he was outside his house watering the cow when Russian troops came by and seized him because he did not have proper identification. His papers were in the house, but Russian troops would not allow him to retrieve them. Another reports that he was held for over a month without charges. A young man says that he escorted refugees from Grozny to a refugee aid center, where he was arrested because his passport was not in order. If the interrogator allows it, family members can be informed that their son or husband is being held. Prisoners answer cautiously, politely; one says that food and medical care are adequate. The prison commandant stands nearby, watching. My memories: darkness, people caged like animals, frightened young men silently awaiting whatever comes, without access to judicial or humanitarian aid.

Once we are outside the car, we question the commandant, a Major Arlov. He says there is only one such camp in the region. (Only one on rails, it turns out. We are told of at least nine other interrogation centers.) Of the 240 persons brought to the camp, 215 were released and 25 were held for further charges after preliminary inquiries. (My guess is that the initial interviews are quick and brutal. Ministry of Interior investigators look for timely tactical intelligence that will lead them to Dudayev or his supporters.) When I ask how many detainees have been brought before the local judicial authorities, Arlov does not know. He is not doing well with questions. Judge Guerra joins us and, not knowing the ground I have covered, repeats many of the same queries. At this point, a Ministry of the Interior colonel emerges from the circle forming around us, grabs Arlov by the shoulders, moves him aside, and says he will answer our questions. (There are several military straphangers in our party; we never learn the names or functions of most. One appears with a tape recorder every time we discuss controversial subjects.)

We ask how long persons can be held incommunicado or in detention centers, without charges being filed against them or counsel provided; and, once charges are preferred, how long persons can be held before a trial. "About nine months" is the answer we receive to each question, in part because Boris Yeltsin, to fight organized crime, has suspended due process provisions of the newly enacted Russian Federation's constitution; and because there are no functioning judicial bodies in Chechnya.

There are reports that, if a detainee has calluses on his trigger finger and a shoulder bruise from a rifle's kickback impact, he will be taken out back and shot. I ask a Russian general if this is true. He avoids the question, saying, "One day I came home from rifle practice. My wife saw my shoulder and asked where had I been that night?"

A week later, I read comments by one of President Yeltsin's representatives who visited the camp with us. Abdulakh Mikitaev says that there is no evidence of brutality or misconduct by the twenty-five-person Ministry of Interior detachment.

"In Afghanistan It Was Mines; Here It Is Snipers"

We visit a Russian military hospital, the first of two in three days. (We never meet any Chechen officials; ours is entirely a Russian-run Potemken Village show, despite repeated requests to extend our mission's scope and duration.) The camp commander, a senior army medical general, says that there have been great improvements in military medicine, principally because of quicker helicopter evacuations. The hospital has treated two thousand patients since it opened in December; it has twenty presently. More than 25 percent of the hospital's injuries are sniper victims. "This is a sniper's war . . . in Afghanistan it was mines; here it is snipers." He tells us that he has not treated any Russian troops for mutilations by enemy soldiers, saying that the army hospital handed over field medical kits to the other side to use in treating Russian prisoners.

That evening we are quartered in a government hotel in Prokhladliy (the cool place), a town of sixty-two thousand persons and six thousand refugees. An armed Ministry of Interior soldier is stationed on each floor. I suspect that someone will search my room daily, but the room is not cleaned in the three days we are there. Occasional signal flares light the night sky, and we hear periodically the whooshing sound of outgoing artillery shells fired randomly into the darkness.

In the evening, the mayor gives us bottles of the locally fabricated cognac, which he says Boris Yeltsin serves at receptions. The third toast is always for "those who are not with us," with the one at the head of the table pouring a small libation into the tablecloth. The most interesting guest this evening is Gen. Eugenov Skobelov, chief, 42nd Army Corps, based in North Ossetia but spread across the Caucasus. A seventh-generation general, his original ancestor introduced order into Central Asia in czarist times. Skobelev is an orphan; his family was wiped out in the Siege of Leningrad. At the toasts, he gives us each a bullet and asks that we keep it as a souvenir of the need for peace rather than war. The general's lower front teeth are covered with gold-colored metallic casing, the same color as the bullet.

What kind of a general was Dudayev, I ask; how did he make his way through Russian army ranks to command an important unit in the Baltics?

"I knew him," Skobelev replies. "We promoted him because he was an ethnic. We had a policy of promoting officers from various ethnic groups whether they were capable or not. In his case, he became a fanatic for power. He seized the oil refineries in Chechnya and plundered them. The employees haven't been paid for months, and retired people haven't been given their pensions. Dudayev took the money."

Still, the Russian portrayal of Dudayev as a power-grasping ethnic ignores an important consideration, Russia's disputed legal claim to hegemony over the Chechen Republic. Dudayev retired as a major general in 1990 and went into politics in 1991. His election to the presidency in his home republic was flawed, but not many elections in the Caucuses meet international standards. Despite massive efforts to apprehend him, the short, mustachioed leader gives interviews to world media. In one he said: "We never signed the March 1992 Federation Treaty, nor have we participated in the new Russian constitution or the Russian parliamentary elections of 1993.

"Chechnya's tragedy is her location. In the eighteenth and nineteenth centuries, we stood in the way of the czars' expansionist designs on Persia and India. Today the real issue is oil. Chechnya's proven premium crude oil and natural gas reserves, as well as the existing pipeline between our country and the Black Sea, are critically important to Russia, the Middle East, and the West."

A Polish Interlude

February 26: When we descend for breakfast in Prokhladliy, we meet two Polish journalists standing in front of the hotel. They accompanied a four-truck Polish aid convoy, causing a Polish-Russian diplomatic incident. Touched by the plight of refugees, the Poles collected food, clothing, and medical supplies in Poland, then drove straight to Grozny, accompanied by a television crew filing daily reports. Russian Federation border authorities give the convoy permission to enter the Chechen Republic, provided that it goes straight to Vladikavkaz, North Ossetia's capital, where the Russian Federation stockpiles aid. Having received permission to turn northward, the Polish convoy heads southward instead, seeking that trusted rarity in a Moslem and Orthodox land, a Roman Catholic priest, to whom they can safely entrust their gifts.

Next the Polish trucks are held for five days at a checkpoint, accused by the Russians of a provocative act and by the International Red Cross of unofficially appropriating a copyrighted symbol. (Convoy members wore Red Cross emblems with "Polish Charitas" on them.) Polish television files daily stories around the theme: "We want to help the people, but we can't make it through the Russian bureaucracy." The Russian Foreign Ministry gets louder and meaner. A spokesman calls the Poles "adventurists" and brands the Polish media's ironic reporting of snafus an "anti-Russian campaign." I ask officials of the local Ministry for Emergency Situations to solve the problem and unload the trucks rather than let the rhetoric escalate, noting that otherwise donors will send their assistance elsewhere. One locally based aid worker remarks, "If people have the choice of giving support to Mother Teresa or this bureaucracy, guess who they'll pick?"

The Chechen Provisional Council

February 26: Umar Avtourkhanov, head of the Chechen Provisional Council, is a weak, inept figurehead fulminating in a decrepit two-story provincial building surrounded by sandbags, guarded by dinosaur-sized APCs (Armored Personnel Carriers) and Rambo-like troops. He says that the provisional council was established by Moscow's decree on December 18, the same time as the massive invasion, and is active in six of the country's seventeen regions.

> In January we convened a Congress of the People of Chechnya, 2,560 delegates attended; 70 percent of the populated settlements were represented. The Congress authorized the work of the provincial council. They demanded that Dudayev resign immediately. In September we created a Government of National Revival; Salambek Khadzhiyev was named prime minister. Twice we made military attempts to remove Dudayev, on November 15 and November 26. We broke through to Grozny's main square but were unequal to Dudayev's forces and retreated. We lost about five hundred men. The Russian Federation authorities considered that we were not up to the struggle, so they introduced troops to restore constitutional order. The prime minister is now in Grozny, responsible for coordinating with regional authorities to restore order. When conditions are right, elections will be held.

Elections are a constant subtheme to our talks. The Russian Federation wants to hold public elections in the Chechen Republic by year's end, to give their actions legitimacy. Our reply is that elections should come after democratic government and a draft constitution are in place. They speak of elections with international observers; we speak of free and fair, openly contested elections with multiple candidates and parties, and neutral ballot counting. We are worlds apart.

The Russian plan's final pillar is reducing the Chechen president's powers to a ceremonial role, thus preventing the rise of a second militant leader, and to delay rebuilding Grozny, keeping political power regionally diffused to avoid the country again becoming a "regional superpower," as one Russian general put it.

We walk through the town's main street, a muddy track, past an impoverished market whose main attractions are plastic buckets of potatoes, strings of garlic, and a few local hard candies wrapped in thick paper. Guards with automatic rifles walk on each side. We enter one door of the local workers' canteen for lunch, as a car delivers the meal's tableware through another door. There is an interminable wait. A youth comes by and tries to sell us a bucket of onions; an old man offers us jars of honey. "When peace comes, I will export it to France," he tells us, counting to ten in French.

We do not know it then, but our helicopters have been standing by for over an hour, waiting to take us to Grozny; Avtourkhanov's ineptitude means that the Grozny visit is now cut to less than an hour because of approaching darkness. Meanwhile, Avtourkhanov prattles on, as we chew bulbous cubes of spongy meat. "Eighty percent of Dudayev's army are criminals, released from prison, plus mercenaries collected all over Russia, men without a past or present, and with no future." I wonder if our hosts have been given plastic laminated cards with talking points to use with foreigners, for many recite variations of the same themes in the same order.

Russian attitudes toward Chechnya have always been divided. For example, during the nineteenth century there developed a view of the southern Caucuses as a romantic, mountainous land of freedom on the far edge of despotic Russia. At the same time, the picture emerged of Chechens as lawless bandits and criminals. The two views were in conflict, but persist to the present. Russia's present attitude of trying to conquer the Chechens by massive force began during the time of General Alexey Ermolov, a military commander and viceroy from 1816 to 1827. It was he who established Grozny (the Russian word meant "threatening place") as an outpost of empire and raided villages, often bayoneting their inhabitants. The Caucasus became known to the Russian military as a "Southern Siberia," a place to assign unruly troops or undesirable generals. Meanwhile, Chechens fought Russians from mountain hideouts, ambushing slow-moving Russian convoys or engaging in lightening raids on Russian settlements—the same tactics they use a century later. A difference is that today's Russian populace is opposed to the war, as seen in the grim footage shown each night on Moscow television, while in czarist times news of casualties and defeats was never carried in the press, and intellectuals grew up on images of heroic mountaineers and simple maidens living a bucolic life, farming when they were not plundering passing caravans. Alexander Pushkin's "The Prisoner of the Caucasus" and a host of lesser works fed such a concept of an alpine kingdom peopled with free but ungovernable mountain bandits. Russian attitudes toward Chechnya remain divided: the Kremlin's party of war ranting for more troops and firepower to subdue the region; the party of peace—articulate in the Duma and among human-rights activists—seeing it as the wrong war in the wrong place at the wrong time, a second Afghanistan conflict. Meanwhile, the Chechen view of Russians has been remarkably consistent through recent centuries: Chechens see themselves as freedom-loving Moslem people forcibly conquered by a brutal northern neighbor. The perceptions each people have of the other remain irreconcilable, and the war goes on.

Grozny Occupied

February 26: Our flight takes twenty minutes at treetop level. The Russian military helicopter throbs like an ancient washing machine; three escort ships cover us. These are the days just before spring's coming, and the land looks as if an angry giant has sunk his nails into the dark earth and clawed a long streak. This is where tanks have dug into grain fields for pitched battles and moved on. Orchard trees near the airport are covered in white—not the white of blossoms, we discover, but of small parachutes slowing the descent of phosphorous shells, allowing night defenders to spot advancing enemy troops. On the runway's sides, Aeroflot planes are snapped apart or bent at odd angles, like the playthings of a disturbed child, who, tiring of them, cracks the planes in two. Fires charred the airport tower, which shows the pockmarks of machine-gun and artillery fire. We hurry through the airport's reception hall, now filled with the vomit-inducing stench of excrement left by troops guarding it.

Six APCs meet us at the door. On top are armed young men, underworld creatures from a Wagner opera, wearing flack jackets, helmets, and camouflage cover, carrying Kalashnikov assault rifles or grenade launchers. It is late afternoon, and the sun is setting; the APCs' oblong, tinted rifle scopes provide our only views of the town, until recently the scene of fierce fighting reported worldwide on television. Our view is distorted by the ultraviolet convex lens; it is like seeing a passing landscape through a submarine periscope. As in a surrealistic film, we see rows of abandoned Russian apartment buildings, many with broken windows and smoke debris around windows and doors; a scrawny mongrel lapping up ditch water; a light gray baby carriage filled with wrapped packages abandoned on a sidewalk; an elderly man limping briskly down a muddy road perpendicular to ours. Some buildings have windows taped with Xs to keep glass from shattering. Others are smudged darkly above the window frames; apartments momentarily became ovens, burning violently when hit by artillery fire. At the battle's height, Chechen troops entered Russian parts of Grozny and fired from apartments; Russian troops responded by destroying their own peoples' dwellings, block by block, flat by flat.

At a forward command post, surrounded by tanks and encircled with sandbags, we meet an enterprising and capable Russian officer, Lt. Col.

Nikolai Yefimenko, who describes efforts to provide aid to the part of town formerly occupied by thirty thousand Russian citizens; all but twelve thousand have fled. He shows us a nearby apartment building where a Chechen sniper is holed up. The sniper killed one of his best men last night. "Dusk is the most difficult time for us," he continues; "then Chechens move about." Street patrols prevent some looting. Soldiers clean up garbage and debris. Intelligence officers evaluate residents' political attitudes. Counterintelligence officers track Dudayev, who that week gave an hour-long interview to a Moscow television station. Obtaining fresh water is a problem for the city, since pipelines are destroyed and putrefying corpses fill several wells. Cemeteries are mined, and, at the conflict's height, people bury their dead in backyards. "When people come in and tell me there is a mine or unexplored mortar shell, I just register it," the colonel says, as he does not have enough troops to clear the mined areas. Distributing humanitarian aid is no problem, since so little of it reaches the battered city. We pile back into our APCs and race to the airport.

If you look from the airfield in a certain direction and ignore helicopters on each side, and if artillery rounds are not being fired, for a moment you see a peaceful rural region. The air is clean and cool, scented by spring earth. The landscape is soft and rolling, and on the horizon stand a farmhouse and barn, empty now, but perhaps you can imagine that a farm family is settling down by lamplight for warm soup and bread. Overhead the first star of evening appears.

It is the day before Ash Wednesday, the beginning of the Christian Lenten season. A verse from the prophet Isaiah is today's daily lesson: "The ransomed of the Lord shall return, and sorrow and sighing shall flee away." Isaiah's words return to me over the next week: "The wilderness and the dry land shall rejoice, the desert shall blossom and burst into song. . . . The ransomed of the Lord shall return with singing. Joy and gladness shall be theirs, and sorrow and sighing shall flee away" (Isaiah 35).

Refugee Voices: "The Ransomed of the Lord Shall Return"

February 26: North of the battle zone in Mozdok we meet with ethnic Russian refugees. Boris Chulkov, director of the federal migration service's local office, is confronted by the twenty persons present. A woman attacks him in a high-pitched voice, shaking her fist, until exhausted: "Why do you want to move us to Central Russia, where it is cold; why do you want to move us anywhere? I was born here; I'm from here; I don't want to go away."

General Tretyakov adds, "I knew your predecessor, and he was three heads taller than you. Don't be false with these people; if you aren't up to this job, go away."

Chulkov, whose profile resembles that of a carved wooden peasant in a Christmas manger scene, is unfazed. His response to everyone is the same: he can offer free one-way transportation to anywhere in Russia, lodging at one of several refugee centers in northern or central Russia, a one-time food package, and 20,500 roubles, roughly five dollars, which the Duma calculates as an average Russian monthly salary. Until recently, he had ten tons of donated canned meat and flour, but it has run out, and Chulkov has no more supplies to distribute.

"I'm Armenian, I'm not Russian, I'm impartial," a woman adds. "Why should we move away at the time of armed insurrection when armed bands are stealing cars, killing drivers, drilling holes in pipelines, and stealing the oil? It's all designed to create a criminal state with its epicenter in Grozny."

"Write about him in your report," Galina Beskrovnaya, a Grozny refugee, says of Father Ivan Makarenko, an Orthodox priest who moved seven people into his simple house. "You say you cannot provide us with any direct help," he begins, "but please influence our government in any way to help us. Anyone who reads the Bible knows that Jesus was sold for thirty silver coins; how can anyone buy anything for twenty thousand roubles? What the government has forgotten is the need for moral support. Many of those who come from Grozny are old and sick; before they ever receive medical service, they must go through a chain of offices. Maybe the Migration Service should be given the power to act directly. You should consider not only the material losses, but the moral losses as well."

Another refugee adds:

> When we came to Nazaran, we had nothing; the driver gave us food and water. We waited in line for two hours to register. I told them that my mother couldn't walk because she had spent a month hiding in a cellar. My son was gray from living underground. Now we live in a train wagon. I have nothing. All we hope for is to return and hope some of our possessions will be left. I am not afraid of work. I am a woman, but I cannot build a house by myself.
>
> We know there are good people among the Chechens, but in the last three years it has been genocide against the Russians. My husband perished; I do not even know where he was buried. I do not

send our child to the school, because they shoot at children. I have a feeling of an absolute lack of security. In Nazaran they gave us nothing; some Baptists gave us humanitarian aid, that was all.

The discussion is hot; accusations fly, fists shake. One refugee yells at others: "Stop this, you are embarrassing us in front of strangers."

February 27: In Vladikavkaz, capital of the neighboring republic of North Ossetia, our time in the war-torn region ends. We sit on a sanitarium bench at the town's edge with some refugees. Their faces are stoical, strong and traced with sorrow. Some sob gently as they talk. An eighty-year-old woman recalls, "I thought I would have a peaceful old age. This is the fourth time I have been forced from my home—in 1925, when I was a child; in 1944, when we were herded to Kazakhstan; in 1992, when I was exiled from North Ossetia in that war; in 1994, when I was forced from my home in Grozny."

I sit with some children, who are hesitant to talk about the war. I am bone-weary by then and tired of arguing with Russian officials. I tell them stories about my dog.

"Is he bold?" they ask. "Does he make jokes?"

I describe Tigger's unsuccessfully chasing a loud crow that hops just ahead of him. We laugh; a handler with tape recorder hurriedly joins us, puzzled.

Other refugees say:

"We thought that, once we were retired, we would have a good rest."

"My two daughters are jobless; one had an excellent library, but it was destroyed. She has 'Chechen Citizen' in her passport and cannot get a job."

"Here is our doctor. She is a great person. She does not ask our nationality and helps us."

"In Grozny, we never knew who was Russian, Chechen, Ingush; I love my aunt, and she is Russian."

"Since we have come here, three women have given birth . . . for what purpose?"

"I have five children. I tried to teach them wisdom, but I don't even have a spoon. I think there will be help for us by the end of the war, but no-one will be alive to receive it."

"Why did the Russians bomb our village?"

"The Russian soldiers said, 'We are not volunteers, we did not know where we were until we got out of the wagons.'"

"I [a woman] am an Ingush Muslim. One day some Ossetian ladies from the neighborhood came and said to me, 'Leave.' I left. My adopted son stays in the house where I lived for thirty-five years, but I cannot see my house."

The Return Flight

February 27: On the return flight to Moscow, six bottles of cognac are produced for eleven of us, and we share food. (Neither food nor drink are served as part of the VIP flight, although the galley crew offers me some tea and dried fish from their personal rations.) I avoid the celebration, word processor plugged into the coffee machine's outlet, writing a draft report. I am asked to give the final toast, with a comment about each of the eleven persons, standing in a circle in the forward cabin as the plane slowly descends toward Moscow's military airfield. Warm hugs are exchanged, and the last of Boris Yeltsin's state reception–quality cognac is consumed as wheels hit the runway. It is 10 P.M. Good-byes are said on the frozen tarmac, and we head for our vehicles, eager to avoid Moscow's cold.

Black Ice in Moscow

February 28: After a long early-morning wait for a driver who never appears, we set out for the Swiss Embassy by subway, only to meet the ambassador heading for the gate in his Swiss-red Volvo. "You have been summoned to the Foreign Ministry," he says. Amberg, our delegation head, must cut short the Moscow program and leave that afternoon for Budapest to brief Istvan Gyarmati, personal representative of OSCE's chairman-in-office, the Hungarian foreign minister. The chairman-in-office will appear the following day in Vienna before OSCE's Permanent Council. I call Gyarmati, who is concerned about what sort of presentation the Hungarian foreign minister, as chairman-in-office, can make to representatives of the fifty-three assembled OSCE member states. I tell him that I will draft a presentation on the plane.

As we head for the airport, Amberg says that the Foreign Ministry meeting was unpleasant. Afanasyevskiy told him, "On the tone of your report depends the future of the Russian Federation's relations with the OSCE." This is because I read to our Russian hosts in the field draft sections of the report, detailing chronic high-level stonewalling and lack of cooperation.

At the airport, Russian customs confiscates Judge Guerra's cash because his entry receipt is filled out but not stamped. We went through customs together, where the clerk did not stamp our customs forms. (A month later, after numerous calls, Judge Guerra's money is returned to the Spanish Embassy in Moscow.)

Budapest and Vienna

In Budapest, Gyarmati is a quick study. He plans to visit the Russian Federation next week and has taken the Chechen crisis on as a personal mission. If he makes the right moves, it could catapult him into the OSCE secretary general's chair, since the incumbent is leaving next summer. Gyarmati shows little interest in the details of our report and asks if the recommendations I made earlier for the restoration of civil order still hold; I say they do. I spend the day working on a draft document, good-naturedly badgering Monika, the hotel business-center manager, to keep the office open late so I can print it.

When we arrive in Vienna, we are told that our presentation, instead of opening the morning's activities, will be delivered unofficially in late afternoon, after the meeting is over. This is because the Russian ambassador asked for a written copy of our report, and we had none. The Russian said that, without a formal document, it would be improper for us to speak officially. "This does not bode well for future Swiss leadership of the OSCE," he added. Our press conference also is canceled; instead, the Hungarians give one on our mission. I have no idea what they say, since we learn about it after the event.

The morning is spent in set-piece speeches congratulating the Hungarian foreign minister on his four-month leadership as chairman-in-office. After the eighth such discourse, white-gloved Austrian waiters should have wheeled in a cake. By late afternoon, when we are finally given the floor, everyone is tired. Amberg falls for the Russian bullying and, instead of chronicling their clear efforts at throwing obstacles in our path, speaks of "confusions" and "misunderstandings." I present the Rule of Law recommendations and, trying to crack the day's sterile boredom, conclude: "May I end with a personal observation? For me the most moving point in our mission was a visit with two groups of refugees. I remember their faces, proud, firm, yet showing traces of suffering. I remember the faces of children, gentle yet wondering 'Why'? At one point, we met an Orthodox priest. A woman refugee told us, 'Put his name in your report, he is sheltering seven of us in his house.' Another told us, 'We are not blaming the young soldiers, they are like a herd of rams sent to be slaughtered.' For the sake of these people, and the afflicted populations like them, we hope for a prompt end to hostilities, immediate steps to speed up the delivery of humanitarian aid, and a prudent effort to introduce governance by Rule of Law."

Finale

No one has any questions or comments for us. The French delegate urges us to be realistic in our recommendations; the Russian repeats that he will withhold comment until a written document is produced. Following the session, I stand at the entrance in case anyone should want to discuss a point he or she did not care to raise in public. None does. The American delegation asks if I could brief them on Moscow and Grozny, but it is late afternoon and the delegation scurries out to a diplomatic reception, saying they hope that we will meet again sometime. The Hofburg Palace ballroom, OSCE's meeting place, is empty, its lights turned out. The white-and-gold Rococo room resembles a provincial opera company's stage, badly needing an infusion of new life. Puzzled as to why anyone would linger, the guard looks at me; I hurry out into the cold evening. In returning to my hotel through the rain, the refugee children's gentle faces return, as does the line from Isaiah: "The ransomed of the Lord shall return, and sorrow and sighing shall flee away."

It remains to write a final report. I spend several hours each day on a draft document. However, I must return to Warsaw on Friday, so Amberg and Filatoff take the manuscript. I know it will lose its perspective, substance, and bite. I feel like a peasant whose horse has been seized by the czar's troops. Amberg says that he wants a "more traditional report" and excises all sections remotely critical of the Russian Federation. He is Swiss, so the body of the report highlights problems of the Geneva-based International Committee of the Red Cross. The four pages of Rule of Law recommendations Judge Guerra and I crafted are reduced to four paragraphs. "Free and fair" elections become "fresh" elections. Later a Russian jurist says that the Rule of Law recommendations, as they appear in this document, are too vague to be useful. I remember Filatoff's self-satisfied grin when I hand my draft report to him. The last time I had seen him was a year earlier when I fell on the steps of Warsaw's Royal Palace and wrenched my knee. He peered down at me briefly through fish-eyed glasses, then moved quickly on.

(Gyarmati returns to Moscow the following week with the Hungarian prime minister and, a few weeks after that, as head of his own OSCE mission. He is denied access to the conflict zone, now moved from Grozny to the southern provincial town of Shali, because the Russians say they cannot assure the group's safety.) Gyarmati says that Russian forces have committed a greater number of human-rights violations than the Chechens, a remark similar to one from his first mission, that Russia's armed response is out of proportion to the situation's military requirements.

Russian Federation authorities, meanwhile, agree to establish a resident OSCE "assistance group"—they will not let it be called an official "mission"—in the Chechen Republic. The assistance group several months later negotiates a cease-fire and talks between both sides. In October 1995, negotiations break down completely. The senior Russian military commander in the region, Lt. Gen. Anatoly Romanov, is gravely wounded when his motorcade is hit by a remotely detonated bomb as it goes through a Grozny underpass. Discussions of a cease-fire, the exchange of prisoners, disarmament of the Chechens, and withdrawal of the Russians are suspended. The OSCE presence is reduced from six to two persons after threats and grenade attacks. Armed incidents on both sides increase.

11

Latvia, Estonia

April 1: In Riga, Latvia, we hold a two-day seminar on "The Judiciary in a Changing World" for forty-five district judges, sponsored by the Latvian Supreme Court. Judge George Marovich from Chicago tells gripping stories of his life on the federal bench, and local judges ask many questions. Our German legal specialist is taken to the hospital on the seminar's second day with what he thinks is a stroke or heart attack but which Judge Marovich correctly diagnoses as the hotel breakfast, heavy on grease. I recall our son Christopher's expression as a small boy in Prague when offered something to eat: "No thanks, I still have half a Czech sausage inside me."

Although spring has come to much of Europe, snow swirls against the slate-gray sky outside my hotel window. Yesterday evening I went to a concert in the Riga Cathedral, a large, stark Baltic Gothic church with hard acoustics. Bach's *St. John's Passion* was performed by an excellent choir, small orchestra, and soloists. The audience was young and intense, bundled in winter coats, some huddled over the painted wooden balcony as if following a sporting event. When the sun went down, cold breezes wafted through the cathedral. I pulled on my hat and gloves and tried to read the German-language inscriptions on eighteenth-century merchants' tombs around the building.

"Save Us, U.N." (Kurdish Refugee Child's Sign, Latvia-Russia Border)

The Latvian Foreign Office is faced with an increasing number of Middle Eastern and Asian refugees who are entering Western Europe as illegal immigrants through Russia and the Baltic States. More than a thousand Kurdish refugees arrived in Latvia in the past year. Russian criminal groups take the refugees' scant savings, promising them access to European countries, where jobs and social welfare benefits await them. In the current case, a hundred refugees, many of them women and children, spent a week being shuttled by train among Russia, Latvia, and Lithuania. "We don't care how long it goes on—we will always send them back," a Latvian immigration official remarks. The Foreign Office lawyer with whom I spoke said that Latvia has high unemployment, a precarious economy, and few refugee facilities.

When questioned, refugees give scant details of names, families, citizenship, and how they came to the Baltics. Many are from Afghanistan and Iraq; some are Kurds. Once they are found in Latvia, they are put on a train back to Russia, where Russian border authorities refuse to accept them. Refugees live in two train cars with one working toilet. Most are women and children. Some paid up to three thousand dollars, a life's savings, to Russian gang members who promised to guide them from their own disturbed countries to Sweden, where they would go on welfare.

The present group boarded a boat for Sweden, but on December 24 it went aground on some shoals in Estonia, after which they were held in an army camp until put on a train. Local attitudes toward refugees often are mean-spirited. When I raise the problem with the head of a human-rights organization, her face hardens: "They thought this was Sweden, but they found out it was Estonia instead."

Sometimes smugglers fly refugees to Poland, charging persons fleeing troubled countries like Iran, Iraq, Pakistan, or the Chechen Republic five hundred to three thousand dollars each to be left on an isolated rural road. A Russian army colonel recently was arrested and sentenced to six years in prison for leading a smuggling ring. The small planes carry cigarettes, narcotics, weapons, and alcohol, as well as refugees, landing in local fields or on strips cleared for them in forests. Crews, known by their first names only, pay local residents small sums to remove rocks from landing areas or to haul planes from mud to hard ground. Once a plane crash-landed; the crew burned it to prevent identification, but its Lithuanian tail markings remained.

Word from Vienna: Russians have blocked a motion allocating funds for the OSCE mission to Chechnya. The Russian ambassador says that he can do nothing without instructions from Moscow. Since the fifty-three-country process works on consensus, his negative vote constitutes a veto. The Russians do not want an international presence criticizing their bombing the Chechen Republic into oblivion. Rather than say so openly, Russia's strategy is to use a variety of procedural ploys, such as "No instructions from Moscow," "The time is not right," and "We cannot assure the mission's safety." In Brezhnev's time, similar stonewalling occurred, but the Russian position was that other countries have no right to interfere in Russia's internal affairs. However, the CSCE accords are so encompassing in asserting that democratic governance represents the political future for Central Europe and the former Soviet Union, that such a position no longer is possible for the Russian Federation.

Russians and Estonians: "Facing Our Common Future in Ide-Virumaa"

April 3: The desolate region of Ide-Virumaa is in Estonia's north, near the Russian border. Once it was grassland and meadows, covered with birch trees and marsh alders, but now there are great piles of waste from formerly secret Russian uranium processing and chemical manufacturing plants, and radioactive waste has trickled into many ponds and streams. The region's residents are about 86 percent Russian and 13 percent Estonian.

Until recently, all information about the town and plant was kept in Moscow. They were not considered part of Soviet Estonia, but today local authorities are responsible for public administration, schools, hospitals, and local order. Attempts to privatize the monster industrial complex have begun, but its technology is hopelessly outdated; conceptually it belongs to the era of the five-year plan, not a market economy. Meanwhile, the residents, many of them well-educated workers and scientists, are unemployed. Where once they governed, they now are aliens in a strange land.

It is in this context that Sarge Cheever, who had been with the OSCE mission to Moldova and now is assigned to one in nearby Johvi, organized a seminar bringing local Estonian and Russian residents together for a weekend to discuss their legal, educational, and economic problems. The animator for this event is a regional Lutheran dean, intellectually impressive but administratively weak, who designed the seminar and then left for a month's tour of Argentina and Chile. His church has purchased a ruined eighteenth-century manor house, part of a huge estate once owned by a German family who lived there until World War II. The two-story building has meter-thick brick walls inside and out, spacious windows on the sea, and a ballroom easily seating sixty persons.

Outside it snows, and a strong wind from the sea blows snowflakes sideways at a building, which is heated only by two porcelain wall stoves, around which participants huddle in coats. I keep my hat on, and my colleague, Arie Bloed, a leading Dutch international affairs specialist, delivers his presentation in his winter coat. The first evening's dinner is bread-and-sausage sandwiches, which we eat huddled by the stove.

Arie and I share a dormitory room in a nearby farmhouse that is undergoing renovation. Two Estonian parliamentarians have the other two beds. One of the occupants, a former world-class discus thrower, has a bone-crunching grip and an all-consuming in-your-face grin; the other sulks and snores.

I build my remarks upon three propositions: (1) not all agonizing human problems are human-rights problems, (2) many problems facing communities like this represent a collision between the law and history, and (3) the law cannot save society. Law can provide norms and boundaries for conduct, but it cannot solve every problem facing society and usher in a Golden Age.

"If you remember one idea, let it be this: organize," I add. "Don't feel sorry for yourselves, don't complain all the time, figure out who is important in Estonian politics and go after them." I describe how Jewish lobbying groups organize in the United States and how Mormons and Pentecostals gain converts in Central Europe. "Take a page from their organizing book," I suggest.

I point to the differences between telephone manners in a Western company that wants business and a Communist bureaucracy that wants to turn it away. A caller may expect to be greeted by a company seeking clients in this way: "How may I direct your call?" Contrast this with the "Nyet" of many Russian phone calls. The "Using the Telephone" section of my "Survival Russian" course contained this useful phrase: "Don't hang up, please; I'm not finished talking yet."

I suggest a minimal definition of human rights, principally the right to free expression, assembly, worship (or not), and several due-process provisions, such as the right to a speedy trial by an impartial court, the right to confront accusers, and the right of access to counsel. Others often add second- and third-generation rights, such as the right to education, health care, apartments, social services, social security, a clean environment, the protection of culture. Such rights belong in individual legal codes. If they are in constitutions, they are almost unenforceable; and some countries simply ignore them, thus weakening their constitutions.

"Typical American answer," remarks a former East German lawyer, now part of the mission. Later the woman, who once worked on the now-defunct German Democratic Republic constitution, tells me that she has applied for the job I will vacate—"the Law and Order post in Warsaw," she calls it.

Estonians Invented the Sauna

April 4: It is bitterly cold, and the conference center is unheated; construction signs are everywhere. The only part of the building adequately renovated is the sauna at the bottom of a dimly-lit, steep-pitched wooden basement staircase. Water seeps through the foundation's freshly cemented edges. In the sauna's corner is a wooden stove which, Aleksei Semjonov tells us, is a sure sign of an authentic Estonian sauna. Aleksei, an ethnic Russian, works with the Estonian government on Estonian-Russian relations. He pours water on the heated black stones, lamenting that he has no beer to pour instead for its grain-like fragrance. Nor are there crushed birch leaves to give off a fresh scent. "You can't have everything," he muses; "we have been independent only four years." Then he waxes lyrical: "Estonians invented the sauna. . . . It is the height of Estonian technology." His English grows more confident. "All other saunas are imitations. During a half-century of occupation, we were not allowed to improve our saunas." Nods of approval, history is vindicated. "Meanwhile, other Nordic countries tried to imitate us, but to what avail?" He shrugs his sweaty shoulders. "Look what the Finns have done with the sauna" (dry irony). "What could the Russians do with a sauna?" Silence.

I break the soliloquy and leave after a brief period in the heated cabin, provoking a comment that the sauna is alien to Americans. Walking along the frozen ground past rusting tractors discarded long ago, I reach our dormitory. Later, as we speed back to Tallinn, I spot an oblong stone-and-earth structure, like a Viking burial mound, outside several large farmhouses. Thin puffs of smoke ascend from some, which, with my new knowledge, I recognize as authentic Estonian saunas.

April 9: Palm Sunday. In Tallinn's Old Town, worshippers carry branches of pussy willows instead of palms. I visit two Lutheran and two Orthodox churches. While the Lutheran congregations sit silently and attentively, the Orthodox Cathedral of Alexander Nevsky and Church of the Transfiguration are as busy as village markets. The service lasts most of the morning. People keep entering and leaving. Some visit each icon, kissing it repeatedly and lighting candles; still others loudly gulp down cups of blessed water from a huge porcelain container. An aged prelate with a jeweled crown covered with purple velvet mumbles a homily, and a black-bearded deacon chants *basso profundo,* after which the altar party, moving about and bowing to each other, disappears in clouds of incense behind the *ikonostasis,* reappearing much later.

Victory in Europe Day

May 7: VE Day, the fiftieth anniversary of Victory in Europe after a war that claimed perhaps fifty million lives. The event was commemorated in London, Berlin, Paris, and Moscow. In London a service at St. Paul's Cathedral was attended by the queen and over sixty heads of state; in Warsaw the British Embassy asked me to hold a service, where the German ambassador read a lesson and reflected on the war's ending. He said the Allied victory freed Germany from fascist control, for which Germans were grateful, and recalled walking near a Warsaw monument to a fallen British airplane crew whose plane went down in a local park while delivering supplies to Polish partisans.

The most conspicuous example of reconciliation in political life in recent times took place when Germany's president, Roman Herzog, visited Warsaw last year at the anniversary of Warsaw's Uprising and asked the Polish peoples' forgiveness for Germany's destruction of Poland. What could have been another civic event of bands and wreath laying became instead one of the deepest possible encounters between nations. Healing began, ancient enmities and disagreements were recast in a new light, benefiting all nations, not only Germany and Poland.

The communion cup I used at the service says in German, "For the hundredth jubilee of the Evangelical Church in Pombsen [Pomerania, northern Poland] from the hereditary mayor, T. G. A. Leinigschen Family, Williamsdorf, dedicated May 1, 1842." The vessel mirrors the simple, clean lines of period German Protestant art, the engraving is in a firm, confident hand—work that might appear in the Buddenbrook's family dining room. (German merchant communities were strong along the Polish coast at that time.) Underneath the chalice's stem someone, with a much lighter hand, almost as if they were in a hurry and used a pin, scratched "Christmas 1916." That was in the depths of World War I when Poland's Protestant north was still under Prussian control. Today, few traces of the German communities remain, Russia's post–World War II removal of any traces of a German presence was done with devastating finality. I wonder how the vessel made its way to Warsaw, who the family was, where the church was located (there is no longer a Williamsdorf), and what the people had gone through across the span of years. The cup had been banged about; when I first lifted it to the sunlight, three tiny holes in its base were visible. Finally, clues led nowhere and mystery remained; as we passed the cup to our small circle on Sundays we recalled another worshipping community sharing joys and sorrows, affirming life's victory over humanity's dark forces.

The Miners' Demonstration

May 26: At noon several hundred Polish miners demonstrate at the Sejm, then parade downtown to the Ministry of Heavy Industry, a grim Communist-era building near ours. They are late in coming; outside, a row of police riot trucks waits. The young officers smoke or sleep in the spring heat. A few with money buy orange soda; Roma fortune-tellers read the hand of one. Some troops stand by in riot gear, gray padding, and helmets, looking like warriors ready to break through the door in a local Star Trek production.

The miners, whose peasant faces evoke those in Zola's *Germinal* or Van Gogh's *Potato Eaters,* are hot and tired when they arrive. They listen attentively as some of their leaders speak with portable microphones, giving speeches at once wavering and bellicose, demanding higher wages and chronicling grievances against privatization. Polish miners are trapped, stuck in a dying industry that for decades has been subsidized. They have legitimate concerns: many mines were sold quickly to foreigners who had little interest in preserving local jobs. Millions of dollars allocated to reeducate workers went to frivolous projects and expensive consultants who stayed at the Marriott Hotel and offered questionable advice to cabinet ministers. To end the demonstration, miners blow whistles and pound plastic hats on the pavement, then they leave. An eerie clamor remains, the historic din of the Polish worker-protesters who stood against Communism long before it crumbled. Today's sound is different. It is a protest against forces of modernization that are turning Poland into a Central European success story. Waiting nearby at the bus stop are young people from technical schools, carrying manuals on computer systems and modern accounting methods in their knapsacks. To them belongs Poland's future.

In a nearby bric-a-brac shop is a local amateur artist's painting of a Silesian town. Coal-mine shafts and elevators cover the horizon, above a drab row of miner's houses. Next is the valley, with a winding blue stream and poplars on each side. Young lovers stroll along the river's banks. Atop a slag heap sits an elf-like miner, puffing his pipe, his features like those of the plaster gremlins for sale at the Polish-German border, looking contented as evening descends on the mining town. No Polish artist would paint such a scene today.

Later, Silesian miners demonstrate at the Sejm, then they lose control at the nearby cabinet offices, where they throw large metal screws and nuts, sacks filled with paint or coal dust; and set off firecrackers and smoke bombs. Police respond; more than twenty police officers and seven demonstrators are injured.

12

Georgia, Moscow, Tajikistan

May 27: 7 A.M. arrival at Warsaw airport for a flight to Frankfurt, then on by unregistered Air Georgia to Tbilisi. "Today you will not travel," says the Warsaw airport guard, who confiscates our money for the two-day seminar we are planning for the Georgian judiciary. Irek Stępiński, our logistics manager, produces stamped, initialed papers from the Polish national bank, and three captains discuss the question for a long time and finally let us proceed. Air Georgia's Russian plane is crowded; passengers may smoke anytime, anywhere, on the plane. We sit on the heated, steamy tarmac, the cabin filled with blue smoke. Someone wheels a bicycle past me down the aisle, storing it at the plane's rear, near bales of goods being imported into Georgia; because of political disturbances, commerce over traditional road and sea access routes has been disrupted.

11 P.M. arrival. We are met by five Supreme Court justices, who take us to Hotel 21, two reconverted Georgian houses on a hill overlooking Tbilisi. They wait outside while a late supper is served us. The judges do not want to impose upon our hospitality and do not have the money to pay for meals independently. (A local judge's salary is five dollars a month.) We would invite them to share a meal with us, but they don't enter the hotel, instead waiting outside until we finish.

Drab as any Georgian building on the outside, inside the rooms at

Hotel 21 are carefully painted white. Walls are hung with old Caucasian carpets with bold geometric designs and dark red-and-yellow vegetable-dye colors. Pieces of old carpets cover pillows on elaborate wire chairs; imaginatively designed brass-and-stained-glass light fixtures could be props from *The Abduction from the Seraglio*. The hotel is the work of Betsy Haskell, the only American operating a business in Tbilisi. A Washington, D.C., entrepreneur who came to Georgia as advisor on economic development and set up several small businesses of her own, including the hotel and Tbilisi Locators, the city's only registered real estate firm. The real estate firm helps the growing Western business and governmental community find lodgings and office space. Fresh strawberries and fruit juice are served us each morning for breakfast. The former editor of a Russian-language publishing house runs the dining room. She could have been the aunt-from-the-country-dacha in a Pushkin play. Her comments are grammatically correct in English, employing words and constructions of a bygone era. Of the street dog waiting at the door, she says, "He is very poor but very friendly." Outside our window, an ancient Russian garbage truck wheezes past each morning; local residents appear curbside and dump small piles of garbage into it.

The Supreme Court building is an imposing structure, the sort of place that might appear on a turn-of-the-century French or Swiss postcard. Built in the late nineteenth century by a Polish architect, it escaped the region's many wars and was tastefully restored. The large four-story building resembles the capital's opera house, designed by the same architect. Our seminar is held in a spacious conference room with an ornate chandelier and elaborate stucco molding; if the door opened and *Tosca* swept into the room, no-one would be surprised. Before World War II, provincial Italian opera companies wandered about the eastern Mediterranean, providing music seasons in places like Yerevan and Tbilisi, both of which were developing world-class musical enterprises of their own.

Georgia's Supreme Court has thirty-nine members; by Western standards, it is an appeals court with civil, criminal, and military chambers, First Deputy Chairman Jimmy Kipiani tells us. A judge's term has been extended from five to ten years. The court's legal department is charged with writing draft legislation, and a research department has been added, as well. Following the tradition employed in many Continental countries, the court gives legal advice to executive and legislative branches, even on issues that soon may appear as court cases. Questions demonstrate a hunger for knowledge of how other judicial systems work and how colleagues would handle different cases. Considerable interest is expressed in the workings of the European Court for Human Rights, how the plea-bargaining process works, how Western prosecutors differ in power from the procurator of the Russian tradition, standards of judicial ethics and comportment, and how judges manage relations with other courts and with the executive and legislative branches.

Judge Edward Rafeedie of the Los Angeles (California) Federal District Court opens the discussion with a complex case involving kidnapping, torture, and extradition in the death of an American Drug Enforcement Agency officer captured and killed in Mexico. American agents seized the person they said was responsible, brought him from Mexico to California with no extradition permit, and tried him before Judge Rafeedie, who ruled the seizure illegal. He was reversed by the U.S. Supreme Court, which took the position that how a person is brought to the United States is not a legal issue; the case begins when they arrive in America. The case was returned to Judge Rafeedie for retrial. During the second trial, the judge dismissed the case for lack of evidence; the defendant was freed, creating a huge public uproar, but Judge Rafeedie believed that this was the only verdict he could return. There is high interest in the case because its ingredients are international crime and the roles of different courts. We return to it often during the two days of spirited discussions.

Each evening we are invited to a dinner by our hosts. For each such meal, a *tamada,* or president of the feast, is named, who orchestrates the evening's toasts, alternating between guests and hosts and adding toasts to absent family members, women present, justice and Rule of Law, love and friendship, and much more. I lose count at fifteen plates and thirty toasts for twenty-six guests. The delicate small dishes of Mediterranean foods are left on the table, in case anyone should want more. A district judge, also an actor, brings four actor-musicians to the gathering; they toss their heads back and sing the rich, earthy minor-chord melodies of the Caucuses, sometimes correcting the pitch by leaning toward one another and adjusting sounds.

One afternoon we visit a private museum in what once were the royal apartments. (What remains of Georgia's royal family lives in exile in Spain.) The artist was a contemporary of Picasso and spent several years in Paris. As might be expected, his work was banned in Stalin's time, but gradually he was allowed to show. A retrospective of his works is planned for Paris next year.

On our final evening, we attend a performance by the children of an educational center, featuring sword dances, dramatic kicking and twirling, lithe village maidens weaving about, drummers and flute players urging the dancers to greater frenzy.

"May God Protect Your Dead"

June 2: As I alight from the No. 117 bus each evening in Warsaw, two elderly women gesture toward portable wooden boxes, on top of which are placed clotted cream, flowers, pickles, garlic buds, and seasonal herbs. Usually the price goes down a third following negotiations. This time, after hard bargaining, I accidentally pay with a new zloty note, ten times the purchase price. With creaky knees, both rise. "May God protect your dead," says one, grasping my hand in her gnarled hands. "May they spend no time in purgatory," her sister adds.

Grand Slam: The Polish State Stud Farm at Janow Podlaski

June 3: The Polish State Stud Farm at Janow Podlaski is a microcosm of Polish history. Charlotte and I visit it with several families from the American Embassy, riding by modern tourist bus along roads traversed in recent centuries by French, German, and Russian invaders. The spacious farm with numerous pastures is on the Polish-Belarus border. Three times it was seized by invading armies.

The world-renowned breeding farm was founded during the Napoleonic era, when prolonged wars wiped out Central Europe's horse population. A hundred good stallions were bought in Russia, arriving in December 1817. The stables were built in 1825 by a famous architect, a designer of palaces in Warsaw and St. Petersburg. Nobility traveling in either direction often broke their voyage with a visit to the horse farm.

During World War I, the horses were seized, taken to Russia and were never heard of again. Russians returned in 1939. Red Army tanks sped across the flat land, surrounded farm buildings, and lined up the staff of one hundred persons along a railing, pointing machine guns at them. Everything that could be removed was seized—horses, fencing, hay, potatoes, etc. Four of the most valuable horses were led in a single line by a groom; frightened by a passing truck, they escaped from the Russian convoy heading east. The groom ran after them, pretending to fetch the horses, but instead he took them into a dense forest, where villagers hid them. Next Germans captured the farm, and eighty horses were transported westward for the German Army. They had the ill-fortune to traverse

Dresden the night it was fire-bombed, and all but two were killed. These were saved when a groom held their reins throughout the attack; one was Grand Slam, who also had fled to the forest a few years earlier.

At World War II's end, Poland's Communist government executed some of the show horses as symbols of capitalistic decadence, while others were turned into work horses. Eventually the state farm was rebuilt and became an international attraction and hard-currency earner. Today it has several stallions, 80 Arabian mares, and 50 Anglo-Arabian mares among its 350 horses. Its annual auctions are attended by buyers from the Arab world, Europe, and the United States. The average horse sells for $20,000 and some for as much as $100,000 (it is currently a depressed market). A few have sold for over a million dollars.

Several mares and stallions parade before us, each a beautiful creature with a distinctive personality. Next we visit pastures and feed apples and carrots to the foals, one of whom butts a sibling out of the way, circles, and returns for the carrot. Several young horses gallop up to investigate us, and mothers nudge their young along. Some show horses prance as if their feet are above the ground. The farm is an enchanted place set in the middle of an otherwise drab region.

On our return to Warsaw, the bus passes many signs in Russian and Polish for "meble," overstuffed, rounded chairs covered in local leather or leather and carpet.

Second Annual Warsaw Judicial Symposium

June 5–10: The judges are from the United States, Armenia, and Latvia; the prosecutors from Georgia and Bulgaria; defense attorneys from Belarus and the Russian Federation. The event is a mock trial, part of the Second Annual Warsaw Judicial Symposium, which has brought fifty judges from sixteen countries for a week's intensive discussions of Rule of Law issues. The event is part of our effort to build a judicial culture in the void left by the former Soviet Union.

Six senior Polish judges present issues relevant to judicial reform from the perspective of a country making a successful transition from authoritarian to democratic governance. Our Western experts are Judge Luis López Guerra, until recently vice president of the Spanish Constitutional Court; Judge Lloyd D. George, a federal judge and specialist in bankruptcy and economic issues from Las Vegas, Nevada; and Judge Cynthia Holcomb Hall of the Ninth Circuit Appeals Court in Pasadena, California, who presides over the trial with courtesy and authority in equal measure.

The mock trial case resembles one working its way through the Polish courts, involving allegations of bid-rigging by a prime minister, who let a generous contract for parliamentary office computers to an old friend, the third highest bidder. A local newspaper calls the prime minister corrupt, and the prime minister files a civil suit for libel against the paper, its editor, and the writer. Witnesses play their roles like vaudeville melodrama actors; and testimony is laced with expressions like "esteemed witness," "honored judge," and "respected counsel." The prosecution is insistent, the defense outraged, the judges cool and professional. By a two-to-one decision (Armenia and Latvia versus the United States), the defendant, a newspaper reporter, is found guilty of civil libel and ordered to print a retraction. No Western court would have found the anodyne editorial libelous, but most Central and Eastern European jurists are satisfied with the verdict, and some think that a stiff fine should be added as well.

We have one week with the judges. The question is what to do in such a brief period? My decision is to concentrate upon steps toward an independent judiciary. All over the former Soviet Union, we hear politicians say, "Democracy is a great idea, but you can't trust the people. If you knew the people we have to work with, you wouldn't trust them either." Our response is, "You don't have to trust the people or their leaders if you design a system of government that is open and accountable; that is what separation of powers and checks and balances mean." Judge George wrote an excellent article on how the American judiciary makes its needs known and conducts its business through the Judicial Conference of the United States. A Polish jurist explains how a similar body, Poland's National Council on the Judiciary, works. A lively interest is shown in standards of judicial conduct and means of judicial discipline and in how judges settle cases short of a trial.

The role of a constitutional court and the binding nature of judgments by constitutional courts are examined from the viewpoints of participating countries. Jurists want to know if individuals can appeal their cases up through the judicial system to the constitutional court. Others ask if the constitutional court should be called upon to give advisory opinions to the executive and legislative branches before an actual case comes before it. In several countries, the constitutional court's decisions are not binding unless accepted by the executive or parliament. Everywhere the judiciary is in a struggle to carve out an independent role, to emerge from the shadows of the old era of "telephone justice" into new times and an independent presence.

In the evening, people from different countries gather in the commons room to continue the day's discussions and swap problems and stories. A Russian judge says, "We have never had an opportunity before to sit down with colleagues from other countries and discuss common problems." An open bar with cold beer and soft drinks eases discussions. Armenian participants cook shashlik one evening, supplemented by choice Armenian brandy. A Georgian jurist introduces colleagues to the art of toasting by a *tamada,* the person presiding over a meal. In addition to the booth interpreters, I assign a student interpreter to stay with each expert at coffee breaks and meals, to facilitate individual discussions. Some of the frankest exchanges come at such times, rather than in formal sessions. The closing reception starts at 6 P.M., outside on a verandah on a cool day in late spring. A Warsaw orchestra plays dance tunes, and the smell of roasting mutton wafts over the gathering. We award plaques to the Constitutional Court of Kazakhstan for courage, the Supreme Court of Georgia for judicial excellence, and the Supreme Court of Estonia for excellence in judicial education.

Each evening the Armenians see us to bed with generous supplies of dark, fiery brandy; each morning Judge Hall has Judge George and me on the road for bird watching at 6:30.

Last Plane to Dushanbe

June 11: Evening at the Arbat Hotel, Moscow. Tomorrow is Independence Day, commemorating the fifth anniversary of what a Foreign Ministry contact told us, with a touch of irony, was Russia's victory over itself. On that date, the Congress of People's Deputies of the Russian Soviet Federative Socialist Republic (RSFSR) adopted a declaration on sovereignty, proclaiming that Russian laws take precedence over Soviet laws. A constitutional commission, headed by Boris Yeltsin, was formed to draft changes to the constitution. Meanwhile, the RSFSR remained part of the Soviet Union until December 1991.

A hot, airless room and squadrons of mosquitoes. I use bug spray, wave towels, and take two showers. Our only relief is two pitchers of cold black cherry juice at breakfast. In the lobby, the traditional Lenin corner has been replaced by the draped Russian Federation and Soviet Union flags behind a statue of a triumphant World War II soldier in winter uniform, helmet extending below his ears, coat collar chin high.

June 12: On the way to Domodedova domestic airport, we pass a Russian tractor pulling two cement-filled wagons haltingly up a steep road.

Hell-black smoke belches, like volcanic eruptions, from a large exhaust pipe directly above the tractor's cabin. On top of the exhaust pipe is a delicate metal hand, like the painted hand seen on the rear of trucks and buses in Moslem countries. The hand, covered with a thick glove of soot, waves lightly, depending on the exhaust fumes' intensity.

Porters meet us in the crowded, dirty airport lobby, race our baggage to the sweltering Intourist cubicle, and charge us one hundred dollars (later reduced to ten). We carry our bags downstairs to the tarmac, where a yellow airport truck pulls up between planes and, for three dollars, takes us to a drab building called "International Hall," its faded yellow sign tilted downward. In the early afternoon we are led upstairs again; a clerk with a faded yellow czarist-era control book lists each passport and visa number in a copybook hand. Bursts of Russian-language announcements rattle like machine-gun fire over the speaker system. After half an hour in the sweltering waiting room, we follow a guard to a bus and a second building, where our passports are stamped. The entire exercise takes three hours. As we board the plane, a clear liquid drips from a wing, like an artesian well oozing water. "Water or kerosene?" I ask.

"Kerosene," replies the armed guard, motioning us aboard. By now the other passengers have been sitting in the unairconditioned airplane for over an hour, looking like malnourished Mexican peasants languishing at a rural bus stop in the midday heat.

The plane's lukewarm beer tastes of the Russian earth; a stewardess sits each bottle on a faded brown towel and lets the foam drip before serving it. A "Style of Switzerland, Schweiz Schokolade, original Swiss guaranteed" chocolate bar from the Syrian Arabic Republic is served. I recall an Irish friend's buying a bottle of whiskey with a grouse on it and the caption "very Scotch whiskey made in Japan." Rectangular pans of Aeroflot blue stewed chicken are heated in the galley. A quarter of a leg, sliced cleanly with a massive cleaver, along with a daub of warm rice, is served to each passenger.

Last year, 302 people died in nineteen internal Russian air crashes, 100 more than were killed in similar crashes the previous year. Poor safety standards and maintenance were mainly responsible. The Russian prosecutor general's office said that most crashes were in small airlines springing up since the demise of Aeroflot, companies that seized Aeroflot's planes but did not have the means or the desire to maintain them.

June 12: Arrival in Dushanbe after a four-and-a-half-hour flight. A hazy, warm summer evening. The plane bounces a few times on near-balding tires. Since engines on the aging Tupolov plane cannot be reversed, we coast to the runway's end, where a youth herding cows watches us. Next we race by car along wide, tree-lined boulevards; roads are almost without cars, buildings without lights. Our destination: the government guest house, three two-story buildings on a twenty-acre compound of fruit trees and buildings in the center of town. Later we walk along the garden path, past an abandoned teahouse, around rows of fruit trees, watching young Russian paratroopers—poverty in uniform—guarding the outer perimeter and power plant. Outside our building, two soldiers sit each night, their World War II–era portable field phone attached to wires dangling from the wall. The night is cool, the air fresh. I fall asleep quickly and am not awakened until 5 A.M., when the sound of gunfire briefly fills the street outside. We are told later it is (a) intended to disperse a large crowd gathering in front of a bakery, (b) drunken soldiers firing into the air, and (c) soldiers signaling to one another.

June 13: We visit a mosque, very much under construction, where an Uzbek *imam* sits in an air-conditioned room with its door open because otherwise the temperature would be too cold. He tells us that about one hundred persons attend Friday prayer services, but up to one thousand persons gather on important festivals. Money to build the mosque comes from Saudi Arabia; Pakistan sends some help. Iraq is interested primarily in oil, not religion; and Iran sends clerics who are unwelcome because they stir up local populations, which are generally peaceful, rural people. In the market we buy spices wrapped in schoolchildren's exercise papers. Nearby are parked Russian tanks and trucks, part of the large Russian force in Dushanbe and near the Afghan border. Tajikistan's dependence on the Russian Federation for economic and military aid has left it, the poorest country of the former Soviet Union, a virtual vassal state.

June 13: Minister of Justice Shawkat Ismailov holds a dinner for us in a restaurant on Dushanbe's outskirts. We are the only guests in the restaurant, probably opened for this single meal. The heads of the constitutional, supreme, and high administrative courts attend; so does the procurator, a stony-faced, shifty-eyed man who says little and looks intently at whoever talks. He reportedly has been given this high position as a reward for leading the attack on antigovernment forces in Dushanbe's civil war three years ago. "Enjoy yourselves from the bounty of our land," the minister says, gesturing toward the plates of dried fish, fresh cucumbers, sliced ripe tomatoes, and shashlik.

"We Shall Overcome"

The problem with Tajikistan's constitution is that it contains no real separation of powers—a point we make often during our three days of substantive talks. Our presenters, in addition to Judge George and me, include Dr. J. A. Frowein, head of the Max Planck Institute in Heidelberg, one of Germany's leading constitutionalists. Frowein identifies several problem articles, including Article 64, which gives the president almost kingly powers: "The President is the protector of the constitution, laws, and rights and freedoms of the citizens; the guarantor of national independence, unity, territorial integrity, stability and continuity of the State, and the ensurer of the functioning of the bodies of state power and Tajikistan's observance of international treaties."

Article 87 says that the courts are independent and subordinate only to the constitution, but Article 49.2 gives the legislature, the Majlisi Oli, the right of "interpretation of the constitution and laws," as was the case with Soviet-era legislative bodies. We urge that the procurator be responsible to the minister of justice, not the legislature. An additional problem: judicial appointments are for only five years, severely restricting judicial independence. Tajiks acknowledge these problems, blaming them on the civil war, their inexperience, and their inability to trust anyone. "We shall overcome," they remark.

At lunch the minister of justice recalls, "We talked among ourselves and said, 'You are good people, tell us your life stories.'" Judge George recounts growing up poor in Nevada but having access to a good education, then the practice of law, which he did successfully for a decade before being offered a position on the federal bench. I recall growing up poor in western Pennsylvania in the post-Depression era but having access to a good education, and being part of a generation believing in what was then called "The American Dream." The minister wants to know the size of our families and what our children do.

June 14: I awake with light shining in my face, a brilliant full moon. Soon a recording from a nearby minaret calls the faithful to prayer, then a chorus of bird song and the Central Asian dawn. Two young Russian soldiers at the guest house's entrance unplug their field phone and walk briskly toward their barracks.

June 14: At the meetings' end, we meet with the president's principal advisor, Abdulrahman Dostoyev; the minister of justice; the ubiquitous procurator; and a handful of close advisors, led by Mrs. R. Museyeva, head of the parliamentary constitutional committee, which goes by the name of Committee on State Building or State Construction and is responsible for writing basic laws, not for roads or bridges.

Dostoyev discusses recent talks with the opposition in Almaty, Kazakhstan. He says that controversy was generated by his remark, "All of us are to blame for the Civil War; it was our generation's fault. Our fathers and grandfathers gave us a good childhood and provided for us, and we did not follow them." He continued, "Everyone was responsible. Some wanted an Islamic state, others wanted a different society. The majority were people who sat on the sidelines, waiting to see who would win. In my view, all three groups bear equal responsibility. That is why all of us should work to rehabilitate our society, from whatever region we come or whatever political tradition."

The conference finishes in late afternoon, so we ride out of town, along a winding road, the main north-south route toward Leninabad. Every few kilometers, busses unload for police checks, or officers supplement their meager incomes by flagging down late-model Western cars for allegedly speeding. Except for a few old Russian trucks belching pale blue smoke, there is little regular traffic. Our translator says that she has not left town in three years because of the civil war. Our destination is a local motel, closed since the war, each room padlocked with a huge lock. In front is a teahouse, a large hall for watching television, and piles of faded blue portable wooden platforms upon which people sat in more peaceful times, legs crossed, sipping tea and conversing for hours. On our return, the driver tours Dushanbe. As cars with melodic horns speed by on each side, he describes each large building: "Opera, ballet . . . Ministry of Bread . . . Ministry of Water . . . Academy of Sciences . . . factory." After each designation, he adds "robota" if the institution is functional or "nie rabotach" if is has ceased to work.

Air Tajikistan: The Anatomy Lesson

June 15: 8 A.M. departure from Dushanbe Airport; the minister of justice sees us off. We talk at length about future cooperation, such as reviewing the draft law on the constitutional court or sending a group of Tajik law writers to Warsaw for an exchange of views with international experts. Professor Frowein offers an internship for a Tajik at the Max Planck Institut, and I arrange for a Tajik intern to join our office.

Finally, time to board. Passengers carry small wooden crates of cherries, peaches, and apricots to sell or give to Moscow relatives. A final dispute with the airlines clerk, as the handwritten ticket lists our departure on flight 6112 instead of 6111, reversing incoming and outgoing flights. I have a center seat, my knees firmly planted in the back of a passenger ahead of me. A German tourist behind me digs his knees into my back; there is no other way. The aged plane is pulled slowly by a yellow truck to a distant runway, past several abandoned Aeroflot planes reclining in a cow pasture. One lacks wheels, another is missing a wing. "Tajik Air" had been painted over "Aeroflot" on some. We taxi past a large garden filled with towering onion plants and surrounded by strands of barbed wire to keep cows away. The garden's door is the blue-and-white door from an Aeroflot plane.

Our return flight takes almost four hours; some Tajik travelers bring food and Chinese thermoses of tea. The meal is the same as on the outgoing flight, except that the chicken is cold, handed out in trays like specimens in an anatomy lesson. Most passengers only nibble and leave untouched the chicken and the blood-colored fatty sausages reminiscent of what is seen under microscopic slides. I spend part of the flight standing in the galley, knees aching from immobility. (The plane is overbooked. Passengers are strapped in all the crew's jump seats.) I read Colin Thubborn's *The Lost Heart of Asia,* looking straight ahead, trying not to glance at the galley kitchen or smell its contents.

Shortly before noon, we arrive at Domodedovo Airport in summer heat and humidity. (Moscow's international airport, Sheremetyevo, was closed for a day last week, its sole operating runway having melted in the heat.) Three dogs (pets are carried on board Russian internal airlines, for baggage compartments are not pressurized) pant furiously and look pleadingly to owners for relief. The baggage carousel is strewn with crushed fruit and burned cigarettes. A small Russian child, her hair cut close to the skull for summer, drags a jointless plastic doll through the grime, singing softly. An ancient worker, medals protected by thick plastic, sits beside an aged wife whose brown face is as lined as the hills outside Dushanbe. His felt hat registers three levels of sweat markings, reflecting, like seismographic markings, different levels of summer heat. Children lie down and cry on the floor. Suddenly I realize that this decrepit, dirty place with handfuls of hanging wires and collapsing light fixtures is a new airport.

Flying Plums

Finally our flight's baggage shoots up a ramp into the air, then crashes onto a conveyer belt. Passengers huddle on both sides of the ramps, trying to grab bags. (Almost all valises and packages are covered in brown paper and tied tightly with string to protect them.) A large square carton of fresh plums shoots over the top and crashes, dribbling fresh fruit along the carousel. Tired, hot passengers reach for Central Asia's bounty. The package circles the conveyer belt several times and remains unclaimed. One of the three heavy-hipped customs ladies screams. I think her child's arm has been caught in the motor. The mechanical grinding stops, and, for a moment, the silence of the dead descends on Domodedovo Airport. Quickly the three customs agents lug the plums to a corner, carefully repackaging them and covering the box with paper; if the Tajik owner does not claim them, a delicious weekend of eating awaits them and their relatives.

I think no more can happen, but the next two hours are spent in crossing Moscow's Ring Road from one airport to another. Our prearranged van is a no-show, but Irek Stępiński finds a taxi driver who will transport the four of us for $150. We wait as the driver subcontracts with a second driver, then speeds off around Moscow's Ring Road on a Mr. Toad's Wild Ride, past a smoke-belching military truck with two flat tires, which is limping along in the slow lane but not giving up.

Bulky women sit by the roadside, Arctic-white limbs exposed to the sun, selling jars of strawberries. A man trots a young horse along the road's berm, the animal's lungs gulping in road smoke. At one spot, at least one hundred red, black, or gold-colored tea kettles are piled in stacks; at another, golden samovars glitter, each with a three-foot L-shaped section of stove pipe. Black-clad soldiers in flack jackets guard bridges and rail crossings. (We learn later that Chechen troops have made a surprise raid deep behind Russian lines.)

Our final obstacle is twenty cars waiting at a railway crossing. Unhesitatingly, our Lada jerks ahead, passing the cars and halting in front of the red-and-white gate as a commuter train clanks past. A large station keeper, clad mostly in a diaphanous summer print smock, holds a yellow flag in her meaty arms, waving at the engineer. She stands, in flat-heeled bedroom slippers and pale blue athletic socks, in front of her station's small garden, an exquisitely arranged bed of orange tiger lilies of the sort Hans Memling might have painted.

Judge George and I are exhausted by the time we reach Sheremetyevo. I have to count my bags each time I set them down; otherwise I will leave one behind. It is five hours until our flight departs for Warsaw. I watch an airport cat descend a nonfunctioning escalator, then wander about the slowly crumbling building. Erected as a showplace of the new Russia, it quickly became a marble mausoleum instead. Television monitors show an aging Julio Iglesias singing love songs. (He is one of several fading Western stars appearing this month in Moscow.)

Suddenly Russians gather around the television set. The elite Alpha unit's crack troops head for a hospital in the southern Russian town of Budennovsk, where several hundred Chechen irregulars are holed up with over a thousand hostages, after shooting up the town police station. Boris Yeltsin appears on the screen from Halifax, Canada, where he is a straphanger at a G-7 meeting, vowing that Russia's response will be swift and final. He adds that Western countries now should support the Russian Federation, instead of asking it to negotiate an end to the Chechen conflict. Within hours, Russian special forces attack the hospital twice and are repulsed. Negotiations begin. These end in a cease-fire and a resumption of the Russian Federation–Chechen talks under OSCE auspices in Grozny.

My body is on automatic pilot; I cannot listen to complicated music tapes. I need something simple and focused and so switch on a tape recording of Victorian and Edwardian ballads sung by Benjamin Luxon, a British baritone—selections such as "The Blind Ploughman," "A Perfect Day," and "Invictus," William Ernest Henley's ode to self-reliance. (I memorized it in high school but have not heard it in decades.) The day's events replay in my head, a Joycean phantasmagoria of aging planes and falling plums, domineering airport clerks and docile passengers, longsuffering Tajiks and bullying Russians:

> In the fell clutch of circumstance,
> I have not winced nor cried aloud.
> Under the bludgeonings of chance
> My head is bloody but unbowed.

One final obstacle: the exit gate to our Warsaw flight. A planeload of irate Italian tourists is in front of us, some gesticulating at customs guards, whose spines are rigid and who withdraw into our baggage-check area and shut the glass doors. Unfazed, Irek Stępiński persuades guards to open another booth. Judge George and I amble on:

> It matters not how strait the gate,
> How charged with punishments the scroll.

I am the master of my fate;
I am the captain of my soul.

Farewell to Warsaw

June 27: On the day the movers come, the embassy political section makes Charlotte the control officer for a one-day visit by Secretary of Defense William J. Perry, who travels with a forty-person entourage.

First, four muscular men, like circus acrobats, bounce from the movers' truck and, as in a fast-forwarded movie, briskly wrap plates, pile clothes, and lug furniture. Four embassy workers, like clowns in a Roman comedy, deliver electric fans to the wrong house.

By early afternoon, the packing is complete, and Tigger and I sit as the German driver, who has spent twenty years moving diplomats and business firms in Central and Eastern Europe, recounts his adventures. They include thirty- to forty-hour waits at the Polish-German border and armed gangs stopping his truck in Russia. His trucker's evaluation of the political-economic emergence of the former Warsaw Pact is similar to that of the *Economist*'s best writers. In late afternoon I make a last walk through the house. Everything is gone except a speck of metal on the study floor—the bullet that General Skobelev, descendent of generations of Russian generals, gave us at a vodka-washed dinner during our trip to the Chechen Republic.

The Old Curiosity Shop

June 28: I went there by accident one day last year during a sudden rainfall. Sometimes during the lunch hour I would wander the streets near our office, visiting art galleries and second-hand shops, record stores and places selling remainders of glass and china sets. "U Bozeny" was a large room filled with bric-a-brac. Sometimes a fine piece appeared, but mostly a procession of the elderly on fixed incomes brought crumpled brown paper bags with a few pieces of family silver or the famous blue-onion pattern of Central European chinaware. Meanwhile, around the corner, New Poles frequented a brightly lit jewelry store for shiny electroplated imitation gold-and-silver sherbet cups and cutlery, signs of affluence and modernity.

Bozenna spoke halting English. Possibly she had studied acting; she would stop speaking at important words and let silence fill in their meaning, although her young assistant spoke good French. Both women were art history majors at Cracow University. Bozenna was the daughter of a prominent surgeon who was killed in the August 1944 Warsaw Uprising; her sister, too, died on the front lines. Bozenna was thirteen at the time, an ammunition bearer and messenger for her part of town. She was the youngest member of the combat unit, except for a twelve-year-old boy, who was killed while delivering messages; a German machine gun sprayed his stomach with dum-dum bullets. "You know what is 'dum-dum,'" she asked, rubbing her hand on her stomach. Then she left the room to cry. While other Poles willingly shared war stories, Bozenna spoke reluctantly, giving only the bare details of what she experienced.

"What Warsaw once was," she remarked, gesturing above her coffee cup. Bozenna would sit at a small table by a sunny window in her otherwise dark shop. When it was filled, it looked like the elegant parlor of a pre–World War II home, resembling the family's apartment on Frederic Chopin Street. Bozenna rarely turned the lights on, unless a German tourist entered. She usually sat, gracefully composed with coffee cup and lit cigarette, reading the Polish translation of a European classic. "In those days the opera was something; our musicians traveled all over Europe. My mother sang with the opera for three years, then her throat." Bozenna rubbed her hand on her throat. I thought that the mother had been garroted, then realized that she had lost her voice. "On Saturday afternoons, my father invited many people; he served sweet wine. People from the opera would sing; we had a Steinway."

Hard as I try, I cannot recall our other conversations. They were mostly about politics and Warsaw life, the president's comings and goings, rumors of cabinet changes, a new production at the opera; such conversation offered a brief glimpse of what life was like among the old Warsaw intelligentsia. I bought a period telephone for one of our children, but Bozenna never tried to sell things, and when she decided to retire and no more new goods came in, the old curiosity shop came more and more to resemble a grandmother's attic.

It happened suddenly. One day last winter, the assistant slipped on the ice and broke her ankle. As she was dependent upon the neighborhood government hospital for treatment, her recuperation took a long time, and two metal pins were placed in her leg. Bozenna was frantic, and frequently the shop was closed for days as she supervised the woman's recovery. I sent some French magazines and toiletries and inquired often about her. When the assistant returned, she grabbed my hands and we mimicked a folk dance, she with her repaired ankle, I with my right knee restored after an operation.

I wanted to visit the two women before my final trip to Tajikistan but didn't. In recent months, most of their trade had come from selling off the remains of an elderly doctor's house. "Once he had everything, now nothing." Bozenna was silent for a moment, gesturing with open, then closed hands: "Once he was a rich man . . . everything. Now he is poor." For my lawyer son, I was interested in the doctor's desk set of brass and dark wood, with a small shelf for quill pens set between square crystal inkwells. Unfortunately I dithered; when I ask about it, she said, "It is gone! He came and took it back. He said it was the one thing he could not part with. It will be on his table when he dies."

During my next-to-last week in Warsaw, I stopped by with presents for both women—instant coffee for Bozenna, a semiprecious-stone necklace from Central Asia for the assistant. Almost everything was gone. The assistant removed a large battered tray from the display window and, selecting three cups from the remaining set of six for sale, made us coffee. She served cream and sugar from the store's last two silver pots.

"I am free," Bozenna said, waiting for the news to sink in. "First I will visit my daughter in Holland . . . then my son in Australia."

I asked, "When?"

"Soon," she continued. "When I make up my mind. I have things to do. I will visit Paris again."

My last day in Warsaw, I came to say good-bye. I did not know many Poles well, and those I did know were on summer vacation. This was farewell, a gesture of closure. Through the grated window, I looked into the darkened shop. Nothing but the chair and table remained; a Polish translation of André Malraux's *Voices of Silence,* which Bozenna was reading when we last talked, was gone. On the door a faded hand-lettered sign listed the shop's hours in a delicate art-historian's hand. Probably it had been made five years ago, when Bozenna, with the fall of Communism, opened her shop.

Above the sign hung a professionally lettered orange and yellow placard with a plastic cutout cruise ship and palm tree: "Coming to Warsaw: Tangoland, opening this August."

A Concluding Essay

Constitutions and Courts

During this two-year period, I traveled to fifteen Eurasian countries, analyzing draft constitutions and holding seminars on judicial reform. Quantitative evidence is hard to come by, but qualitatively I am convinced that, despite their flaws, the constitutions represent good beginnings for the furtherance of civil society and that the judiciaries have high numbers of competent professional jurists who increasingly fulfill their mandates with distinction.

The 1990s represent the constitutional decade for Central and Eastern Europe, the Russian Federation, the Baltics, and the states of Central Asia and the Caucuses. (It is impossible to find a correct term to encompass the geographic region covered by OSCE's programs. It is more than the former Soviet Union or Russian Federation, for the Baltic states always maintained their hope of independence from Russia, despite being conquered. Central Asian countries extend the region beyond Europe, and the Caucuses have strong ties to Europe and the Middle East.)

Within a few years, these states have moved from tightly controlled authoritarian political systems to more pluralistic forms of government with constitutions, political parties, a semblance of free media, and beginnings of market economies. If there are relapses, such as the closing of Kazakhstan's constitutional court by the president, or the dismissal of the chief judge of Albania's supreme court for political reasons, they should be seen in the broader perspective of these countries' evolution. During the Cold War, Russian diplomats at various times gave me copies of their constitution to provide assurance that dissidents, Jews, Baptists, and non-Russian minorities were not being persecuted; on paper, buried in a lengthy and unenforceable document, they had constitutional rights. Until recently, such constitutions were almost useless archival documents which ruling Communist parties referred to infrequently, either to claim legitimacy or to squelch criticism. Today, however, constitutional language is everywhere—despots act in the name of constitutional order, dissidents resist because of the constitution. Even if rulers use rather than observe constitutions, the vocabulary of constitutionalism remains the norm.

Constitutions

Most of the documents I examined show evidence of competing ideas and probably will not have long shelf lives. If the average Latin American constitution survives for approximately seven years, there is no indication that the constitutions of the countries I visited will fare much better. But that is not as disturbing as it might appear. It is wrong to expect these constitutions to endure as long as the American constitution, which was written at a particular historical moment; had it been drafted a decade earlier, in the unsettled times of the Revolution, it would have been a different document. Had it been written a few years later, in the populist Age of Jackson, it would be considerably different from what it was. Americans are fortunate to have a constitution last two centuries; elsewhere, far shorter durations are the norm.

Part of the problem facing the new constitutions is the uncertainty of their intended audiences. Are they drawn up for the benefit of people, governments, or professional jurists? Since these are new nations, usually the documents contain preambular language about the country, its sovereignty, and its status as a democratic state ruled by law. Most documents sandwich in long sections about legislative or executive powers. Here the discerning eye looks for indices of separation of powers and checks and balances, which often are more apparent than real. Different functions may be sorted out, but rarely are powers truly separate. I asked a Central Asian legislator who is also a cabinet minister about this.

"If you knew the people we have to deal with, you would not trust them with power," he replied.

I said, "You don't have to like or trust the people, but if you have separation of powers, an independent judiciary, and an open political process, you will have a government of laws and not people."

"We're not ready for that yet," he replied, giving a response I heard often in the two years I traversed the region.

Many constitutions have escape clauses that provide opportunities to suspend the document by invoking war powers or emergency powers, or that allow for rule by presidential order or executive decree. Some constitutions sew together compromises of the moment, and it is a good thing that they can be amended relatively easily, often by a two-thirds legislative vote, for many of the issues they leave ambiguous will become clearer or lose their importance with the passage of time. Parenthetically, only a handful of these documents are the products of finished legal drafting. Many lack symmetry among parts; in most, the judiciary's role is sketched only vaguely. Several countries presently are writing laws on the organization of the judiciary. After all, the American judiciary was launched with a single sentence in the Constitution: "The judicial Power of the United States, shall be vested in the one supreme Court, and in such inferior Courts as the Congress may from time to time ordain and establish" (Article III, Section 1).

Key questions are avoided with phrases that indicate the topic will be "subject of further clarification by law." Sometimes a concept is left vague, garlanded with adjectives which leave the notion murky but call attention to it in solemn language. The disadvantage of such formulas is their vagueness; the advantage is that they often refer to topics too controversial for present resolution, such as the status of a troubled ethnic region.

Rights

No issue is more important and yet more tentatively dealt with in many constitutions than the question of rights. How broad should a constitutional statement of rights be? Should it be limited to justiciable rights, like those affecting free speech, free assembly, and due process? Or should rights include vaguer aspirational rights as well, such as the right to the protection of one's cultural heritage, to a proper education, or to a clean environment? Some commentators, like Professor Herman Schwartz of American University, who has worked extensively in the region, argue that such aspirational rights belong in a constitution because they indicate the direction in which a society might head.

The difficulty with a constitution caught in the middle between enforceable and aspirational rights comes with something concrete like the demand for proper medical care. Can a citizen in a Central Asian country sue the government for not providing adequate clinics, doctors, or hospitals? Faced with such insoluble dilemmas, some courts say they will not enforce statements of rights when they cannot provide proper remedies. While such a solution may shock some Western jurists, its merit in developing countries is obvious. The society's goals remain intact, the court takes on cases it believes it can adjudicate without bringing down legislative and executive branch jeremiads upon itself, and remaining issues are left, hopefully to be addressed at a later time when possibilities of their being resolved are more favorable.

Legislatures and courts of once-Communist countries face a dilemma. Social rights, especially workers' rights to wages, pensions, and medical and other benefits, have been inherited from Communist days. Reducing or removing such long-established rights would be a highly unpopular step, so they remain in the constitution.

Self-Determination and the Place of International Law

There are several vexing questions these constitutions have not anticipated, such as the self-determination aspirations of groups like the Crimean Tartars, or the status of the Chechen Republic, or the rights of ethnic and religious minorities, including the dispersed Russian populations in now-independent countries.

Many of these constitutions accept the supremacy of international laws and treaties over domestic law. This acceptance will become increasingly important as such countries draw closer to Europe, especially in the human rights area, where the international provisions allow citizens of a given country to appeal to the European Court of Human Rights in Strasbourg. I asked several jurists why their countries give precedence to international law and treaties over domestic law. "We have not had time to write our own laws on subjects like human rights," a Russian judge told me; "besides, we want to become part of Europe, and these are European standards. Considering our past, we thought it best to accept them as they are." The shadow of Europe looms large for these countries, and acceptance into the European community is a powerful incentive for most to adopt international human-rights standards.

Ratification

The question of how a constitution is ratified by and for the people is open-ended. Ideally, the document should reflect citizens' hopes, turned into a final version by their representatives and then presented to the citizens for ratification. Several difficulties are inherent in this idealized model. First, citizens' aspirations can contradict one another, i.e., conservative farmers and industrial workers may have quite different desires. Second, citizen apathy is notorious, even in developed countries, and there is a risk that cynicism will pervade and the people will not vote, thus defeating the constitution's passage. How could it be otherwise in states that have been under the yoke of Communism, where communication is poor and possibilities for participation in civic culture through political parties and interest groups were only embryonic.

The constitution writers in the Republic of South Africa reached an ingenious solution: they held lengthy consultations with constituent groups, then the constitution was drafted, and finally the draft was reviewed by the constitutional court for conformity with the earlier discussions.

Subjecting the entire document to a popular referendum is fraught with peril. Everyone will identify those provisions most objectionable to her or him, and the longer and more detailed the document, the greater the potential for opposition, as in the draft Polish constitution, in which the Roman Catholic Church's once-privileged position is considerably diminished. The founders of the United States, fearing the potential tyranny of the majority, used a ratifying convention as a screening device. Some countries have preferred to have the legislature ratify the constitution by a substantial vote. The disadvantage of such a system is that in most countries legislatures of the 1990s are transitional bodies, with substantial numbers of their members being veterans from Communist party days. Parenthetically, although the German constitution is one of the most admired models for these countries, it never was put to the people for a vote but instead was ratified by the legislature.

Constitutional Courts

Constitutional courts in these countries will be harbingers of how effectively democratic society is being instituted, for to these courts will come the major political and judicial questions facing a people. The model adopted by most countries of this region will be close to the French or the German constitutional court, but the Spanish Constitutional Court has an obvious appeal. Spain is a civil law country that emerged from a recent Fascist past to a democratic present, while wrestling with issues like Basque separatism and Catalonian regionalism—questions that interest constitution framers in Moscow, Bishkek or Tbilisi who face similar problems. Likewise, the Italian model has influenced countries of the former Yugoslavia, and an Austria model has appealed to some nations of the former Austro-Hungarian empire, such as Hungary. Many of these emerging courts resemble that of John Marshall, created when the *terra incognita* of how far judicial review and the court's authority will extend is being mapped in each country.

Most courts struggle for a role and for adequate space, salaries, and staffs. Some questions they face include these: Can individuals petition directly to courts on the constitutionality of cases, as they can in Hungary? Are courts' opinions binding or advisory? Can courts take direct jurisdiction in a case, or must they wait for the legislative or executive branch to bring it to them?

Another issue is the form in which court opinions are issued. In many countries, they are contained in a short document that avoids discussing the court's reasoning or including dissenting opinions. At this crucial hour, when formative jurisprudence takes shape, it is desirable to know "the mind of the court" in each country and to share opinions among countries, for many courts wrestle with similar cases.

While few politicians welcome the prospect of sharing power with constitutional courts, many see in the successes of the Hungarian and Polish constitutional courts a contribution to political stability in otherwise turbulent times. Despite problems and setbacks, the picture clearly is a positive one for the future of such courts. Ironically, the two countries with the most advanced constitutional courts, Hungary and Poland, have yet to adopt new constitutions. Hungary operates with several major amendments to its 1949 constitution, Poland with the so-called 1992 "Little Constitution."

The Polish Experience

The evolution of Poland's Constitutional Tribunal is instructive. Originating in the repressive Communist era in response to growing popular demand for a more democratic society, the tribunal slowly but surely, over the next decade, expanded its powers and competence until it became a force to be reckoned with. In response to increasing public clamor for a less authoritarian political system, the Communist government created the court—which became operative in 1986—but severely hobbled its powers. For example, it could review no laws more than five years old; thus the important declaration of martial law of 1981 was excluded. Moreover, its decrees could be overturned by a two-thirds parliamentary vote, an option that rarely was invoked.

Despite such an inauspicious beginning, this judicial body changed with the times. After the regime's 1989 collapse, its role expanded, and a newer generation of more professional judges replaced an earlier era's loyalists. Polish apparatchik were among the Communist world's most grimly authoritarian bureaucrats, and the court gradually struck down many of their extralegal decrees and gradually expanded the protections afforded human rights and due process. Professor Lech L. Garlicki, a recently appointed judge, described the court's relationship with Parliament as being "like a tennis match," with the court cautiously seeking to expand jurisdiction, while the legislative branch showed considerable hesitation in accepting an expanded role for the judiciary. Still, the inescapable conclusion is that parliamentarians are becoming increasingly conscious of the constitutional dimension of their acts, especially following the lengthy debates about the new constitution. More than fifty parliamentary members participated in the constitutional commission. Its frequent public hearings on constitutional questions and widely circulated expert studies contributed to a greater awareness of constitutional issues in both government and the media.

Judges

Independent judiciaries were not a feature of the Communist past. Judges were poorly paid minor civil servants, gray and barely visible among the silent, stoop-shouldered *nomenklatura* making their way along the streets of Prague or Budapest. Ivan Klima, whom we knew to be a witty, merry person, chronicles the dreary life of one such minor jurist in Prague in a recent novel, *The Life of a Judge*. The book vividly portrays the era of "telephone justice," when party officials telephoned judges, delivering verdicts before cases were heard. When I used this phrase in a conversation with Garlicki, he became animated. "It was more than that," he said. "Judges would anticipate what the party wanted without any conversation. Often they would make the sentences more severe and ask, 'Is ten years adequate, Mr. Chairman? Twelve years?' Certain judges were known to be unwavering party loyalists. When we saw who would be hearing the case, we knew what the outcome would be before the trial was held." A judge from Azerbaijan told of having a black and a red telephone next to his desk. When the red phone from party headquarters rang he stood at respectful attention while answering it, so long was the party's reach.

Constitutional evolution and improvements in judiciaries' status must be viewed in tandem with political change in these emerging societies. It is judges who interpret laws and settle disputes between contending branches of government, between citizens and governments, or among citizens. If judicial evolution does not keep pace with other steps in a societies' evolution, writing constitutions becomes a futile exercise. Judges need to have long tenure and not be subject to covert or overt political pressure. Their salaries, benefits, and retirement systems must be adequate for them not to be susceptible to bribes and influence-peddling. Clerks, secretaries, law books, and support staffs are needed to make a judicial system work. I visited courts which lacked electricity much of the day and others where proceedings went unrecorded because the clerk had no paper. Only a few courts had word processors, and those that did usually had no more than one or two machines.

As a correlate of increased Western European contact with Central and Western Europe, there probably never has been a class of legislators and judges from transitional societies more exposed to the ideas and experiences of other countries than the emerging generation of Central and Eastern European leaders. Hundreds have visited the West, and European and American jurists have held seminars, consulted with colleagues, taught university courses, and exchanged documents. During the two years I traversed the region, television screens often displayed the O. J. Simpson trial, but it was the least of the questions we discussed. Judges wanted to know everything from how plea bargaining and alternative dispute resolution worked to what are the retirement benefits for judges in other countries. "How do you enforce your decisions?" was a question we heard constantly. "And how is a judge protected from violent or vengeful persons?"

Civic Culture

Building a civic culture—a culture that includes respect for, and widespread open participation in, the political system—is a task facing the countries of Central and Eastern Europe. This begins with citizen respect for and confidence in government. Each emerging country of this region represents a different history and ties with the West. Countries like Hungary, the Czech Republic, the Baltic states, and Poland knew Western legal and institutional systems before their conquest by Russia. I remember in one country urging the constitution writers to reserve a room in the Ministry of Justice where the archives of their deliberations might be kept and the draft constitutions displayed for schoolchildren and scholars. Future generations have the right to revisit the deliberative process that produced the initial post-independence constitution, unfinished as it might be.

If a constitution takes several years to write, building a civic culture takes decades, perhaps a century, to realize. Respect for a constitution comes if it works fairly and speedily, which in turn depends on the presence of a competent, independent judiciary. Another ingredient of civic culture is peoples' attitudes toward the law. In more mature democratic societies, courts are clogged with litigants, and a lawsuit or threatened lawsuit is in the arsenal of many citizens. While it is easy to argue that Western courts are used too much by citizens, in these emerging states the wish is that citizens would use the courts more. However, this requires a change in popular attitudes. Historically in such countries, the courts were repressive arms of the government, and the citizen who questioned state practices or became too obvious might be visited by the police. Additionally, there were no market economies and consequently no tradition of commercial dispute resolution or robust civic life. Many people "mentally immigrated," putting their societies out of their minds. An important publication of Prague's Charter 77 dissidents, called *Latchkey*, symbolically divided the world into insiders and outsiders.

Free media, bar associations, law schools, and nongovernmental groups such as human-rights associations and legal-aid societies all contribute to building a civic culture. No issue is more vexing than the place of free speech. Judges have shown me articles which I, as a former journalist, found embarrassing for their inflammatory tone and dearth of facts. Still, the advantages of a free press far outweigh its disadvantages. It can keep a government honest by exposing scandals and improper conduct, and it can be the voice for new ideas and legitimate political debate. Politicians in emerging countries have used constitutional provisions to silence potential opposition. Often this comes from invoking a "defamation of character or good reputation" clause, including monetary and penal sanctions. Such clauses, almost impossible to enforce and rarely used in Western countries, are held like swords over the heads of critical journalists in Central and Eastern Europe.

An equally important question is how to regulate formerly state-owned media in countries where minute control was exercised over everything from the content of television broadcasts to newsprint supplies. Should media institutions be privatized or remain as quasi-state-owned and -controlled bodies? What is their legal status to be in a new political and economic climate?

Elections

Citizen access to elections also is fundamental in building a civic culture and a democratic society. Who can vote? Who can be a candidate? How free to form are political parties? (Some constitutions screen out the political opposition that has fled to Moscow, Frankfurt, or New York by including a ten-year residency requirement for candidates.) How free to form are civic groups representing citizens' interests? (Some laws on free association require so many signatures from so many districts that it is almost impossible for an association to form.) How free are media to discuss political issues? Is the electoral process under the scrutiny of political parties and independent observers, from initial balloting to final vote counting? (In some countries, independent scrutiny of vote counting ends at the local polling place, after which ballots are trucked off into the night for a final tally behind closed doors.)

Unless there is easy citizen access to the political process—primarily through voting and participation in political parties—democratic aspirations are frustrated, citizen apathy and cynicism multiplies, and participation in national life ebbs. The way is left open for special interest groups to control political life, for corruption to spread, and for talented young people to turn their interests elsewhere than to careers in government.

Federalism

As these countries become more stable, many are beginning to look at possible federalist solutions to their internal political problems. The key issue is: how much power is the center willing to yield to constituent parts? Generally, it is easy to reach agreement that local or regional government should have authority to build public works, roads, schools, and medical facilities, and to support agriculture, fisheries, and forestry. But should they raise their own taxes? police their territories? make their own laws? grant special status to ethnic or religious minorities? These important issues are only beginning to be raised, yet federalist solutions are likely to become increasingly important in addressing regional issues in the decades ahead.

The Convergence of Civil and Common Law Traditions

All over the region we witness the convergence of civil-law and common-law traditions. Court structures in these emerging countries will continue to reflect a civil-law design but increasingly adopt common-law features, such as jury trials and an adversarial system of court proceedings. The multiplication of laws and decrees makes increased information-retrieval skills a necessity for jurists.

Likewise, there is a growing interest in case law, and already the jurisprudence of the European Court of Human Rights gradually is being applied throughout the region. I once asked an experienced judge from a formerly Communist country if he used case law in reaching his decisions. "All the time," he replied, "but I disguise it when I write my opinions. We are not quite ready to acknowledge the importance of individual cases yet." Basically, in subject matter covered by Roman law, such as property, contracts, and torts, the civil-law tradition and its codes stand; but in new areas, such as intellectual property, environmental, banking and finance, and human-rights law, the case-law tradition becomes increasingly important.

Combatting the Criminal State

The determined efforts of western and Eurasian jurists to build states governed by democratic norms are seriously threatened by crime and corruption, spreading like wildfire across the steppes. Combatting crime and corruption is a foreign policy issue countries will face in the next century of the magnitude of the Cold War in the twentieth century and global expansion a century earlier. Criminal gangs in the Russian Federation and neighboring states grow at over twice the speed of multinational corporations, but instead of strengthening indigenous economies, gangs destroy them. Money comes from international sales of narcotics and armaments, to which the smuggling of illegal immigrants and the selling of women and children into prostitution are added. Like the Italian Mafia a generation ago, today's Russian gangs are quickly buying into legitimate businesses like hotels, newspapers, and television stations, and purchasing expensive real estate in New York or Florida. Extortion is as common in Moscow as it was in Chicago in the 1920s, and gangland killings are commonplace. Police, government, an judicial corruption is endemic—how could it be otherwise when a Moscow judge makes between $350 and $650 a month and a police officer, even less? Codes of public ethics remain in their infancy. At one seminar we held, local judges saw no conflict in being judges as well as paid legal consultants to banks and businesses.

The international criminals are rich, brutal, and resourceful, but many of their networks are fragile and their methods, crude and obvious. If and when a legal infrastructure is in place, backed by competent, well-paid, well-staffed police and judicial agencies, it will be possible to combat these criminals effectively. In Moscow, a colleague was left behind accidentally at Moscow University. The occupants of a new Lincoln Continental offered him a ride back to town. (They wore cowboy boots, blue jeans, had H.-R.-Haldeman haircuts, and were dressed in Marlboroman sheepskin coats.) Wanting to thank them for the lift, my colleague asked the driver if he could assist them. "No thanks," was the reply, "but if you see any late-model Mercedes Benzes, let us know." In Riga, I watched one night at the local McDonald's as a large American car pulled up, and the occupants, dressed similarly to their Moscow counterparts, ordered six carry-out meals, the combined cost being more than most Estonians' monthly salary. It was absurd to see gang members parading around the lobbies of principal hotels, calling one another on cellular phones. In even a desolate place like Tiraspol, Moldova, gang members' BMWs driven by young hoodlums in signature leather jackets, gold chains, Italian silk shirts, and American jeans sped up and down the town's main street. Seeing many new cars with "D" stickers (for "Deutschland") on their rear bumpers, I remarked, "It's strange to see so many German tourists in Tiraspol in winter." A local resident responded, "Those are not tourists; those are stolen cars," adding that the cars were stolen in Germany, then transported eastward in trucks covered with cabbages or potatoes.

Conclusion

Against the backdrop of this region's convulsive history, the era of constitution writing represents a passing moment. As it succeeds and an independent judiciary emerges, the foundations will be laid for government by rule of law to flourish, with its attendant political and economic benefits, respect for human dignity, political stability, and economic prosperity. The task is daunting, and the constitutions, even in their unfinished forms, reflect the state of political discourse in various countries—but also, no less, peoples' hopes, aspirations, and fears. Compared to the summary decrees of czars, khans, commissars, and emperors, most of these constitutions are liberal, progressive documents, the likes of which this part of the globe has not seen before. The constitution drafters and judges deserve praise for their demonstrable successes. They also deserve the assurance that colleagues from other countries will continue working with them in sorting out the challenges ahead.

Index

Belarus, 111–16; elections, 111–12, 114–16; Kebich, Vyacheslav, presidential candidate, 111; Lukasenko, Alexander, Belarus president, 111; Minsk, life in, 111–15

Beran, Zdeněk, Czech artist, 149–50

Berlin, visit to, 37-38

Biskek, Kyrgyzstan, 117–21, 152–53, 154–56

Bisset James, Canadian diplomat-refugee official, 184

Blandu, Florentina, CEELI lawyer in Moldova, 19

Bloed, Arie, Dutch human rights-OSCE expert, 206

Brezhnev, Leonid, xvii, 205

Brzezinski, Ian, legislative advisor to Ukrainian Parliament, 130

Budapest CSCE annual meeting, 132–34, 153–54

Bulgaria, stop in, 110

Ceauşescu, Nicolae, Romanian dictator, 64

Central and Eastern European Law Initiative (CEELI), 19

Chalupecky, Jindrich, Czech art critic, 149

Chechen conflict. *See* Chechen Republic; Russian Federation

Chechen Republic; Avtourkhavov, Umar, chair, Chechen Provincial Council, 192–94; Chulkov, Boris, Russian refugee coordinator, 196–97; Dudayev, Dzhokar M., Chechen leader, 89-90, 180–82, 191–92; Grozny, visit to, 193–96; Gyarmati, Istvan, personal representative of OSCE Chairman-in-Office on Chechen Crisis, 184, 199–202; hu-

manitarian aid distribution problems, 178, 181, 184, 192; human rights problems in, 175, 179–80, 188–90; Khadzhiyev, Salambek, leader, Chechen Government of National Revival, 175, 195; Makarenko, Fr. Ivan, Russian Orthodox priest helps refugees, 197, 200; military aspects of conflict, 179–80, 187–88, 190–92, 195–96; mission to, 178–202; Mitkitaev, Abdulakh K., deputy from North Caucasus, 186–87, 190; Paskoushev, Khumit Atnevich, Chechen banker describes war, 185; prisoners, status of, 179–80, 188, 190; Prokhladliy, Chechen city, 190–93; refugees, 182, 196–200; report on Mission to OSCE, 200–201; Russians block mission's work, 181–84, 186, 199–202, 205; Shepshov, Col. Gen. L. P., chief of staff, Russian Army in Chechen Republic, 188; Skobelov, Gen. Eugenov, Commander, 42nd Army Corps, Russian Army, 197, 225; "Stolypin" interrogation trains used in Chechen Republic, 189–90; Tretyakov, Boris S., Russian General, mission escort, 186, 188, 197; Tsagolov, K. M., Russian general-civil administrator, 165, 187; Yefimenko, Lt. Col. Nickolai, Russian commander in Grozny, 195, 196

Cheever, Sarge, American diplomat with CSCE, 19, 205–207

Chernyaskaya, Elena, Ukrainian entrepreneur, 130–32

Chisinau, Moldova, 17-18

Chulkov, Boris, Russian refugee coordinator, 196–97

European Commission for Democracy through Law, 66–68. *See also* Venice Commission for Democracy through Law

Falandysz, Lech, Polish president's constitutional advisor, 93–95, 177
federalism, 21, 237–38
Fillatof, Pierre, French diplomat, 178, 201
Frowein, Prof. Dr. J. A., German constitutionalist, 220–21

Gagauz Republic (in Moldova) 18, 24–25
Gantchev, Gancho, OSCE mission head, Tajikistan, 138
Garbuz, Vladimir, Transdnistrian *agent provocateur*, recants testimony, 52
Garlicki, Lech L., Polish constitutional court judge, 99, 154
George, Lloyd D., U.S. federal judge, 99–100, 158, 215–16, 223–24
Georgia, 86–93, 211–14; constitution, 66–67, 88, 90–93; Georgian-Russian relations, 93; Schevernadze, Edouard, Georgian president, 90–93, 162; state of judiciary, 211–14; Tbilisi, 86–88, 211–14
Giysov, Kadriddin, Chair, Central Elections Committee, Tajikistan, 140
Glover, Audrey F., Ambassador, ODIHR Director, 33, 77
Guerra, Luis López, Vice President, Spanish Constitutional Court, 97, 154–57, 164, 178, 183, 201, 215–16
Gutnichenko, Larisa, Deputy Chair, Supreme Court of Kyrgyzstan, 120–21, 161

Gyarmati, Istvan, Personal representative, OSCE Chairman-in-Office on Chechen Crisis, 199–202

Hall, Cynthia Holcomb, U.S. federal judge, 158, 215–16
Harremoes, Erik, Head, Council of Europe legal department, 60
Haskell, Betsy, American entrepreneur in Georgia, 212
Havel, Vaclav, Czech dissident writer, then president, xviii, 145, 148
Helsinki Accords (1975), xvii–xviii
Helsinki Foundation, human rights organization, 126
Howard, A. E. Dick, American constitutional expert, in Poland, 45, 93–95
Höynk, Wilhelm, OSCE Secretary General, 29, 74–76, 132–33
Huber, Conrad, Office of High Commissioner on National Minorities, 119
human rights: Chechen Republic, 179–80, 184–85, 188–90; Kazakhstan, 83–84; Kyrgyzstan, 83–84, 154–55; Moldova, 19, 51–52; Russian Federation, 172
Hurowitz, Edward, American Ambassador to Kyrgyzstan, 119–20

Ilascu, Ilie, Tiraspol human rights activist, 51–53, 64
individual vs. group rights, discussion of, 84, 155, 206–207, 230–231
International Foundation for Electoral Systems (IFES): in Tajikistan, 142; in Ukraine, 129
international law, precedence of over

Marovich, George, U.S. federal judge, 203

Marutse, Rait, Chair, National Courts of Estonia, 169–70

Meyrat, Thierry, head of delegation, International Committee of the Red Cross, Russian Federation, 184–85

Mihm, Michael, U.S. federal judge, 99–100, 154–56, 161

minorities, status of: Baltics, 171; Estonia, 171, 205; Kazakhstan, 81, 85; Latvia, 67–68; Lithuania, 68, 171; Moldova, 18, 24–25, 51–52; Poland, 70

Mitkitaev, Abdulakh K., Russian Federation duma deputy from North Caucasus, 186–87, 190

Moldova, 16–25, 51–64; conflict with Dnister Soviet Socialist Republic, 51–64; Council of Europe visits, 60; Garbuz, Vladimir, Tiraspol *agent provocateur,* recants testimony, 52; human rights monitoring mission, 51–64; Ilascu, Ilie, Tiraspol human rights activist, 51–53; Ivanova, Olga, chief judge, Tiraspol Supreme Court, 58–59; Romanian interest in, 62–64; Smirnov, Igor, Transdnistrian leader, meeting with, 53, 60–62; Snegur, Mircea, President of Moldova, 53; "Tiraspol Six" murder and human rights trials, 51–53, 57–62; Voznian, Ian, Moldovan attorney for Ilie Illascu, 59–60

Moore, John Norton, American law professor, 49

Musoyeva, Rafika, Chairman of the State Construction, Republic of Tajikistan, 221

Mylenasz, Zdenek, Czech dissident economist, 147

Nazarbaev, Nursultan, President of Kazakhstan, 79, 82

Office for Democratic Institutions and Human Rights, ODIHR, missions to: Chechen Republic, 178–202; Estonia, 169–71, 205–208; Georgia, 86–93, 211–14; Kazakhstan, 78–85, 151–52, 156; Kyrgyzstan, 152–55; Latvia, 167–69, 203–204; Moldova, 20–25, 55–64; Tajikistan, 134–43, 217–25; Warsaw Judicial Symposium, first annual, 98–100, Warsaw Judicial Symposium, second annual, 215–17

Organization on Security and Cooperation in Europe, OSCE, 153–54. *See also* Conference on Security and Cooperation in Europe, CSCE

Orlov, Oleg P., member of Memorial human rights organization, 184

Pakowski, Wojtech, Polish artist, 74

Palach, Jan, Czech student, self-immolation of memorialized, 149

Paliszewski, Jacek, Polish diplomat, ODIHR staff, Warsaw, 33

Parfait, Alan, British diplomat, 178

Pashin, Sergey, Russian legal reformer, 172–73

Paskoushev, Khumit Atnevich, Chechen banker describes war, 185

Penner, Dr. Gary, American embassy physician, Warsaw, 42

Pickering, Thomas, American ambassador to Russian Federation, 180–81

Poland: constitution, 69, 93–95, 232–34; constitutional tribunal, 43, 232–33; Falandysz, Lech, presidential advisor on constitution, 93–95, 177; Garlicki, Lech L., Polish constitutional court judge, professor, 99, 154; Howard, A. E. Dick, American constitutionalist visits, 45, 93–95; Kolodzeijczyk, Piotr, defense minister, 72; Kwasniewski, Alexander, political leader (later president), 69; NATO, 72–73, 154; Pakowski, Wojtech, artist, 74; Polish State Stud Farm, Janow Podlaski, 214–15; refugees, 70; Walesa, Lech, Polish president, 68–69. *See also* Warsaw

Quinn, Charlotte, American diplomat, 19, 33–35, 41, 225
Quinn, Frederick, xvii–xix, 21–22, 30, 41 44, 49–50, 133–34, 224–27

Rafeedie, Edward, U.S. federal judge, 211–14
Rakhmanov, Immomali, presidential candidate, then president, Tajikistan, 135–36, 141, 143
ratification, 232
Rogov, Igor, Deputy Chair, Constitutional Court, Republic of Kazakhstan, 123
Romania, 62–64, 96–98; Badenter, Robert, French Constitutional Court president, 97; Bucharest, 53–54, 62–64, 96; constitutional court seminar (Venice Commission sponsored), 96–98; Dracula's Castle visit, 97–98; Guerra, Luis López, Spanish Constitutional Court Vice President,

97; Moldovan relations, 17–18, 62–64; Peoples' Palace, 96–97
Russian Federation: Afanasyevskiy, N. N., Deputy Foreign Minister, Russian Federation, meetings with, 181–82, 199; airports, 12–17, 221–25; Bakhmin, Viaceslav I., head, International Humanitarian and Human Rights office, Ministry of Foreign Affairs, 182; Bissett, James, Canadian diplomat-refugee aid worker, 184; Bolshoi theatre, 174; Chechen Republic, OSCE mission to, Moscow meetings, 178–202; Chulkov, Boris, refugee coordinator, 196–97; constitutional court, status of, 172; Duma representatives, meeting with, 185–86; human rights in, 172–73; Ivanov, I. S., Deputy minister for National and Regional Political Affairs, Russian Federation, 183–84; judges, status of, 171–73; jury system, introduction of, 173; Khadzhiyev, Salambek, leader, Chechen Government of National revival, 193; Kovalev, Sergi, Russian Human Rights Commissioner, 179, 188; Kovalev, Valentin A., Minister of Justice, Russian Federation, discusses Chechen conflict, 183; Latvian-Russian relations, 169; law reform, 172–73; life in, 171, 174–77; Meyrat, Thierry, head of delegation, International Committee of the Red Cross in Russian Federation, 184–85; Ministry of Foreign Affairs, meetings with, 181–84, 199–200; Mitkitaev, Abdulakh K., Russian Duma deputy from North Caucuses,

Kadriddin, Chair, Central Elections Committee, 140; Hoffman, Gwen, IFES elections expert, 142; Ismailov, Shawkat, Minister of Justice, 219–20; Musoyrva, Rafika, Chairman of the State Construction, Republic of Tajikistan, 221; OSCE Mission to Tajikistan, 137–40; presidential campaign televised, 141; presidential elections, 138–43; Rakhmanov, Immomali, presidential candidate, then president, 135–36, 141, 143

Tbilisi, Georgia, 86–88, 211–14

Teague, Elizabeth, Office of High Commissioner on National Minorities, 119

Tevrizian, Dickran, U.S. federal judge, 100–108

Tigger, German shepherd, 3–6, 35, 69, 127–28

"Tiraspol Six" Murder Trial, 51–64

Tretyakov, Gen. Boris, Russian escort officer in Chechen Republic, 186, 188, 197

Tsagolov, Gen. K. M., Russian general-civil administrator in Chechen Republic, 165, 187

Turkish workers in Germany, 69–70

Ukraine, 129–33; Chernyaskaya, Elena, 130–32; Crimean problem, 130; electoral system, 129; International Foundation for Electoral Systems (IFES), 129; Kiev, 129–32; political conflicts, 129; relations with Russian Federation, 130

Venice Commission for Democracy through Law, 66–67

Vitruk, Nicholi, acting president, Russian constitutional court, 172

Voznian, Ian, Moldovan attorney for Ilie Ilascu, 59–60

Walesa, Lech, 68–69

Warsaw: American embassy, description of, 39–40; apartment, 3–5; bus, description of, 7–8, 51; Count Kinski's Treasures (fantasy), 46–48; crime as problem, 4–5, 151; diplomatic Life (entertainment), 12; Easter, 73–74; farewell to, 225–27; Good Friday, 73; house, 35–36, 45–46; Howard, A. E. Dick, American constitutional expert visits Warsaw, 45, 93–95; life in, 3–12, 26–27, 38–39, 45–46, 51, 65–66, 151, 208–10, 214; miners' demonstration, 209–10; neighborhood, 3–5, 36–37, 39–40, 128; Pakowski, Wojtech and Anna, 74; Palace of Culture and Science, 10–11; Polish Political Science Association, 9–10; popular taste in books, 76; Remembrance Sunday, 48–49; Russian market, 6–7; slaughterhouse as metaphor for political society, 10; train robberies, 151; Warsaw Judicial Symposium, first annual, 98–100; Warsaw Judicial Symposium, second annual, 215–17

Wyman, Lowrey, legal reform specialist in Kazakhstan, 100

Yefimenko, Lt. Col. Nickolai, Russian Commander in Grozny, 195–96